THE DUAL ENROLLMENT KALEIDOSCOPE

THE DUAL ENROLLMENT KALEIDOSCOPE

Reconfiguring Perceptions of First-Year Writing and Composition Studies

EDITED BY
CHRISTINE DENECKER
AND CASIE MORELAND

UTAH STATE UNIVERSITY PRESS
Logan

Published by Utah State University Press
An imprint of University Press of Colorado
245 Century Circle, Suite 202
Louisville, Colorado 80027

Printed in the United States of America

ASSOCIATION of UNIVERSITY PRESSES

The University Press of Colorado is a proud member of the Association of University Presses.

The University Press of Colorado is a cooperative publishing enterprise supported, in part, by Adams State University, Colorado State University, Fort Lewis College, Metropolitan State University of Denver, University of Alaska Fairbanks, University of Colorado, University of Denver, University of Northern Colorado, University of Wyoming, Utah State University, and Western Colorado University.

∞ This paper meets the requirements of the ANSI/NISO Z39.48-1992 (Permanence of Paper).

ISBN: 978-1-64642-252-4 (paperback)
ISBN: 978-1-64642-253-1 (ebook)
https://doi.org/10.7330/9781646422531

Library of Congress Cataloging-in-Publication Data

Names: Denecker, Christine, editor. | Moreland, Casie, editor. | Farris, Christine, 1949– writer of foreword.
Title: The dual enrollment kaleidoscope : reconfiguring perceptions of first-year writing and composition studies / edited by Christine Denecker and Casie Moreland.
Description: Logan : Utah State University Press, [2022] | Includes bibliographical references and index.
Identifiers: LCCN 2022019873 (print) | LCCN 2022019874 (ebook) | ISBN 9781646422524 (paperback) | ISBN 9781646422531 (ebook)
Subjects: LCSH: Dual enrollment—United States. | English language—Rhetoric—Study and teaching (Higher) | English language—Composition and exercises—Study and teaching (Higher) | Teachers—Training of—United States. | High school students—Education (Higher)—United States. | College credits—United States.
Classification: LCC LC146.54 .D83 2022 (print) | LCC LC146.54 (ebook) | DDC 371.2/1973—dc23/eng/20220617
LC record available at https://lccn.loc.gov/2022019873
LC ebook record available at https://lccn.loc.gov/2022019874

Cover photograph by Casie Moreland

To the memory of Katie McWain.

Greg, Gabe, and Luke; Myla and Dutch—
this book is also for you.

CONTENTS

FOREWORD

Composition in a New Light and a Different Place

Christine Farris

A kaleidoscope uses angled mirrors to create a symmetrical reflection of an object. With each twist, the initial image is disrupted and transformed. New patterns emerge, no two alike. Fragmentation and change are built into a kaleidoscope—an apt metaphor for the complex workings of dual enrollment (DE) composition, as its offerings multiply, producing new arrangements and challenges.

Over a decade has passed since Kristine Hansen and I published our National Council of Teachers of English (NCTE) volume, *College Credit for Writing in High School: The "Taking Care of" Business.* It has been almost that long since the Conference on College Composition and Communication (CCCC) task force I chaired surveyed the membership and authored the first 2012 CCCC "Statement on Dual Credit/Concurrent Enrollment Composition: Policy and Best Practices," revised in 2019 as a joint statement with the NCTE, Two-Year College English Association (TYCA), and Council of Writing Program Administrators (CWPA).

In that time, the number of dual enrollment partnerships has skyrocketed. While some programs originated as alternatives to AP and others as jumpstart opportunities, dual enrollment, broadly conceived, has been folded into "college and career readiness" initiatives nationwide. In efforts to increase college enrollment, lower tuition costs, and shorten the pathway to degrees and jobs, more state policymakers have mandated that dual enrollment courses be available and/or required for high school graduation. Pearson, the textbook and test publisher, has launched Accelerated Pathways, brokering access to thousands of online dual enrollment courses and providing "success coaching" and "transfer assistance." With this growth has come more responsibilities across the high school–college divide and challenges posed by the social

https://doi.org/10.7330/9781646422531.c000a

and economic inequities laid bare by the effects of the COVID-19 pandemic. Students are struggling to stay on track, and college enrollments have dropped.

Christine Denecker and Casie Moreland's book examines what the twists of the dual enrollment kaleidoscope have wrought. The twenty-one authors' findings and conclusions, drawn from DE research and practice in a variety of state and institutional settings, move beyond the concern most often raised in decades past—whether the high school version of composition is correspondingly "rigorous"—to contend with the intended and unintended consequences of dual enrollment's rapid growth.

This collection demonstrates how dual enrollment throws into relief issues that were there all along: the purpose of first-year writing in the liberal arts curriculum and beyond, inequitable access, unfair labor practices, and the vexed relationship between high school and college English. Authors investigate areas with serious implications for DE's future, including the possibility that dual enrollment courses, imbedded in a larger web of inequities, impede rather than facilitate successful transition to college (Schneider, chapter 1, this volume).

In the early 1990s, when I became the faculty liaison for composition in Indiana University's Advance College Project, I knew that the aim—a mirror image of the campus course in high school—was unrealizable. By then I had worked in a variety of programs aimed at bridging disciplines, institutions, and grade levels. I learned, often the hard way, that these initiatives work best when there is willingness to understand the different cultures in which we teach and acknowledgment of the many factors that combine, like so many shards of glass in a kaleidoscope, to shape students' writing proficiency and long-term academic success, not just acquisition of credits.

In my thirty-year association with dual enrollment, what emerges time and again—whether I'm working with DE teachers and students, reviewing new DE programs in my state, or reading the chapters in this volume—is the indispensability of professional development for high school instructors responsible for teaching college writing courses. Policymakers committed to low-cost K–16 reforms often disregard differences in curriculum and expertise across the high school–college divide, particularly regarding general education courses like English that "anyone can teach" and that can be gotten "out of the way" to make room for career preparation.

Higher education accreditation organizations are now requiring that DE instructors hold master's degrees or graduate certificates in the content area they teach, a commendable move that should include coverage of tuition. In addition to graduate courses (available online from many vendors), partnering postsecondary institutions need to provide professional development particular to each dual enrollment course: comprehensive, discipline-specific, faculty-led training and mentoring, not just generic one-day orientation to DE policies.

I have been fortunate to work with an established forty-year-old dual enrollment program. Indiana University partners with 170 high schools across Indiana and four other states. It is accredited by the National Alliance of Concurrent Enrollment Partnerships (NACEP), which it helped found in 1999. The program subsidizes DE composition teachers' participation in a week-long summer seminar (with available graduate course credit) that familiarizes them with a required sequence of assignments focused on analysis of texts typical of disciplines across the curriculum. During the week, presentations by veteran DE teachers go a long way to assure teachers that they and their students can handle the curriculum.

In emphasizing collaboration over "re-education," annual review days for all DE composition teachers have become mini-conferences, featuring sessions led by experienced DE teachers who share successful classroom strategies and innovative approaches to reading and writing assignments.

Teachers often report that their experience with dual enrollment has changed the way they teach their other English courses. Many have told me how they incorporate source-based analysis and argument in their ninth through eleventh grade classes. As several authors in this volume suggest, we should not wait until the end of high school to introduce skills and habits of mind that ease the transition to college-level work. Furthermore, DE need not be the only venue in which high school and college English faculty collaborate on a coherent reading and writing curriculum.

To that end, in the last decade I've been involved in several professional development projects not connected to DE. In two summer school sessions, I arranged clusters of graduate and undergraduate courses that brought together high school teachers, English TAs, and pre-service education majors to read the same texts, design writing assignments, respond to student papers, and research pedagogical issues while they taught, tutored, and observed composition classes.

I also co-directed a two-year project with ninth through eleventh grade English and history teachers in high schools the state had identified as "underperforming," based on the low number of college-bound graduates. In tandem with Common Core revisions to state standards for English/language arts, we designed pairings of literary and "informational" nonfiction texts that raised compelling questions addressed in a series of low-stakes writing tasks (Farris). Local collaborations of this sort, I believe, can benefit teachers and students as much as, if not more than, pushing college back into high school.

While comparability studies of college admission and completion and studies of writing proficiency are built into the justification for and continuation of DE programs, I hope that the proliferation of dual enrollment in a multitude of settings continues to prompt scholarship *specific to composition studies*, to which, as Denecker and Moreland argue, the field as a whole must pay attention.

I hope to see more teacher accounts and formal studies that explore, for instance, how younger students respond to aspects of the curriculum that differentiate college from high school, such as analysis and evaluation of ideas in difficult texts. I want to know more about how dual enrollment teachers revise their traditional role from that of broker for college standards they think lie ahead to that of facilitator of inquiry in the here and now of a college course. Such investigations matter in efforts to generate more state and institutional support, not just for unfettered expansion of dual enrollment but for the development of quality instruction that meets student needs for the long game, particularly if dual enrollment is replacing other first-year support programs on campus.

As the CCCC Policy Statement and David Jolliffe (xii) suggested a decade ago, the fact that more students begin college with first-year composition completed calls for a different sort of advanced writing course or at least transition-to-college workshops. The field needs to more fully acknowledge these changes in college culture, and our journals and conferences need to make successful models available as, like it or not, college credit for writing in high school becomes the new normal.

WORKS CITED

Conference on College Composition and Communication. "Joint Position Statement on Dual Enrollment in Composition." CCCC, 2019. https://cccc.ncte.org/cccc/resources/positions/dualenrollment. Accessed July 25, 2020.

Conference on College Composition and Communication. "Statement on Dual Credit/Concurrent Enrollment Composition: Policy and Best Practices." CCCC, 2012. https://cccc.ncte.org/cccc/resources/positions/dualcredit. Accessed December 14, 2012.

Farris, Christine. "Reclaiming English's Disciplinary Responsibility in the Transition from High School to College." In *Improving Outcomes: Disciplinary Writing, Local Assessment, and the Aims of Fairness*, edited by Diane Kelly-Riley and Norbert Elliot. MLA, 2021, pp. 121–132.

Hansen, Kristine, and Christine R. Farris, eds. *College Credit for Writing in High School: The "Taking Care of" Business.* NCTE, 2010.

Jolliffe, David. "Foreword: Tough Questions for Thoughtful Educators." In *College Credit for Writing in High School: The "Taking Care of" Business*, edited by Kristine Hansen and Christine R. Farris, NCTE, 2010, pp. vii–xiii.

ACKNOWLEDGMENTS

Over the past several years, we have worked with others to foster and participate in a Composition Studies Dual Enrollment community through the CCCC DE Special Interest Group, DE workshop, and DE Comp listserv. This edited collection is an outgrowth of that community and all those who discuss, research, advocate for, and critically evaluate dual enrollment's place in composition studies. We want to acknowledge and thank that community for inspiring, supporting, and challenging us in compiling this edited collection.

Specifically, we want to thank the collection contributors; we appreciate the perspectives their voices add to this work, and we are grateful for the time they invested in this project. Thanks, too, goes to Christine Farris, as well as Keith Miller and Shirley Rose—not only for providing the foreword and afterword (respectively) to this collection but also for their own contributions (published and unpublished) to the nascent academic conversation on dual enrollment.

The process required many hands, and we are grateful for the guidance of Rachael Levay (acquisitions editor), the peer reviewers who provided rich feedback, and all those who touched this project from an administrative standpoint. We would also like to acknowledge the University of Findlay, Western Oregon University, and Willamette ESD for their continued recognition and support of our scholarship.

Most important, we want to thank the DE composition students who are the center of the DE kaleidoscope. It is their image that brings into focus and gives purpose to this conversation.

THE DUAL ENROLLMENT KALEIDOSCOPE

Introduction
THE DUAL ENROLLMENT KALEIDOSCOPE

Christine Denecker and Casie Moreland

To be honest, we are not entirely sure how we feel about dual enrollment (DE). That might seem like an odd confession given that DE is the focus of much of our scholarly and professional efforts. On the one hand, we see in DE the promise of academic and social access for marginalized students, as well as the opportunity to re-envision and reinvigorate secondary education. Ideally, we see in DE the possibility of achieving a robust K–16+ continuum where instructors work collaboratively across artificial boundaries of high school and college to provide engaging, challenging, and relevant learning opportunities that will enrich lives, economies, and communities. On the other hand, we also see the potential for DE to contribute to political pandering, watered-down curriculum, credits for dollars, and "turf wars" as universities feel forced to cede courses to their secondary counterparts. Simply put, DE and the responses it evokes are complicated. Its perceived as well as actual repercussions vary as much as its names (e.g., Dual Credit, Concurrent Enrollment, Early College High School), its modes of delivery (at the college, online, in the high school), and those who teach it (college professors, adjunct instructors, high school teachers). To be clear, DE should not be confused with Advanced Placement (AP) or International Baccalaureate (IB), which also deliver college-level curricula. The difference is that (at least conceptually) DE courses *are* actual college courses, not just "college-level" courses.

In terms of first-year composition (FYC), DE has the complexity of a kaleidoscope's refractions: it is here, there, and everywhere. And as it grows, DE is blurring, or to borrow from Christie Toth, making more "porous" those theoretical and physical spaces between high school and college education. That statement stands—not as an alarmist's view but as a fact. Those of us who work with or in DE FYC bear witness to the

https://doi.org/10.7330/9781646422531.c000b

steady migration of college composition courses into the high school experience. In Kristine Hansen and Christine Farris's 2010 edited collection, *College Credit for Writing in High School*, Miles McCrimmon asks: "What if college-level writing truly extended its territoriality into high school" (222)? Ten years later, McCrimmon's question is no longer a "what if." DE FYC is happening. What is missing is the intentionality behind McCrimmon's question. In other words, what if composition studies took a more proactive role in shaping the DE FYC narrative?

The September 2020 special issue of *Teaching English in the Two-Year College* is a good step in that direction; however, the decade-long gap between major publications such as *College Credit for Writing in High School* (which is not solely about DE) and the 2020 "Dual Credit Programs" issue of *TETYC* suggests that DE FYC conversations continue to remain marginal among writing program administrators (WPAs) and English department chairs. That is not to say that other studies and manuscripts on DE are nonexistent; a list of "relevant research" in the field accompanies the Conference on College Composition and Communication's (CCCC's) "Joint Position Statement on Dual Enrollment in Composition." A closer look at that list, though, reveals that of the thirty-seven manuscripts included, just ten focus on DE composition—the rest are broader and more generalized in scope. Similarly, just six DE composition presentations were part of the 2019 CCCC program (one of those presentations was eventually canceled); likewise, the proposal for a 2019 DE composition workshop was rejected and a subsequent workshop was accepted then dis-invited when COVID concerns caused the 2021 conference to be scaled back. Considering Joyce Locke Carter's remarks in 2016 that "it's not hard to imagine a world where FYC no longer takes place in college" (384), those of us living DE composition daily have, frankly, hoped for more engagement from the field.

We believe that those in DE FYC spaces should not be the only ones discussing DE's impact on composition studies: the field cannot actively shape the narrative if it does not participate in the conversation. DE, with its many facets, serves to hyper-illuminate struggles, inconsistencies, and ongoing challenges within FYC. It disrupts long-held beliefs of who should take and who should teach college writing. It forces us to reflect on the place of writing instruction within the academy and the purposes as well as the value of first-year composition. Most important, DE forces the field into the uncomfortable position of acknowledging other ways of defining and carrying out college composition instruction. These refracted images merge to form the DE "kaleidoscope." Just as kaleidoscopes reconfigure objects in their view, so too does DE change our "vision" of FYC. This edited collection serves as a starting point for elevating the voices of those doing DE work—those who historicize, legitimize, scrutinize, critically analyze, align, and assess DE composition. It serves as a call for readers to recognize that DE FYC conversations are, in fact, FYC conversations that affect the entire field.

For those new to the DE FYC conversation, it may be surprising to note that as early as 1937, the University of Chicago admitted high school sophomores to college in a unique program meant "to accelerate the educational process" (College in High School, *Expanding* 5). College writing in particular has been available as a DE choice since the first formalized program began in 1955, which is explored more deeply in Moreland's *The Impossible Plan: A History of Dual Enrollment in an Era of White Complacency*. Three years earlier, the Ford Foundation's Fund for the Advancement of Education sponsored an "Advanced Standing" program at Kenyon College in Ohio (Jones), which eventually became the first Advanced Placement (AP) program; however, as other institutions developed their own Advanced Standing programs, DE emerged as an alternative choice (Radcliffe et al. 19). By the mid-1960s, Simon's Rock, a Massachusetts women's school, merged the junior and senior years of high school with the first two years of college; successful students graduated with both high school diplomas and associate's degrees (College in High School, *Expanding* 5). This "middle-college" concept grew in the New York region in the 1970s, and by the 1980s, dual enrollment "began to take shape and expand" with Minnesota leading the way (6). Helen J. Estes published the first scholarly manuscript on DE programs in 1959, but thirty years passed before any serious academic attention was given to DE writing instruction. It wasn't until 1991 that the field would take a critical look at DE's impact on composition. That year, in *Writing Program Administrators* articles, David E. Schwalm called dual enrollment "a threat to our student's chances of developing college-level literacy" (51), and Michael J. Vivion suggested increased scrutiny of DE writing courses (56–57).

It would be another twenty years (2010) before Hansen and Farris's groundbreaking collection in which Chris Anson argued that DE options were "already firmly established in the U.S. educational system and are growing in popularity" (247). As of 2021, all states offered some form of DE (Kelley and Rowland Woods n.p.). A recent longitudinal study by the US Department of Education estimates that about 34 percent, or one-third, of all American high school students participate in dual enrollment options (Shivji and Wilson 1). According to Katherine

Mangan, "The number of part-time students under 18 enrolled in community colleges nearly doubled" from 2007 to 2017, and "most of those were students enrolled in high school" (n.p.). On average, nearly 15 percent of all current incoming community college students are dual enrolled: this from a 2017 Community College Research Center study (Fink et al. 1). And while the numbers are rising in two-year institutions, the college-in-high-school trend is also impacting four-year institutions, resulting in "declining enrollments in first-year courses in core subjects" (Mangan n.p.). Furthermore, if Texas can serve as a barometer for national DE growth, then we should all take notice. In a fifteen-year span (2000–2015), the number of high school students participating in dual enrollment rose 650 percent (College in High School, *Unlocking* 6). Admittedly, this increase in participation reflects the Texas state mandate that all high schools provide twelve credit hours of college to high school students. However, the approach in Texas is not unique, as at least "twelve states require all high schools and eligible postsecondary public institutions to provide dual enrollment opportunities" (Education Commission of the States n.p.). And in 2019, eighteen governors included earning college credit while in high school as part of their annual addresses (College in High School, *Unlocking* 4). In some states, students have the opportunity to graduate from high school with an associate degree or job-related certification at little or no cost (Barshay n.p.).

Statistics do not exist on the numbers of students enrolled in DE worldwide. However, DE stretches beyond US borders. Organizations such as the International Partnership of Education Research and Communication (IPERC) match American higher education institutions with international high schools to provide dual enrollment opportunities around the globe. For example, St. Louis University partners with IPERC to provide an Advanced College Credit Pathway (AACP) for international students. Through this pathway, students "earn transferable college credits while attending high school in their home country" (IPERC n.p.).

The recent rapid expansion of DE should come as no surprise, since DE is marketed as a way "to reduce time needed to get a degree, save money on college costs, and prepare students for collegiate success" (Thompson n.p.). In addition, research demonstrates positive impacts on college enrollment and degree completion among students who participate in DE (College in High School, *Recommendations* 1). However, DE as a whole lacks consistency in its design, management, and delivery (Fink et al.; Speroni; Education Commission of the States; Weissman).

Variance exists among states regarding eligibility for student participation, with widely differing parameters for age, grade level, and grade point average. Likewise, the cost of DE (and who bears that cost) differs per state, as do mandates regarding professional development of instructors and accreditation (Fink et al.; Education Commission of the States). Recorded accounts of current disparities in enrollment for students of color also exist, which counters proponents' claims of DE as a way to grant college access for "all" (Moreland and Miller). In 2019, the National Center for Education Statistics reported a higher number of white and Asian students with college-educated parents taking DE courses as compared to their peer groups (Shivji and Wilson 1). Similarly, in 2018, the US Department of Education's Office for Civil Rights revealed disparity in enrollment, with higher numbers among white students as compared to African American and Latino students (Fink n.p.). Granted, NACEP provides best practices for when DE delivery is in the high school setting and advocates "prioritizing equity in dual enrollment" (NACEP n.p.). Still, just 131 programs are accredited nationally ("NACEP Accredited Programs" n.p.). Furthermore, when it comes to DE composition, research demonstrates that "much variation is evident particularly in regard to *who* is responsible for oversight and *what* oversight entails" (Stancliff et al. 3, original emphasis). And while equity and oversight in DE programs need not be mutually exclusive, the former becomes an even heavier lift when the latter is not in place.

The confounding aspects of who is responsible for DE FYC and what oversight requires, coupled with the dearth of DE FYC scholarship, is where we (Chris and Casie) found ourselves when writing our dissertations: Chris in 2007 and Casie in 2018. Chris's decade of teaching high school English before transitioning to postsecondary writing instruction had a marked impact on her entrance into the academy and DE composition work in particular. Since the initial courses she taught in her faculty position were on-campus DE writing courses (then called Post-Secondary Enrollment Options), she was, to borrow from Katie McWain, concurrently "inhabiting high school and college discourse communities" (421). In many ways, like her students, she was transitioning from high school to college writing instruction in real time. Furthermore, as she simultaneously worked on her PhD, she found herself living out much of what she was reading in volume 1 of Patrick Sullivan and Howard Tinberg's *What Is "College-Level" Writing?* Like Merrill Davies, she had to acknowledge moments of high school teaching when she had been "Whistling in the Dark." During faculty meetings, her mantra was that of Peter Kittle: "It's Not the High School Teachers' Fault." And "Bam," the title of Amanda Winalski's contribution to Sullivan and Tinberg's collection, best summed up her experience moving from high school to college writing instruction. In short, like Winalski, she "had to reevaluate [her] definition of a successful college writer" (307). The experience led to her dissertation, "Toward Seamless Transition? Dual Enrollment and the Composition Classroom." During her research, Chris relied heavily on experience, the language of the secondary/postsecondary writing "divide," generalized DE scholarship, and Rhonda Catron's 2001 dissertation, "Dual Credit English: Program History, Review, and Recommendations," due to the gap in DE composition research.

For her part, Casie began teaching DE FYC as an adjunct faculty member in 2011. Without teacher training, Casie sought scholarship pertaining to best practices for dual enrollment FYC, as she quickly found that teaching writing in a high school setting can be quite different from teaching FYC on a college campus. In a search for scholarship that might support her teaching efforts, she found fewer than thirty sources, eleven of which were in Hansen and Farris's landmark collection. Fast forward to 2016. Casie began working on her dissertation, a project that questioned the historical origins of DE within the context of the Civil Rights Movement and the *Brown v. Board of Education* I and II rulings of 1954 and 1955: where did the programs begin? Why did they begin? Who were the programs intended to serve? Who benefited monetarily? What were the gateways and barriers to participation among students? While Casie found that dual enrollment writing courses had been available for what is now over sixty years, DE composition had never been the focus of historical narratives in rhetoric and composition studies. Some composition historians (Thomas P. Miller, Nan Johnson, James Berlin, Robert Connors, and others) make nods to the development of Advanced Placement courses, the Committee of Ten (set to standardize the high school curriculum), and other details that certainly influenced the eventual development of DE FYC; however, DE composition as its own entity is absent from our field's history. Thus, as Casie wrote her dissertation, she found herself facing a difficult task: entering a conversation with huge gaps.

To be fair, the field's national organizations—National Council of Teachers of English (NCTE), Council of Writing Program Administrators (CWPA), and Conference of College Composition and Communication (CCCC)—have all issued statements on the preparation and support of dual enrollment writing instructors, specifically in regard to teacher qualifications, discipline-specific training, ongoing professional development, and site visits. These statements certainly equate to "action" versus a "call" *if* put into practice. *But that is a big if.* As much as these statements have the best intentions, no evidence or assurance exists that the guidelines they contain are being integrated among the already labor-intensive responsibilities of teaching and administering writing instruction. So we are left to ask: who is carrying out DE FYC training, professional development, and oversight? Where this work is being done, how are these faculty being compensated, supported, and even trained themselves? Is the field ready to take the next step of professionalizing DE FYC by "lobbying for monetary compensation . . . and protecting them [DE instructors] from exploitation" (Denecker, "Closing" 83)? Are we ready to include the voices of DE instructors "in disciplinary conversations at institutional and national levels" (83)?

For us, the marginalization of DE FYC is indicative of the positionality of those who most often carry out the work: community college instructors, high school teachers, contingent faculty, and teaching assistants—voices not often central to academic conversations in our field. Their perspectives, like variegated patterns in a kaleidoscopic lens, shift the shape and the reality of DE FYC. It is in examining the reconfigured shards of their perceptions that a new amalgamated picture of first-year writing emerges. Thus, we open this collection with the argument that DE first-year composition courses must be viewed from diverse vantage points to assemble a clearer picture of DE's current and future impact on composition studies.

OVERVIEW OF CHAPTERS

In section one, Perspectives of the "Gap": Theorizing the Divide, authors explore the long-held tensions between high school and college writing and use DE as a vehicle for questioning the ways the gap has been perpetuated, mythologized, bridged, and sustained. In chapter 1, Barbara Schneider utilizes a social justice lens to scrutinize whether DE is truly closing the gap among socioeconomic groups through equitable composition offerings. She concludes that educators, politicians, and taxpayers may be better served to reconsider DE and shift the focus away from DE to improvements that might benefit *all* students early in their education (pre-K) instead of *some* students during later levels of learning (secondary schools).

For their part, Amy Lueck and Brice Nordquist trace and theorize the high school–college "gap" in their chapter. Specifically, the authors use the lens of DE to consider how the historical and perpetual rearticulation of secondary/postsecondary relations extends into current debates regarding DE FYC where scholars argue for the need to work across the divide, warn against the proliferation of DE, or claim the impossibility of bridging the high school–college writing gap. Within these complex and often conflicted discussions, the authors argue, the divide is re-inscribed on all sides.

In chapter 3, Joseph Jones reflects chronologically on the historical, curricular, material, and political spaces between school and college. In doing so, Jones demonstrates how Arthur Applebee's explanation of the "common school" is reprised through DE FYC and argues that college English has "long imposed" itself on high school English. Furthermore, Jones contends that while dual enrollment certainly manifests new iterations of the high school–college divide, DE also creates opportunities for genuine secondary/postsecondary collaboration.

In section two, Perspectives of Alignment: Building High School–College Partnerships, contributors investigate the unique types of professional development used to support and align the work of DE FYC faculty in their various spaces of instruction. In chapter 4, Katie McWain, Jackie Hoermann-Elliott, and Jennifer Hadley discuss the "careful tightrope walk" of DE observations. The authors—who hail from both secondary (Hadley) and postsecondary institutions (McWain and Hoermann-Elliott)—argue that site observations grounded in shared goals can be productive tools for supporting cross-level collaboration in DE partnerships and for examining the ways postsecondary knowledge has historically held privilege over secondary knowledge. By drawing on experiences in a state and institutional context, McWain and her colleagues posit that site observations provide a means whereby WPAs and other DE administrators might better understand and even ameliorate the problematic optics of DE partnerships.

Melanie Burdick and Jane Greer's chapter 5 builds on the previous work of both Denecker and McWain to explore the ways DE teachers respond to professional development opportunities. Their work—a mixed method study of surveys and focus groups with high school teachers—includes narratives that demonstrate how secondary teachers navigate a complex landscape of professional development opportunities in search of support for the DE writing instruction they are charged with providing. Burdick and Greer's findings support literature that calls for increased theoretical and pedagogical training for DE teachers who are left to navigate the differences between the demands of high school English and those of college writing.

Scott Campbell follows with an exploration of how DE FYC has the potential to shift what defines composition as a field "even beyond" high school contexts. Campbell uses assemblage theory to analyze the unique positions of contingent DE faculty and argues that academic contingency (or edge labor) is a factor of curricular drift and de-territorialization. In questioning the "elasticity" of FYC, Campbell claims that DE can help describe FYC, not just deliver it. He urges those in the field to recognize that the teachers of DE FYC, like most contingent faculty, pursue goals and define productivity in ways that make use of, but are not subsumed by, expectations of their tenure-line counterparts.

In chapter 7, Annie S. Mendenhall and David Gehler describe the perspectives of college DE faculty who work in high schools and examine how these instructors face material and social challenges to meet the student learning outcomes (SLOs) of DE FYC. According to Mendenhall and Gehler, the challenges these instructors face may have less to do with their knowledge of high school spaces and more to do with the sense of isolation they feel in carrying out DE FYC work. Likewise, since traveling DE faculty operate in college and high school spaces simultaneously, their experiences provide general insight into trends reshaping FYC instruction.

In section three, Perspectives of Legitimacy: Is DE FYC Really FYC?, authors provide various viewpoints on the legitimacy and repercussions of DE as a way to earn credit for college writing. Dominic Ashby and Jill Parrott's work presents a fresh discussion of issues of equivalency versus identicality of DE FYC and probes stereotypically held perceptions and biases about dual enrollment. They base their claims on a comparative analysis of aggregated assessment data from traditional and DE writing courses derived from a region in Kentucky that includes seven of the thirty most poverty-stricken counties in the United States. The authors argue that DE writing courses embedded at high schools cannot possibly provide an *identical* experience to that which occurs on college campuses. However, they go on to say that DE FYC could provide an *equivalent* educational experience based on quality instruction, rigor, and outcomes.

In chapter 9, Miles McCrimmon provides examples of how DE is often devalued and utilizes the success of Reynolds Advance College Academies (J. Sargeant Reynolds Community College) to advocate for DE composition programs. McCrimmon details surveys from DE alumni and argues that the relocation of FYC into high school spaces should be embraced instead of feared, as the move might serve to expand composition's reach and influence.

In chapter 10, Tyler Branson considers how DE policies fit into the broader public discourse about education in the United States. Using a policy lens, Branson details findings from his research as a participant-observer in an urban Ohio DE composition classroom. There, he found that instructors and students engage in complex day-to-day rhetorical negotiations to navigate, enforce, and often resist DE policies in meaningful ways.

Cornelia Paraskevas and Leigh Graziano outline legislation and review the details of the Willamette Promise—one of Oregon's regional dual enrollment programs—in their contribution. Offering replicable practices for DE FYC programs that ensure equity for teachers and students, the authors suggest taking a social justice approach to DE through the use of a proficiency-based assessment model for college writing to ensure equity.

In section four, Perspectives of Student Success: DE FYC for All?, contributors utilize the DE FYC lens to interrogate DE's claims of access for all from various vantage points, including state, historical, and student perspectives. Nancy Knowles opens this section by providing a different perspective from the other side of the state of Oregon. Instead of simply defining DE "success" as student matriculation to college (as some scholars do), Knowles teases out the complexity of this claim by examining the results of Oregon's Eastern Promise. Her findings—which demonstrate low pass rates among DE writers—contrast with DE success narratives in which high school students flourish in DE spaces and then matriculate to college. Knowles's research leads her to argue that since DE programs are not going away and success is not always apparent, it is especially important that rhetoric and composition studies engage with DE FYC conversations.

In chapter 13, Erin D. Scott-Stewart focuses on DE students' feelings about themselves as writers. Using a mixed methods approach, Scott-Stewart provides evidence of how former DE students experience FYC curriculum. Specifically, she measures DE students' self-efficacy in writing as compared to peers from other credit pathways. Ultimately, her findings suggest a relationship between race/ethnicity on performance in DE writing courses.

Finally, Anna Bogen explores the defensive posture of those in the field regarding DE FYC. Bogen posits that the defensive approach is an untenable one, as scholars have yet to truly define FYC as a larger entity. She then gives voice to the struggles of high school DE FYC teachers as they grapple with perceptions of professional legitimacy among their postsecondary writing instructor peers. With a focus on notions of "shame" and "blame," Bogen uses community college DE student responses to demonstrate how students are often caught in the middle of the college writing debate.

As the chapters in this edited collection demonstrate, DE FYC is complicated and variegated. The DE FYC conversation has surprisingly deep roots and even deeper gaps. It is a conversation that continues to evolve. It is a conversation that warrants attention. As colleges vie for student enrollment, DE has become grounds for recruitment. In fact, the Education Advisory Board (EAB) lists dual enrollment first on its recommendations for "How to Retain and Recruit Six Student Populations" and advises community colleges in particular to "*capitalize on the double-edged sword of dual enrollment*" (Hussak n.p., original emphasis). EAB even highlights the tactic of one college that has made "dual enrollment part of the default curriculum for all local high school students" (n.p.). As previously mentioned, in some states, DE students are graduating from high school with associate degrees ("Record Number"; Kimberling). To that point, the University of North Georgia reported a record number of DE students earning associate degrees in May 2020—a 42 percent increase from 2019 (Devine). In Illinois, the Illinois Articulation Initiative (IAI) assures that associate degrees earned by DE students are transferable to public and private schools within the IAI consortium (Kimberling). Spokane Community College in Washington has also seen growth in DE thanks to a 2019 state law that aligns "high school courses with a technology pathway in college" (Ashford n.p.). The result? High school students pursue an associate of applied science degree, which includes an English course (not college composition) "geared to concepts on the job" (n.p.). Similarly, career-tech models are expanding across New York, New Jersey, Texas, Louisiana, Maryland, Connecticut, Rhode Island, Colorado, and Illinois (College in High School, *Expanding* 3).

Alongside these recruitment efforts, the COVID-19 pandemic stands to impact DE growth as well. Uncertainty about high school content delivery, the availability of extracurricular activities, and fears of "falling behind" educationally may drive high school students to pursue dual enrollment opportunities (Ashford n.p.; Kimberling n.p.). According to the American Association of Community Colleges, Montgomery College (Maryland)—which was already "aggressively recruiting" DE participants—saw a 300 percent increase in dual enrollment for fall 2020 as compared to fall 2019 (Ashford n.p.). In terms of summer 2020 numbers, Austin Community College's (Texas) DE enrollment rose 28 percent. At Cuyahoga Community College (Ohio), the increase was 20 percent, and Tallahassee Community College (Florida) saw a 71 percent jump (n.p.). In effect, what may have begun as a subtle paradigmatic shift in education has now intensified.

So where does that leave us? Just as kaleidoscopes reconfigure an image from multiple perspectives, DE FYC provides composition studies with reflecting images of what first-year writing was, is, and can be. As a field, it is our responsibility to examine the refractions, intensify the conversations, and take ownership of the DE FYC narrative.

WORKS CITED

Anson, Chris. "Absentee Landlord or Owner-Tenants? Formulating Standards for Dual-Credit Composition Programs." In *College Credit for Writing in High School: The "Taking Care of" Business*, edited by Kristine Hansen and Christine R. Farris. NCTE, 2010, pp. 245–271.

Ashford, Ellie. "A Surge in Dual Enrollment." *Community College Daily*, American Association of Community Colleges, Sept. 8, 2020. https://www.ccdaily.com/2020/07/a-surge-in-dual-enrollment/. Accessed Sept. 8 2020.

Barshay, Jill. Hechinger Report. "Research on Early College High Schools Indicates They May Pay for Themselves in the Long Run." Feb. 24, 2020. https://hechingerreport.org/research-on-early-college-high-schools-indicates-they-may-pay-for-themselves-in-the-long-run/. Accessed May 11, 2022.

Carter, Joyce Locke. "2016 Chair's Address: Making, Disrupting, Innovating." *College Composition and Communication*, vol. 68, no. 2, 2016, pp. 378–408.

Catron, Rhonda. "Dual Credit English: Program History, Review, and Recommendations." 2001. Virginia Polytechnic Institute and State University, PhD dissertation.

College in High School Alliance. *Expanding New York's College in High School Programs*. College in High School Alliance, Nov. 2020. https://www.bard.edu/news/web-resources/BEC-Expand-College-Whitepaper.pdf, PDF file. Accessed Dec. 1, 2020.

College in High School Alliance. *Recommendations for the Biden-Harris Administration to Support Dual Enrollment and Early College High Schools*. College in High School Alliance, n.d. https://static1.squarespace.com/static/589d0f90ff7c507ac483988e/t/5fce848be80877332032bc52/1607369870255/College+in+High+School+Alliance+Transition+Memo+for+Biden-Harris+Administration.pdf, PDF file.

College in High School Alliance and Level Up Coalition. *Unlocking Potential: A State Policy Roadmap for Equity and Quality in College in High School Programs*. College in High School Alliance and Level Up Coalition, n.d. https://static1.squarespace.com/static/589d0f90ff7c507ac483988e/t/5d9be31d3dc97713cd06b40a/1570497323864/UNLOCKING+POTENTIAL+-+A+State+Policy+Roadmap+for+Equity+and+Quality+in+College+in+High+School+Programs-1.pdf, PDF file.

Conference on College Composition and Communication. "CCCC Position Statement on Preparing Teachers of College Writing." CCCC, 2015. ncte.org/cccc/resources/positions/statementonprep. Accessed Aug. 7. 2019.

Conference on College Composition and Communication. "Joint Position Statement on Dual Enrollment in Composition." CCCC, 2019. https://cccc.ncte.org/cccc/resources/positions/dualenrollment. Accessed July 25, 2020.

Davies, Merrill. "Whistling in the Dark." In *What Is "College Level" Writing?* edited by Patrick Sullivan and Howard Tinberg. NCTE, 2006, pp. 31–35.

Denecker, Christine. "Closing the Gap? A Study into the Professional Development of Concurrent Enrollment Writing Instructors in Ohio." *TETYC*, vol. 48, no. 1, Sept. 2021, pp. 66–87.

Denecker, Christine, "Toward Seamless Transition? Dual Enrollment and the Composition Classroom." 2007. *English Ph.D. Dissertations*. 47. https://etd.ohiolink.edu/apexprod/rws_etd/send_file/send?accession=bgsu1194187966&disposition=inline. Access date June 27, 2022.

Devine, J. K. "Record 20 UNG Dual-Enrolled Students Earned Degrees in 2020." *UNG Newsroom*, University of North Georgia, May 21, 2020. https://ung.edu/news/articles/2020/05/record-20-ung-dual-enrolled-students-graduated-in-spring-2020.php. Accessed Sept. 11, 2020.

Education Commission of the States. "Dual Enrollment: All State Profiles." ECS, 2020. http://ecs.force.com/mbdata/mbprofgroupall?Rep=DEA#:~:text=Participating%20postsecondary%20institution%3A%20Three%20states,are%20primarily%20responsible%20for%20tuition. Accessed Aug. 6, 2019.

Estes, Helen J. "College Level English in High School." *English Journal*, vol. 48, no. 6, 1959, pp. 332–334.

Fink, John. "How Does Access to Dual Enrollment and Advanced Placement Vary by Race and Gender across States?" Community College Research Center, Nov. 5, 2018. https://ccrc.tc.columbia.edu/easyblog/access-dual-enrollment-advanced-placement-race-gender.html. Accessed March 6, 2021.

Fink, John, Davis Jenkins, and Takeshi Yanagiura. "What Happens to Students Who Take Community College 'Dual Enrollment' Courses in High School?" Community College Research Center and National Student Clearinghouse Research Center, Sept. 2017. https://ccrc.tc.columbia.edu/publications/what-happens-community-college-dual-enrollment-students.html. Accessed March 10, 2021.

Hansen, Kristine, and Christine R. Farris, eds. *College Credit for Writing in High School: The "Taking Care of" Business.* NCTE, 2010.

Hussak, Larisa. "How to Retain and Recruit Six Student Populations." Education Advisory Board, June 26, 2018. https://eab.com/insights/blogs/community-college/how-to-recruit-and-retain-six-student-populations/. Accessed Sept. 8, 2020.

International Partnership of Education Research and Communication (IPERC). "Global Higher Education." IPERC, 2020, https://www.iperc.org/highereducation. Accessed Sept. 4, 2020.

Jones, Joseph. "The Beginnings of AP and the Ends of First-Year College Writing." *College Credit for Writing in High School: The "Taking Care of" Business*, edited by Kristine Hansen and Christine Farris. NCTE, 2010, pp. 43–67.

Kelley, Bryan, and Julie Rowland Woods. "50-State Comparison: Dual/Concurrent Enrollment Policies." *Education Commission of the States*, August 6, 2019. https://www.ecs.org/dual-concurrent-enrollment-policies/. Accessed Aug. 12, 2019.

Kimberling, Ronald C. "Expand Dual Enrollment Programs for Pandemic-Challenged High School Students." *Independent Institute*, Aug. 27, 2020. https://www.independent.org/news/article.asp?id=13234. Accessed Sept. 12, 2020.

Kittle, Peter. "It's Not the High School Teachers' Fault: An Alternative to the Blame Game." In *What Is "College Level" Writing?* edited by Patrick Sullivan and Howard Tinberg. NCTE, 2006, pp. 134–145.

Mangan, Katherine. "Rise in Dual-Enrollment Courses May Help Community Colleges, but Minority Students? Not as Much." *Chronicle of Higher Education*, Feb. 7, 2019. https://www.chronicle.com/article/Rise-in-Dual-Enrollment/245642. Accessed Aug. 7, 2019.

McCrimmon, Miles. "Contesting the Territoriality of 'Freshman English': The Political Ecology of Dual Enrollment." In *College Credit for Writing in High School: The "Taking Care of" Business*, edited by Kristine Hansen and Christine R. Farris. NCTE, 2010, pp. 208–226.

McWain, Katie. "Finding Freedom at the Composition Threshold: Learning from the Experiences of Dual Enrollment Teachers." *Teaching English in the Two Year College*, vol. 45, no. 4, 2018, pp. 406–424.

Moreland, Casie. *The Impossible Plan: A History of Dual Enrollment in an Era of White Complacency.* SUNY, forthcoming.

Moreland, Casie, and Keith D. Miller. "The Triumph of Whiteness: Dual Credit Courses and Hierarchical Racism in Texas." In *Haunting Whiteness: Rhetorics of Whiteness in a*

"Post-Racial" Era, edited by Tammie Kennedy, Joyce Middleton, and Krista Ratcliffe. Southern Illinois UP, 2016, pp. 182–194.
National Alliance of Concurrent Enrollment Partnerships. "NACEP Accredited Programs." http://www.nacep.org/nacep-accredited-programs/. Accessed July 28, 2020.
National Alliance of Concurrent Enrollment Partnerships. www.nacep.org/. Accessed July 5, 2022.
Radcliffe, Shirley A., Winslow R. Hatch, and Office of Education (DHEW), Washington, DC. *Advanced Standing: New Dimensions in Higher Education, Number 8.* ERIC Clearinghouse, 1961.
"Record Number of Students Earn Two Diplomas." *The Republic: AZ Central*, May 19, 2015. www.azcentral.com/story/news/local/phoenix/2015/05/19/record-number-students-earn-diplomas-cbt/27407173/. Accessed Aug. 7, 2019.
Schwalm, David E. "High School–College Dual Enrollment." *Journal of the Council of Writing Program Administrators*, vol. 15, no. 1–2, 1991, pp. 51–54.
Shivji, Azim, and Sandra Wilson. "Dual Enrollment: Participation and Characteristics." US Department of Education, Washington, DC. National Center for Education Statistics, 2019.
Speroni, Cecilia. "High School Dual Enrollment Programs: Are We Fast-Tracking Students Too Fast? An NCPR Working Paper." *National Center for Postsecondary Research*, Dec. 2011, pp. 1–72.
Stancliff, Michael, Erin Whittig, Lisa McIntyre, Shirley Rose, and Duane Roen. "Collaborative Assessment of Dual Enrollment: The View from Arizona." *Journal of Writing Assessment*, vol. 10, no. 1, 2017, pp. 1–13. journalofwritingassessment.org/article.php?article=117. Accessed July 20, 2019.
Sullivan, Patrick, and Howard Tinberg, eds. *What Is "College-Level" Writing?* NCTE, 2006.
Teaching English in the Two-Year College, vol. 48, no. 1, September 2020. Special Issue: Dual Credit Programs, editors Caitlin Larracey and Holly Hassel.
Thompson, Alec. "Dual Enrollment's Expansion: Cause for Concern." *National Education Association*, 2019. www.nea.org/home/71701.htm. Accessed July 20, 2019.
Toth, Christie. "Unmeasured Engagement: Two-Year College English Faculty and Disciplinary Professional Organizations." *Teaching English in the Two-Year College*, vol. 14, no. 4, 2014, pp. 335–353.
Vivion, Michael J. "High School–College Dual Enrollment and Composition Program." *Journal of the Council of Writing Program Administrators*, vol. 15, no. 1–2, 1991, pp. 55–60.
Weissman, Sara. "Dual Enrollment Works, but Who Is It Working For?" *Diverse*, April 9, 2020. https://diverseeducation.com/article/172340/. Accessed Sept. 11, 2020.
Winalski, Amanda. "Bam." In *What Is "College Level" Writing?* edited by Patrick Sullivan and Howard Tinberg. NCTE, 2006, pp. 302–308.

SECTION ONE

Perspectives of the "Gap"

Theorizing the Divide

1

AND YET THE GAP PERSISTS

Barbara Schneider

Dual enrollment (DE) is an educational reform movement motivated largely by the desire to efficiently increase the number of college degrees earned by citizens of the United States. Proponents argue for multiple goods accruing to participating students. DE allows for an easier transition from high school to college and makes it more likely that students will attain a college degree; because it distributes the financial burden for those college credits among school districts, schools, and participating community and four-year colleges, DE reduces the overall cost of college to successful participants. This last claim is especially important as it is amplified as a means of increasing the number of low-income and underrepresented minorities who hold degrees. As economist Richard E. Haskell puts it in his analysis of Utah's dual-credit enrollment (DCE) and Early College High School (ECHS) programs, "State level policy directives specify the targeting of underrepresented students for such programs in an effort to narrow the observable and growing education gap contributing to troublesome differences in productivity, income, health and wealth for these students and their current and future households" (144). This appeal to the value of social justice is repeated in program materials, conference proceedings, and justifications for continued funding.

The appeal to social justice resonates particularly with composition instructors, where a disciplinary commitment to open participation, sensitivity to the biases of language, and advocacy for equity are enmeshed in the establishment of the field. And composition feels the impact of DE disproportionately. According to the Texas Phase II study by Trey Miller and his colleagues, composition courses accounted for more than 20 percent of the courses taken by eleventh and twelfth grade students, a full 7 percentage points ahead of history, the closest competition (Miller et al., "Phase II" table 1.2, 36). In the Oregon study, College Algebra had the highest course enrollment, followed by Composition 1,

https://doi.org/10.7330/9781646422531.c001

Trigonometry, Composition II, and History (Pierson, Hodara, and Luke appendix E, table E1). Composition studies, then, has a far greater stake in DE than other fields, both more to gain and more to lose.

In what follows, I propose that DE programs fall short of their claims to reduce the equity gap. This is evidenced through a review of recent statistical studies that examine high school students' attainment of college credit through the lens of social justice to situate composition studies within the national terrain of DE. I then examine three critiques of DE programs that call into question the wisdom of our rapid acceleration of DE programs. None of these studies, however, provides clear direction for writing program administrators who are invested in the social justice claims ostensibly forwarded by these programs. I close by proposing that my claim that the programs fall short be tested locally. I suggest that the disparate impact analysis adapted by Mya Poe and colleagues and Casie Moreland for evaluating the validity of writing assessments be applied to the analysis of program outcomes to gain the clarity needed to make sound judgments regarding the growth of DE.

Advocates for pursuing DE to help realize what some scholars call the "completion agenda"[1] now have multiple studies, many sponsored by state boards regulating higher education, that provide some evidence for these claims. These studies begin to fill the research gap that has led many engaged in composition studies, including myself, Kristine Hansen and colleagues, and others, to be skeptical of these programs. What these statistical studies show is that students who participate in DE programs are indeed more likely than non-participating peers to complete both a high school and a college degree and to reduce the time it takes to earn that degree. Some of the studies include ECHS, which makes using their results difficult (Berger et al.; Edmunds et al.), but ECHS is not a focus of this study. However, the success of those schools suggests revisions for DE, and I will return to them later.

In a study of Illinois high school students, Bob Blankenberger and his colleagues found that students who participated in dual-credit programs were 7 percent more likely to achieve a postsecondary credential and 8 percent more likely to earn a bachelor's degree, proposing that "the results of this study offer further evidence of the benefits of dual credit participation on postsecondary completion" (260). While DE improved the odds of degree achievement for students at all but the most selective institutions, the impact of DE was most significant for students who began their postsecondary careers at community colleges rather than at more selective institutions. Twenty-eight percent of DE students earned a bachelor's degree compared with 19 percent of their non-DE peers.

Since 40 percent of Illinois students begin their college careers at community colleges, the ability of DE programs to improve degree completion is "crucial to meeting state completion goals" (260). The study's differentiation of results for types of postsecondary institutions provides a new level of insight into who stands to benefit the most from DE programs, and it should inform program design and funding decisions.

The Illinois study also revealed that "the smallest impact was found for students starting at very competitive institutions, where the results were not significant" (Blankenberger et al. 260). In fact, depending on the state, some selective schools—public and private—do not accept DE credit or transcript-accepted credits as general electives. Others restrict credit awards to those courses taken on a college campus, the smallest percentage of course offerings nationally; and some defer credit decisions to the student's major department. This is a finding that could have implications for family decision-making as well as for honesty in recruitment.

For example, a student taking a DE first-year writing (FYW) course at a high school in Ohio taught by a qualified high school teacher will not receive any credit if he or she subsequently enrolls at a selective institution, such as Cleveland's Case Western Reserve University: "Any such courses taken prior to the student's graduation from high school must be . . . taken in the company of matriculated college students, and organized and taught by college faculty. In addition, to be considered for transfer credit, such courses must not have been used to fulfill high school graduation requirements" (Case Western University n.p.). In contrast, Ohio public universities must accept DE (known as College Credit Plus, or CCP, in the state) per a state transfer agreement.

Case Western is not alone in its decision to limit the credits it accepts from DE programs. A quick spot-check of *US News and World Report*'s 2018 top ten national universities shows that all of them restrict the acceptance of college credits earned through DE to some degree.[2] DE, then, does not reduce the time to degree and the cost of college for students headed to selective institutions, something not routinely included in recruiting materials for DE programs.

Furthermore, limitations to the Illinois study should be noted. First, the study does not disaggregate how the dual-credit hours were earned—at a high school, at a partner higher education institute, or in an Early College High School. Results from ECHS vary considerably from DE programs, so the inclusion of ECHS data muddles the results. More important, the researchers use race, gender, and household income to create match groups, and their enrollment data show significant participation gaps. In addition, the results are not disaggregated for degree attainment. Decision-makers, therefore, cannot use the Illinois study to determine if DE in that state is closing the equity gap.

In a similar study conducted on data collected from Oregon public high schools, community colleges, and four-year public colleges, US Department of Education researchers note the state's explicit aim to address questions of social justice: "This report also addresses stakeholders' research priorities by presenting findings on equity in participation rates . . . The state has invested extensively in accelerated college credit programs that seek to increase the number of underrepresented students earning college credit" (Pierson et al. 1). The authors differentiate between "dual credit," where students earn both high school and college credit by taking college courses at their high school, and "dual enrollment," where students earn both high school and college credit by taking college courses at a community or four-year college.[3] Only those two categories are included in their analysis, thereby eliminating the variables introduced when ECHS is included. The US Department of Education study also points to increased high school degree and postsecondary enrollment compared with similar students who do not participate in DE programs. The study reports that 71 percent of dual-credit students who graduated from high school enrolled in college compared with 59 percent of all graduates. While that outcome is ostensibly positive, the report highlights the participation gap between white and Black students. Through the use of demographic data from all students enrolled in Oregon high schools and expected to graduate between 2006 and 2013, the study found that 25.7 percent of white men and 33.3 percent of white women participated in DE, while just 10.5 percent of Black men and 17.4 percent Black women participated, as did just 14 percent of Latinx men and 21 percent of Latinx women (Pierson et al.).

TEMPERING THE SUCCESS CLAIMS

The authors of the Oregon study exercise laudable caution in the claims they make for the causal relationship between successful participation in the accelerated programs and subsequent degree completion. In at least two points in the study they note, "This study cannot determine whether dual credit participation contributed directly to these outcomes" (Pierson et al. 15). The "Dual-Credit Education Programs in Texas: Phase II" study does try to identify the causal relationship between participation and college degree attainment (Miller et al., "Phase II").

The Phase II study, conducted by the American Institutes for Research (AIR), is a follow-up to the Phase I study conducted by the RAND Corporation. Two of the leading researchers, Trey Miller and Holly Kosiewicz, participated in both studies; and both studies drew from the same data provided by multiple sources, including Texas public high schools, community colleges, and four-year institutions. The Phase II authors note that the first study mandated a quick turnaround of just six months and was designed to provide information most significantly on the correlation among DE participation, high school graduation, and college enrollment and completion (Miller et al., "Phase II"). The Phase II study was conducted over the course of a year and addressed six areas not fully addressed in the first phase: (1) a causal impact study, (2) a racial disparities study, (3) an HB 505 study, (4) an advising study, (5) an academic rigor study, and (6) a cost study (12). Of those areas of study, items 1 and 2 are of most interest when considering DE as a program aimed at social justice.

The Phase II study provides an important corrective to earlier claims for the extent of improvement in outcomes. Using an econometric approach called an "instrumental variable identification strategy" (Miller et al., "Phase II" 50), the study pursued the same questions as Phase I but sought to determine if DE was the cause of increases in high school graduation, college enrollment, and completion. The Phase I study showed much higher attainment of all three marks for participants (Miller et al., "Interim Report"). Using the causal model, the Phase II study found that high school completion for DE participants was 83.8 percent, while the rate for non-participants was 83.1 percent—a difference not statistically significant in this case (Miller et al., "Phase II"). The causal impact of DE on college enrollment was more positive, with 56.4 percent of participants enrolling in college compared with 54 percent of non-participants enrolling—an increase that is modest but still significant. That causal impact, however, is significant only at the community college level, where DE participants enrolled at 31.5 percent compared with 29 percent for non-participants, and is almost negligible at the four-year level, where the difference between the two groups is just 0.7 percent. College completion, which the study identified as "completing a four- or two-year degree or any certificate program at a public or private nonprofit college in Texas within ten years of a student's junior year of high school" (56), was very modestly improved by participation in DE. Just 1.1 percent of participants were more likely complete a credential than non-participants. All of the other measures—upward transfer from a community college to a four-year college, reduction in time to degree, number of credit hours earned—show similar, very modest, and often not statistically significant improvements for participants.

DISCLOSING THE GAP

More important, using this model to examine the impact of participation for students disaggregated by race and income shows that DE increases college completion for white students by 2.7 percent but does not increase completion for Black and Brown students. The news is even worse for students at an economic disadvantage, where eligibility for free or reduced-price lunch is used as a proxy for low income: "The results suggest that the effect of dual-credit participation varies considerably by the student's economic status, with large positive effects for most outcomes among those who are ineligible [for free lunch] and large negative effects for most outcomes among those who are eligible" (Miller et al., "Phase II" 62). College enrollment increased by 5.5 percent and college completion increased by 4.5 percent for students who are not eligible for free lunch, but "participating in dual-credit education significantly decreases college enrollment by 3.2 percentage points for students and significantly decreases college completion by 6.7 percentage points for free or reduced-price lunch eligible students" (62). In other words, at least in Texas, students who are well supported enjoy much improved outcomes, while those students whose families struggle financially are actually left worse off by participation in DE.

A further analysis of the Texas Phase II data "suggest[s] that the negative results for free and reduced-price lunch eligible students were likely due to the fact that free and reduced-price lunch eligible students were more likely than ineligible students to have lower eighth grade standardized test scores that hindered their success in dual credit education courses" (Miller et al., "Phase II" 62). Alternatively, most eligible students who managed to score at least one standard deviation above the mean benefited from participation. Clearly, the statistics indicate that students who struggle financially have to score significantly better than their wealthier classmates to enjoy the benefits DE can provide.

The researchers also looked at multiple factors to determine the cause of lower participation in DE by students from underrepresented racial and ethnic groups. What they found is that no single factor—not access to DE courses, not academic preparation, not income, not access to Advanced Placement (AP) and International Baccalaureate (IB) coursework, not high schools attended, not access to tuition and fee waivers—can account for the significant gap in participation between white students and racial and ethnic minorities. Difference in access accounts for almost no difference in participation, while each of the other factors accounts for some but never all of the difference. Running a model that accounted for all of the variables "implies that if underrepresented minorities were equally prepared academically, had similar incomes to and attended similar schools as white students, then gaps in DC participation would be quite small" (Miller et al., "Phase II" 30). In other words, if all things were equal, it would close the gap—but all things, of course, are not equal. And not only are they not equal, they are not equitable, and the gap appears to be growing.

What these studies also show is that the very students targeted by these programs—underrepresented minority and low-income students—are not reaping the benefits at the same rate as white students of sufficient economic means. In fact, the gaps between participating cohorts map directly onto the gaps seen in persistence and degree completion at campuses nationwide. According to RAND's interim report, DE participation rates of white students peaked at about 30 percent in 2011 and declined to 26 percent in 2015. DE participation rates of Black students peaked at about 13 percent in 2009 and declined to about 10 percent by 2015. DE participation rates of Hispanic student peaked at about 20 percent in 2011 and declined to approximately 16 percent by 2015 (Miller et al., "Interim Report" 22). For the latest year reported here, 2015, the dual-credit gap between white and Black students in the state of Texas was 16 percent, while the gap between white and Hispanic students was 10 percent. In the Pell report on college participation, we see the gaps replicated on a national scale. Pell's longitudinal study of college participation, 1990–2016, shows the participation gap between white students and underrepresented students not only persisting but growing (Cahalan et al. 34). Pell reports that in 2016, 66 percent of white students enrolled in college immediately after leaving high school, while 59 percent of Hispanic students and 51 percent of Black students did so. That leaves a 7 percent and 15 percent gap, respectively. In 1976, about 41 percent of white students who left high school enrolled in college immediately, while 34 percent of Hispanic students and 33 percent of Black students did so. Those are gaps of 7 and 8 percent, respectively (34).

Couple the evidence that the college participation gap between white and Black students is increasing with the evidence that participation in DE has a negative impact on students whose families struggle financially, and I can only conclude that DE as it now stands provides substantial advantages to white students whose families are financially stable and does not live up to its promises for students already disadvantaged by race or economics.

EFFECTS BEYOND CREDIT ACCUMULATION

The inability of DE programs to narrow the equity gap has drawn fire from critics. Erik Gilbert, in a commentary in the *Chronicle of Higher Education,* argues that the ongoing exodus of the well-supported students from first-year courses is significantly affecting the tenor of general education. Offering an anecdote about the declining enrollment in his first-year honors history course, he attributes the exodus of middle-class white suburban students—those most likely to earn college credit in high school and to attend public universities—to DE. The result, he proposes, is that white middle-class students gain advantage through DE, while students discouraged from participation by socioeconomic factors that limit access and participation must spend more time and money for the same degree. To improve equity, he proposes, "the best, but politically difficult, solution would be to eliminate concurrent enrollment and AP programs" (4). In other words, Gilbert argues, if DE's positive effect for those students embraced by its publicly stated aim is slim and its contribution to a widening gap is observable, it should be halted. While Gilbert is deliberately provocative and guilty of over-generalization, his statement succeeds in focusing attention on unintended consequences. And he is not alone in his critique.

The efficacy and rigor of DE are certainly questioned by the previously mentioned elite institutions that restrict or reject DE credits. The American Association of Colleges and Universities' (AAC&U) critique, made most extensively in the 2012 special issue of *Liberal Education,* also called the rigor of the courses into question, but the studies cited in the present report—particularly the Texas Phase II study—might allay those fears. But according to a 2020 report by Kelly Field in *EducationNext,* concerns about the rigor and quality of dual enrollment courses in Texas have led both the former and current commissioners of higher education to call for a slowdown in the growth of Texas's booming dual enrollment programs. Former commissioner Raymond Paredes told the reporter that "the state 'has oversold the potential of dual credit courses'" (Field n.p.). Current commissioner Harrison Keller noted that because the state of Texas admits the top 10 percent of all graduating seniors to its selective public universities, high school dual enrollment instructors face a real temptation to dilute course content to assure high grades, questioning whether the rigor of the courses was consistently maintained (n.p.).

The AAC&U's critique, however, goes beyond the rigor question. It focuses on three dangers to the future of higher education posed by the completion agenda, in which DE participates: the shift away from the kind of liberal education that prepares students for full participation in a global economy based on knowledge creation, the pressure to employ more and more contingent faculty to deliver first-year courses, and the change in standards from a baccalaureate degree to any postsecondary credential for what counts as an improvement in national educational attainment. This last critique speaks most clearly to the claim for social justice. Contributor Gary Rhoades argues that when the completion agenda counts the attainment of any postsecondary credential as success, it thereby exacerbates the growing equity gap. It does so by diminishing the role of community colleges in preparing students for baccalaureate degrees and emphasizing their role in workforce development: "This has meant promoting a narrow conception of community colleges, which have long been the principal destination of working-class, first-generation, and Latino students . . . The result is that these institutions, which have long been instruments of upward social mobility, are being turned into dead ends for students who seek ultimately to obtain baccalaureate degrees" (n.p.).

Scott Evenbeck and Kathy E. Johnson extend his argument and propose that the progress made in narrowing the equity gap by some higher education institutions through the employment of high-impact practices articulated by Mary-Ann Winkelmes and her colleagues (as well as many other retention measures) is undermined by DE programs that cannot provide the kind of wraparound supports that lead to success for students from the most vulnerable groups. At present, most summer bridge and first-year learning communities are designed to put students in cohort groups that take common general education courses. With increasing numbers of students taking general education courses during high school, campuses are scrambling to find new ways to build curricula for those early start and learning community cohorts. Some students find themselves without a cohort or are only participating in those common courses they haven't yet taken. The sense of community these programs seek to foster can be made more fragile when many students are only half in. This is an outcome, however, that, once recognized, can be amended by local programming.

Low-income students who manage to accumulate college credits while in high school and arrive on campus with thirty or more credits may be more vulnerable to some of the pitfalls associated with financial aid. To be clear, DE programs do not touch a student's financial aid, and if all goes well, their financial aid is not at risk. However, if students struggle in their DE courses, their resulting high school GPA may be lower; if they still struggle when they reach college, they may fail to maintain the 2.0 GPA federal financial aid mandates. If they replace those grades by repeating the courses, they may find that they fail the Satisfactory Academic Progress (SAP) test, which requires that they earn at least 67 percent of the credits they attempt. It is not an immediate threat, but carrying a GPA below 2.0 trips up an estimated 10 percent of students per year.[4] Students already facing bad odds may find themselves at even greater risk of not graduating from college.

PROPOSALS FOR REALIZING THE SOCIAL JUSTICE PROMISE

DE programs, as they now stand, are not delivering on the promise of social justice. To be fair, however, those programs have been tasked with the impossible. They are asked to overcome entrenched socioeconomic inequities that simply will not yield to college credit accumulation. Should they, then, as Gilbert provocatively suggests, be halted, or can such programs be revised in ways that can correct course?

Some possibilities for revision can be found in the kind of wrap-around services offered by Early College High Schools whose very differences from DE persuaded me to leave them out of this analysis. Their success in helping first-generation, underrepresented, and financially under-resourced students far exceeds the success of DE programs. Part of that success is attributed to the academic and financial advising they offer, their test preparation services, and their careful monitoring of students. Replicating those services could help, but this comes at a cost to the institutions offering them. Another possibility lies in the ability of colleges and universities to dramatically revise their on-boarding services for new, direct-from-high-school students. Expectations for learning cohorts, transition services, and advising all have to be reexamined in the face of growing DE programs so the progress made by successful retention initiatives is not lost. One possible example is the OnRamps program at the University of Texas in Austin. Responding to concerns about teacher and student preparedness, the flagship campus offers a five-course teacher preparation for dual enrollment instructors to attune them to university-level expectations, as well as a host of student support services for dual enrollment students.

Others argue that social justice and higher learning would be better served if we stopped DE and redirected our time and money. Some advocates for pre-K programs suggest that money spent on DE might be better spent far earlier in a student's life and would go further toward remedying the achievement gap that appears as early as kindergarten for low-income children. Earlier interventions could also affect the eighth grade-level assessments that are key to DE participation in many states and decrease the need for multiple other interventions over a student's career.[5] Particularly compelling is a longitudinal research project that demonstrates that early intervention programs sustained through grade 3 have lasting effects into early middle age, and not just on educational attainment. Arthur J. Reynolds and his colleagues—noting that "low educational attainment (i.e., high school credential or less) is a major risk factor for all 7 health metrics of the American Heart Association (e.g., hypertension, smoking, and obesity), economic disparities, criminal behavior, and mental health problems" (248)—conclude that Early Childhood Intervention (ECI), established during the pre-K years and sustained through grade 3, contributes positively to not only educational attainment but also health and well-being overall. Situated at the beginning of a student's education journey, these programs may be better positioned to overcome the socioeconomic inequities DE is asked to address in the last few miles of that journey.

In their comparative study of student performance in writing during their first semester, Hansen and her colleagues ask: "What if, instead of pushing more and more college learning into high school, we set the bar for graduation from high school higher, and laid the foundation deeper? What if we had challenging courses like AP and IB in high school but didn't allow double counting of high school courses for college credit" (82). Hansen and colleagues appear to side with Gilbert's provocative suggestion that we halt DE, but what they actually argue is ultimately that high school curricula be invested with more rigor. Pending that, they suggest that students who earn credit for writing in high school take more writing courses at higher levels and that writing program administrators advocate for more and richer campus writing experiences for all students, recognizing that writing develops over time and with maturity.

The suggestion that universities add more writing courses may cancel out the cost savings earning college credits in high school is supposed to achieve and is likely to raise the hackles of proponents anxious to get students through college and into the job market quickly. Many of these completion proponents are those who subscribe to what David Jolliffe, drawing on Brian Street, calls the "autonomous" model of literacy. That model proposes "that literacy consists of a fixed set of skills that are 'neutral' and 'universal' " (x), not dependent on context, and that, once acquired, they remain stable. Jolliffe, alternately, understands literacy as a social practice that develops over a lifetime, is always contextualized, and requires ongoing critical reflection. Jolliffe does not advocate doing away with DE or any of the other ways of earning college credit before coming to college. What he is suggesting is that colleges and universities do more to address those students entering with writing credit. He does not suggest more courses but instead workshops, focused interactions, or "whatever configuration seems reasonable—so that they can learn about the culture of reading and writing that successful students inhabit at the college or university" (x). He proposes that these workshops might yield reflective journals that would provide insights for both high school and college faculty about the literacy development of young adults.

While I think all of these suggestions are worthwhile, none has high potential to quickly reduce the equity gap DE is currently exacerbating. Eliminating DE might stymie the expansion of the gap, and pre-K programming might reduce it for the next generation. Revising writing programs might yield better education but may not reduce the equity gap. More important, these proposals are beyond the reach of a writing program administrator's grasp. What I propose instead is within that grasp. While I have argued here that DE is expanding the equity gap, I think that proposal should be rigorously tested. And I further propose that it be tested by the disparate impact analysis used by the Office for Civil Rights (OCR) to uncover unintentional bias. Poe and colleagues and Moreland have suggested using this analytical method for evaluating the validity of writing assessments. I suggest that writing program administrators apply that same method to evaluate program outcomes. In all of this, I am mindful of Brian Huot's advice about assessment: it must be valid not only in its content and its construct but also in its consequences (178).

Moreland utilizes disparate impact analysis (a tool used by the OCR, a method for investigating civil rights that has been forwarded by Poe and colleagues as a validation tool) to determine if assessment practices that admit students to DE and FYC courses at a large Arizona community college are valid. She argues that when the consequences of such assessment tools result in racially disparate treatment of students, the tool must be investigated to uncover unintentional bias. Her attempt to carry out analysis of the ACCUPLACER Writeplacer® at her research site, however, was frustrated by a lack of "data publicly available or internally compiled," which, Moreland argues, is a violation of students' civil rights (177). Correcting for that kind of data collection and analysis is something writing program administrators are positioned to do.

The large-scale statistical studies reviewed here were limited by a number of factors: match groups created using income, race, and gender but results reported only by institutional outcomes; results from differently configured programs collapsed into one set of outcomes; and confounding variables too numerous to be fully addressed. To get the kind of clarity necessary to determine if our own offerings of DE courses are narrowing the equity gap or just exacerbating it, we are going to have to do it with an eye to measuring what really matters: tracking and measuring the effects locally, from placement and admissions through alumni results. We need to gather and record the admissions and placement data that make access possible, and we must conduct local research if we discover a participation gap at that end of the pipeline. We must gather and record course success data and investigate any disparities we find in DFW rates, course persistence measures, and credit hour enrollments. We must track participating students from their high school graduation through their subsequent college enrollment and measure time and credit hours to graduation. If, collectively, those of us charged with delivering FYC on our campuses and collaborating with regional high schools delivering FYC in their schools kept and analyzed our own disaggregated data at every catch point along the continuum, we would be in a better position to answer whether we should halt or work to improve DE.

If we find that our practices routinely render whole groups at a disadvantage, then we must halt. But if some schools are narrowing the equity gap in their locations, perhaps they could then share those results in a community of practice. And if we decide we should continue, then we should also, it seems to me, continually assess not only the content and quality of our courses but also our collaborations as they are clearly laid out in the CCCC's position statement on dual and concurrent enrollment, the National Council of Teachers of English (NCTE) position statement on preparing college faculty, and the National Alliance of Concurrent Enrollment Partnerships (NACEP) standards for concurrent partnerships. We should make our ongoing assessment of the effects of DE as rigorous and as routine as we currently make our assessment of our retention and graduation efforts. Only then can we make honest claims about social justice.

NOTES

1. The AAC& U used this term in a special issue of *Liberal Education* in 2012 titled The Completion Agenda, and AAC&U president Carol Geary Schneider used the term to describe "completion and productivity initiatives . . . for improved degree production" (6).
2. *US News and World Report* listed these institutions as the ten best national universities in 2018: Princeton University, Harvard University, Columbia University,

Massachusetts Institute of Technology, Yale University, Stanford University, University of Chicago, University of Pennsylvania, Northwestern University, and Duke University.

3. The report gathered publicly available data from Oregon public universities and colleges for the purpose of describing accelerated college credit options in the state, but for all other questions, it linked Oregon Department of Education data for the five cohorts of high school students expected to graduate between 2006 and 2010 with community college data. Most statistics, then, are based on partnerships between high schools and community colleges.
4. The Learning Policy Institute authors, Meloy and colleagues, reviewed more than twenty academic studies designed to measure the short- and long-term effects of participation in pre-schools that met many of the National Institute for Early Education Research (NIEER) standards. After acknowledging that findings in longitudinal studies are in some cases inconsistent, it determined that quality pre-schooling could return seventeen dollars for every dollar invested.
5. Fastweb, an internet-based scholarship research site, estimates that 10 percent of students lose financial aid because of failing to maintain the required minimum grade point average. Local statistics at one Midwest public university show a higher percentage, particularly among underrepresented and Pell-eligible students (Randolph).

WORKS CITED

Berger, Andrea, Lori Turk-Bicakci, Michael Garet, Mengli Song, Joel Knudson, Clarisse Haxton, Kristina Zeiser, Gur Hoshen, Jennifer Ford, and Jennifer Stephan. *Early College, Early Success: Early College High School Initiative Impact Study*. American Institutes for Research, 2013. www.air.org/resource/early-college-early-success-early-college-high-school-initiative-impact-study-2013. Accessed Nov. 8, 2018.

Blankenberger, Bob, Edirc Lichtenberger, and M. Allison Witt. "Dual Credit, College Type, and Enhanced Degree Attainment." *Educational Researcher*, vol. 46, no. 5, 2017, pp. 259–263. /doi.org/10.3102/0013189X17718796.

Cahalan, Margaret, Laura W. Perna, Mika Yamashita, Jeremy Wright-Kim, and Sureima Santillan. *Indicators of Higher Education Equity in the United States—2018 Historical Trend Report.* Pell Institute for the Study of Opportunity in Higher Education, Council for Opportunity in Education (COE), and Alliance for Higher Education and Democracy of the University of Pennsylvania (PennAHEAD), 2018.

Case Western University, Office of Undergraduate Studies. "Study at Other Colleges and Transfer Credit." n.d. https://case.edu/ugstudies/academic-policies/study-other-colleges-and-transfer-credit. Accessed March 2021.

Conference on College Composition and Communication. "CCCC Position Statement on Preparing Teachers of College Writing." CCCC, 2015. ncte.org/cccc/resources/positions/statementonprep. Accessed Aug. 7, 2019.

Edmunds, Julie A., Fatih Unlu, Elizabeth Glennie, Lawrence Bernstein, Lily Fesler, Jane Furey, and Nina Arshavsky. "Smoothing the Transition to Postsecondary Education: The Impact of the Early College Model." *Journal of Research on Educational Effectiveness*, vol. 10, no. 2, 2017, pp. 297–325.

Evenbeck, Scott, and Kathy E. Johnson. "Students Must Not Become Victims of the Completion Agenda." *Liberal Education*, vol. 98, no. 1, 2012, p. 12.

Field, Kelly. "The Rise of Dual Credit." *EducationNext*, vol. 21, no. 1, 2020. https://www.educationnext.org/rise-dual-credit-more-students-take-college-classes-high-school-degree-attainment-rigor/. Accessed Nov. 1, 2021.

Gilbert, Erik. "How Dual Enrollment Contributes to Inequality." *Chronicle of Higher Education*, Nov. 5, 2017. www.chronicle.com/article/How-Dual-Enrollment/241668. Accessed March 2021.

Hansen, Kristine, Brian Jackson, Brett C. McInelly, and Dennis Eggett. "How Do Dual Credit Students Perform on College Writing Tasks after They Arrive on Campus: Empirical Data from a Large-Scale Study." *WPA: Writing Program Administration*, vol. 38, no. 2, 2015, pp. 56–92.

Haskell, Richard E. "The Effects of Dual-Credit Enrollment on Underrepresented Students: The Utah Case." *International Journal of Economics and Finance*, vol. 8, no. 8, 2015, pp. 116–165.

Huot, Brian. *(Re)Articulating Writing Assessment for Teaching and Learning*, 1st ed. Utah State UP, 2002.

Jolliffe, David. "Foreword: Tough Questions for Thoughtful Educators." In *College Credit for Writing in High School: The "Taking Care of" Business*, edited by Kristine Hansen and Christine R. Farris. NCTE, 2010, pp. vii–xiii.

Meloy, Beth, Madelyn Gardner, and Linda Darling-Hammond. "Untangling the Evidence on Preschool Effectiveness: Insights for Policymakers." Is Licensed under a Creative Commons Attribution-NonCommercial 4.0 International License. In *Untangling the Evidence on Preschool Effectiveness: Insights for Policymakers.* Learning Policy Institute, 2019. learningpolicyinstitute.org/product/untangling-evidence-preschool-effectiveness-report. Accessed Mar. 3, 2019.

Miller, Trey, Holly Kosiewicz, Courtney Tanenbaum, Drew Atchison, David Knight, Beth Ratway, Scott Delhommer, and Jesse Levin. "Dual Credit Education Programs in Texas, Phase II." *American Institutes for Research*, Dec. 2018. http://www.60x30tx.com/media/1428/dual-credit-education-programs-in-texas.pdf. Accessed May 11, 2022.

Miller, Trey, Holly Kosiewicz, Elaine Lin Want, Elizabeth VP Marwah, Scott Delhommer, and Lindsay Daugherty. "Dual Credit Education in Texas: Interim Report." *RAND Corporation*, 2017. www.rand.org/pubs/research_reports/RR2043.html. Accessed Jan. 3, 2019.

Moreland, Casie. "Chasing Transparency: Using Disparate Impact Analysis to Assess the (In)Accessibility of Dual Enrollment Composition." In *Writing Assessment, Social Justice, and the Advancement of Opportunity*, edited by Mya Poe, Asao Inoue, and Norbert Elliot. WAC Clearinghouse and UP of Colorado, 2018, pp. 171–199. wac.colostate.edu/books/perspectives/assessment/. Accessed Jan. 1 2019.

Pierson, Ashley, Michelle Hodara, and Jonathan Luke. "Earning College Credits in High School: Options, Participation, and Outcomes for Oregon Students." United States, Department of Education, Institute of Education Sciences, Regional Educational Laboratory Program. March 2017. https://ies.ed.gov/ncee/edlabs/projects/project.asp?projectID=433. Accessed Jan. 3, 2019.

Poe, Mya, Norbert Elliot, John Aloysius Cogan, and Tito G. Nurudeen. "The Legal and the Local: Using Disparate Impact Analysis to Understand the Consequences of Writing Assessment." *College Composition and Communication*, vol. 65, no. 4, 2014, pp. 588–609.

Randolph, Kathryn Knight. "Losing Financial Aid for Unsatisfactory Academic Progress." Fastweb. Oct. 25, 2021. https://www.fastweb.com/financial-aid/articles/students-lose-financial-aid-for-failure-to-make-satisfactory-academic-progress. Accessed Nov. 1, 2021.

Reynolds, Arthur J., Suh-Ruu Ou, and Judy A. Temple. "A Multicomponent, Preschool to Third Grade Preventive Intervention and Educational Attainment at 35 Years of Age." *JAMAPediatrics*, vol. 172, no. 3, 2018, pp. 247–256.

Rhoades, Gary. "The Incomplete Completion Agenda: Implications for Academe and the Academy." *Liberal Education*, vol. 98, no. 1, 2012, pp. 18–25. https://www.aacu.org/publications-research/periodicals/incomplete-completion-agenda-implications-academe-and-academy. Accessed January 2019.

Schneider, Carol Geary. "Where Completion Goes Awry: The Metrics for 'Success,' Mask Mounting Problems with Quality." *Liberal Education*, vol. 98, no. 1, 2012, p. 6.

University of Texas at Austin, Office of Strategy and Policy. "OnRamps." N.d. onramps.utexas.edu. Accessed March 2021.

US Department of Education, Institute of Education Sciences, What Works Clearinghouse. *Transition to College Intervention Report: Dual Enrollment Programs*. 2017. https://ies.ed.gov/ncee/wwc/interventionreport/671. Accessed February 2019.

US News and World Report Best Colleges Rankings. 2018. www.usnews.com/best-colleges/rankings/national-universities. Accessed Apr. 20, 2019.

Winkelmes, Mary-Ann, Allison Boye, and Suzanne Tapp. *Transparent Design in High Education Teaching and Leadership: A Guide to Implementing the Transparency Framework Institution-Wide to Improve Learning and Retention*. Stylus Publishing LLC, 2019. EBSCOhost, search.ebscohost.com/login.aspx?direct=true&db=eric&AN=ED594987&site=eds-live. Accessed Jan. 3, 2019.

2

DUELING ENROLLMENTS

Historicizing the High School–College Divide

Amy Lueck and Brice Nordquist

It is late April, and the locker-lined halls of Robinson High herald the graduating class of 2018. Flyers remind seniors to attend assemblies and register for graduation, and display cases feature copies of college acceptance letters alongside class portraits. As warning bells speed the traffic of students through hallways, Mary Wilson's fifth-period dual enrollment (DE) writing class is buzzing with commerce. Students sporting newly minted graduation T-shirts disregard the final bell and continue to circulate around the room making deliveries, collecting cash, and taking orders. Their classmates stuff shirts into bags or slip them over their heads and search for names on each other's backs. While commencement is still more than two months away, Mary's students are surrounded by signs of the end.

In an attempt to bring her class to order, Mary, a veteran English teacher, interrupts the graduation chatter with a familiar admonition: "You've been taking college courses; you've been doing college work. Spring senior year doesn't actually happen during your freshman year of college. You're 75 percent of the year there. You still have 25 percent to finish, but you're acting like you're done. You're almost there—keep going." The reminder to students that they are all still enrolled in a college course despite the stream of events signaling the end of their senior year is met with a mix of exasperation and resolution. The work of college does not slow or stop for skip days, prom, assemblies, or senioritis. Outside the confines of DE, their time as high schoolers may be winding down, but within this frame, the finish line is still distant on the horizon, and the payoff of their work in the form of college credit is far from secure.

Mary's attempt to realign her students with an imagined space-time of college represents a key element in the discursive work of dual enrollment: the perpetual effort to simultaneously collapse and uphold the

https://doi.org/10.7330/9781646422531.c002

distinction between high school and college. What is currently happening there, on a near or distant campus, should simultaneously happen here; in this case, in an under-resourced, "at-risk" public high school. At the same time, insisting that college is not high school becomes a key component of performing college in high school. While Mary and her students are well aware of the complexity and unpredictability of "doing college work," whether in high school or in college, they often pause in moments like these to collectively recommit to the pursuit of "college-level" effort and production.

This pursuit relies on a flattened abstraction of both the high school and college as sites of practice. To be replicated, a college course must be imagined as stable, singular, and therefore exportable. For instance, in projections like Mary's, college is conceived as a purer workspace with fewer material constraints and social relations to impede progress. And this abstraction is used to narrow the focus and raise the stakes of college work in high school so the decontextualization of one situation enables the decontextualization of the other: "Spring senior year doesn't actually happen during your freshman year [of college]." While it may be routine enough to produce abstractions of labor in another place and time (in fact, these are regularly provided in the form of standardized syllabi, course objectives, assessments, and the like), it requires a great deal of effort to intellectually separate one's work in the present from its own cultural, material context. But this is exactly the sort of effort DE demands of Mary and her students. Aligning work in high school with representations of college work requires them all to engage in the continual production, management, and correction of spatiotemporal discontinuities.

This abstracted understanding of secondary and postsecondary institutions is reflected in writing pedagogies that produce formulaic abstractions of writing. That is, insofar as the college is conceptualized as a singular, stable target location, so must college writing be conceived as such: as a singular, stable, replicable process that can be taught in roughly the same ways regardless of who and where the participants are. The misalignment of such formulaic writing pedagogies with the ethos of writing courses among college and university faculty has been a significant—and thus far unresolved—point of tension.

Because DE courses tend to flow from tertiary to secondary schools, the burden of reconciling this tension in daily practice falls primarily on high school teachers and students, while the labor of reconciling curricular differences falls on university administrators responsible for brokering the transfer of courses. Of course, much has been made of this brokering of equivalencies in rhetoric and composition and, particularly, scholarship on writing program administration (Hansen and Farris; Tinberg and Nadeau; Malek and Micciche). This scholarship tends to evoke contextual differences, like the ones mentioned above, to assert the impossibility of truly equivalent writing courses and to argue against the managerial and efficiency-driven impetus of their exchange.

Citing these differences, what critiques of DE share in common with attempts such as Mary's to enact replicability is an assumption of the essential distinction between high schools and colleges as sites of practice. In fact, this distinction becomes a defining feature. Articulated through metaphors of containment, depictions of the high school and college writing classroom are subsequently presented not according to the practices that constitute them but by the boundaries and borders between them, both real and imagined. Emphasis on the difference between high school and college poses a distinctly ironic problem for DE students and teachers who must re-inscribe differences between high school and college writing through performances of college writing in high school.

Since the early twentieth century, high school and college have been persistently imagined as stable and self-apparent entities in this way. Even as we continue to debate the purposes of each, one assumption seems clear: the high school is not the college, and the college is not the high school. Consequently, college writing is not high school writing. Because we rely so heavily on this distinction for our definitions of each, it is unsurprising that many are unsettled by the prospect of undermining these distinctions through DE and other "competing brands" of college composition available to high school students, such as Advanced Placement and International Baccalaureate (Hansen).

In this chapter, we examine the discursive construction between high school and college as institutions and its effects on writing practices for teachers and students. As we argue, this discursive divide has real, material consequences. It informs (and constrains) writing practices and pedagogies, becomes a barrier to access (particularly when operationalized in testing procedures), contributes to dropout and attrition, exacerbates unequal power and resources in communities, and justifies hierarchical relations between high school and college faculty and staff. In short, the metaphoric gap becomes a foundational assumption in disciplinary ideologies, managerial systems, and writing pedagogies.

This is not to say that differences between structures and practices in high school and college are only illusory. Research exploring students' transitions from high school to college writing has revealed differences between secondary and postsecondary writing instruction and the challenges these differences can create for students (Addison and McGee; Brockman et al.; Denecker; Hannah and Saidy; Patterson and Duer; Reiff and Bawarshi; Wilder and Yagelski). Such differences range from the types of writing students are asked to do (DeStigter) to the syntactic features students will be expected to use (Brown and Aull) to the terms teachers use to assign and talk about writing (Hannah and Saidy). Along with these scholars, we acknowledge these and other material and social differences between practices in high school and college. However, we also contend that such differences are reproduced and thus sedimented in our scholarly and pedagogical practices for the sake of discipline building and *boundarying*. Following linguistic anthropologists Susan Gal and Judith T. Irvine, we identify boundary-making devices as methodological, curricular, administrative, and pedagogical practices shaping and shaped by "ideologies that highlight disciplinary differentiation in situations of scholarly competition for institutional or public approbation, legitimation, and support" (971). We would add that all scholarly competition is imbricated in economic competition. In other words, compositionists participate in and benefit from the production of "the divide" in the form of disciplinary status and economic security and often fail to acknowledge its consequences for high school and college students and teachers. The trusted distinction between institutions and stages of education is also maintained, in part, through our disciplinary boundarying activities.

In contrast to this accepted distinction, we take as given the understanding that, both historically and in the present, high schools and colleges are constituted through practices that have overlapped significantly in symbolic and material ways. By deconstructing definitions of high school and college and the metaphors of containment they rely on, we seek to invigorate debates, research methodologies, curricula, and pedagogies around DE composition. We hope to shift the conversation away from one of transference or articulation between the high school and college and toward a more dynamic sense of emergence and negotiation as practiced in our writing programs and classrooms. That is, rather than think about DE as mediating stable entities of high school– and college-level writing practice and pedagogy, we want to attend to the theoretical practices and frameworks that have shaped these institutional responses historically and into the present. Drawing on the concept of boundarying in particular, we render visible scholars', administrators', teachers', and students' roles in the discursive construction of the "high school–college divide" through their productions and contestations of "college-level writing" in high school classrooms.

Following these lines of inquiry, we begin with a brief overview of the ways metaphors of spatiotemporal containment have historically served to reproduce oppositions between the high school and college. Beginning with the emergence of the multipurpose high school in the nineteenth century, we trace the idea of the "high school–college divide" as a central definitional assumption in educational discourse and curricular planning that denies the reality of recursive and overlapping practices across sites of learning. We then consider how this historical and perpetual rearticulation of relations extends into current debates around dual enrollment in rhetoric and composition. In these debates, critics, advocates, and the majority of scholars in between tend to either argue for the need to work across the divide to improve designs and implementations of DE composition or warn against the proliferation of DE by emphasizing the difficulty—in some cases, the impossibility—of bridging the divide. Within this complex and often conflicted discussion, the divide is taken for granted and thus re-inscribed on all sides.

INHERITANCE: INVENTING THE HIGH SCHOOL–COLLEGE DIVIDE IN THE NINETEENTH CENTURY

Educational institutions are, of course, not natural or necessary formations but instead products of motivated discourse and action, the meaning of which shifts continually over time. Tracing how our present-day institutional forms emerged historically helps us lay bare the metaphors that shape our current practice and recover the possibility of other arrangements and conceptualizations. What has *college* meant, and how has it related to the high school and the teaching of writing? It will be helpful to go back to the beginnings.

The American college of the eighteenth and nineteenth centuries was not a place so much as a curriculum—the Classical curriculum, which featured Latin, Greek, and mathematics—largely taught by recitation. Schools that pursued this curriculum could apply for charters to be recognized as colleges, and few, if any, that engaged other subjects would have been recognized as such. Rather than discrete classes for which students might receive credit, college courses in this arrangement indicated a course of study across all subjects for a full three or four years. Emphasizing the metaphor of process and movement that the term implies, the college *course* was defined by its practices: the process of "disciplining the mind" through the study of Classical languages and literatures over a span of time. And that practice occurred in various locations, including, once they were established in the nineteenth century, some large urban high schools.

The newly emergent American high school, by contrast, was a complex and disruptive innovation, of which little else was agreed upon other than that it was to encompass the highest level of study within a public school system (though there were exceptions even to that rule). Without a tradition to build on, the educational practices engaged at the high school tended to be diverse. In some larger cities, the comprehensive high school offered a full Classical curriculum, and some conferred bachelor's and even master's degrees on students, such as the male high schools of Philadelphia, Baltimore, and Louisville (see Labaree; Reese; Lueck). Regardless of whether their aspirations were so elevated, the high schools in most cities were not in a subordinate or preparatory role in relation to the college but instead posited an alternate vision of higher learning for the broader public. That vision was manifested most pointedly in what was called the English (also called the Latin-Scientific) curriculum, which emphasized English-language and science instruction and often excluded Greek. This more "practical," modern curriculum—associated particularly with the public high school and the academy[1]—was hailed as better preparing the broad citizenry for their lives than the traditional curriculum of higher learning. To the extent that colleges maintained a classical orientation while high schools adopted these more modern curricula, some tensions did emerge. As the school board in St. Louis explained it, "It is somewhat startling to learn that there are two systems firmly established in our land confronting each other with radically different theories as to a proper course of study. Such hostility could not but develop sooner or later into an open contest" (*Nineteenth Annual* 54–55).

In fact, though, the tension was more complicated than a contest between "two systems firmly established." Instead, many large high schools actually offered the Classical curriculum alongside one of the more modern curricula, just as most colleges would eventually adopt something more akin to the English curriculum—including composition courses—by the last quarter of the century. So, from their earliest beginnings, high schools were interested in extending their curriculum into the highest branches of knowledge, whatever that might be. Meanwhile, colleges have also long complicated their own status by offering preparatory branches with enrollments that often outnumbered the enrollments in their college courses (Leslie; Fleming). And yet, the metaphors of containment—based in reference to the two competing pedagogical models of the Classical versus English curriculum—have persisted, taking on a geospatial and territorial valence as they have shifted to referring not to the curricula but instead to the two ostensibly competing institutional sites: the college and the high school.

Contributing to this way of understanding separate institutions was the fact that high schools have long been discussed and conceptualized as highly local. Supported by local taxation, most emphasized relentlessly the benefits to their home communities, defining themselves in relation to those communities and their students far more than by institutional categories or titles. Thus, for many cities, providing college education in the high school was all but expected (for white males) and valued for the fact that it curtailed the "necessity" for students "to continue study elsewhere," as the Baltimore school board explained (*Twenty-Ninth Annual*). So, in many instances, the nascent "divide" between high school and college was a geographical one, referring to the physical relocation (one might even say dislocation, from the perspective of high school administrators) of students who, given the limited resources of many public schools, had to go "elsewhere" to continue their studies.

The divide has also been fundamentally racist and sexist. Reflecting well-established patterns of resource allocation, the fact is that schools in less affluent locations and those serving non-dominant (particularly non-white and female) student groups were significantly less likely to be able to offer a full array of courses in the "higher branches," even if local school boards allowed them to do so. Though there was still great variability across individual institutions, the trend by the end of the nineteenth century was that high schools without the resources to provide a further course of study began to shift their educational missions from "extension of" to "preparation for" advanced studies, while some better-resourced schools protected the value of the high school credential by designating differential collegiate and non-collegiate tracks (see Labaree; Lueck). At the same time, local and national committees (particularly on behalf of colleges and universities) worked to formally articulate high school and college educational practices as credentials in a hierarchical and sequential system, abstracting and commodifying educational experiences in the process (VanOverbeke; Labaree). That is, the aim at the end of the nineteenth century was to solidify the two sites of practice by defining them in relation and contradistinction to one another—to make the college sequentially successive to the high school curriculum, such that students would continue on to college only after completing the full high school course of study. This new arrangement promised to serve the interests of both institutions by reducing competition for students without addressing the continued disparity in resources and the ongoing fluidity of these categories for the most privileged students and institutions.

The Committee of Ten, convened at a meeting of the National Education Association in 1891, is one of the most widely recognized efforts to effect this arrangement (*Report of the Committee of Ten*).[2] In their separate reports to this committee, representatives from each subject area were tasked with drafting recommendations on how to achieve uniformity of instruction across schools and determine appropriate subject-specific admissions criteria for colleges. As is apparent from the second part of this charge, a hierarchical and sequential ordering was already built into considerations of high school and college by this time, as was the presumption that the collegiate curriculum would be dislocated from the site of the high school and only selectively available to students, as regulated by an admission examination.

The committees' responses reinforced that arrangement. Significantly, the reports outlined subjects to be studied in the form of tables, proposing units of time spent on each subject and eschewing consideration of "scope or intensity" of the study or other concerns about actual pedagogical and educational practice. The tables were justified as representing "with tolerable accuracy the proportional expenditure which a school is making on a given subject, and therefore the proportional importance which the school attaches to that subject" (38), but this heuristic became ossified as the primary means of discussing discrete "courses" in the curriculum, understood through the "question of educational expenditure" (38). Thus, rather than a *course of study*, the four-year curriculum was identified as a *programme of study*, composed of discrete subject areas—emphasizing the administrative unit rather than an ongoing educational process—and that program was to be clearly bounded and contained from overlap with that of the college.

In this way, an enacted understanding of educational practices transmogrified into a spatial and relational arrangement of (and distinction between) institutions by the end of the nineteenth century, reinforced by tables and graphs that helped to order education and transform it from an individual experience into a replicable, scalable system. It is through these national standardization efforts that the college became distinguished fully from the high school on a definitional level—that is, the high school was established as spatiotemporally beneath and prior to the college experience, defined by its relative position not in relation to the common schools (as an extension of academic work into the "highest" branches) but in relation to the college (as preparatory and subordinate). Hence, what might have been a more fluid and recursive process of preparation and development became a highly regulated and sedentarized abstraction of learning when these institutions were formally decoupled, with the college admission exam operating as a key boundarying mechanism.

However, the discursive and material efforts to accomplish this distinction have not resolved or removed the rich internal variety of experience and practice within and across these sites of learning. Instead, US high school and college relations have been marked by an unbroken pattern of overlap and imbrication over the course of their history, including persistent debate about curricular programs and institutional boundaries in relation to admissions exams, general education requirements, and "junior colleges," to name but a few key examples. Though this hierarchical alignment and distinction has never been fully achieved, it is through this effort to distinguish purposes and roles that the value of containment and corresponding spatiotemporal metaphors for imagining high school and college relations has emerged and continued to exert pressure into the present. One form this containment has taken is the required first-year composition course, which (whether taught in the high school or college) functions as a key gatekeeping mechanism upholding—indeed, defining—the boundary between high school and college writing practices.

REPRODUCTION: MAINTAINING THE SPACE-TIME BETWEEN

Despite this rich history of imbrication and mutual constitution, it is the conception of "two systems firmly established" that persists in the narratives of rhetoric and composition, with implications for our writing pedagogies across educational sites. For instance, Howard Tinberg and Jean-Paul Nadeau begin their article on composition in an era of dual enrollment by imagining "the space between high schools and colleges" as a historical "site of contestation" (704). In their history of territorial conflict, the National Council of Teachers of English (NCTE) was established to prevent the aforementioned subordination of high schools by protecting their sovereignty against elite colleges seeking to colonize and convert them into training grounds for higher branches of learning. In their article, this conflict reemerges over a century later around the proliferation of DE courses and their questionable efficacy in producing and predicting "college readiness" and in maintaining the integrity of the "college experience." Tinberg and Nadeau call upon the NCTE and its college associations to work together as a "bridge between the worlds that dual-enrollment students inhabit" (706). In this spatial imaginary, high school and college are discrete, stable, and self-evident worlds naturally separated by a host of identifiable contextual and cultural differences. Consequently, dual enrollment composition is figured as an unnatural union, a "transplant" of "college-level experience" into high school (711).

The spatial metaphors of crossing Tinberg and Nadeau draw upon to represent relations among secondary and tertiary institutions are commonplace in rhetoric and composition and secondary education. In scholarship on DE composition and other topics related to articulations, alignments, and transitions, students and courses cross thresholds and straddle worlds (Denecker; McWain; Sommers and Saltz), traffic across borders (Malek and Micciche), bridge divides (Taczak and Thelin; McCrimmon), and mind gaps (Edmonds and Squires; Hoffman et al.). These metaphors of spatial containment and separation are employed interchangeably from all sides of the DE debate. They communicate an enduring confidence in the stability of institutions and stages of education and thereby reduce complex, co-constitutive relationships to questions of bridge building—regardless of whether they can be built (or resisted), what they should look like, where they should be located, and how we should go about building them. This discourse of bridging re-inscribes bounded places and gaps between them.

According to Gal and Irvine, we build and re-inscribe these boundaries through a number of intertwined semiotic processes, which they describe in terms of *iconicity*, *recursiveness*, and *erasure*. In our scholarship, program and curricular development, and pedagogy, we often transform practices that *index* contexts of high school and college into *iconic* representations of high school and college—as if particular practices or features could reveal the inherent nature or essence of an institution and the people and things that help constitute it (973). We also *recursively* project oppositions that allow us to create distinct disciplinary identities and professional selves at different levels of contrast (974). As evidenced in Mary's discursive construction described earlier, "college-level" work and writing can only be imagined in opposition to an iconic representation of "high school–level" work and writing. Finally, our practice often renders invisible the activities, events, people, and processes that disrupt ideologies of division. In other words, we often *erase* or ignore resonances, traces, and replications of practice across seemingly discrete stages of education.

In these ostensive, rather than performative, definitions of institutions and associated practices, such as academic writing, we nail down what we know for the production and reinforcement of disciplinary boundaries and locate the objects of our knowledge in slices of time anchored to specific spatial formations; that is, grade levels, stepped standards, vertical alignments, and similar formations. As feminist geographer Doreen Massey might suggest, we "convene spatial multiplicity into temporal sequence" (61). College writing is not high school writing because these phenomena are located in separate slices of time or stages of development mapped onto curricula and administered by disciplinary experts in set locations. Despite the recursive nature of the English curriculum, which returns to the practice of similar concepts or skills iteratively across the years of study, our standards and language of educational leveling assert a progressive movement across stages.

These stages are reinforced with appeals to ostensibly predictable relations among age, grade level, and cognitive, curricular, and social processes of development.[3] As Tinberg and Nadeau proclaim, "Educators would generally agree, given what we know about learning and development theory, that curriculum should be increasingly challenging for students. For this reason, we assume that postsecondary courses are more challenging than those courses in which students have been enrolled previously" (715). Based on this assumption, they suggest that the increasing demand for dual enrollment could reveal a lack of rigor in instruction: "If high school students can handle college courses, what does that say about the challenges presented in those courses? Is recalibration in order" (715)? In other words, shouldn't we consider increasing the rigor of dual enrollment college writing courses and the college composition courses they're intended to replicate so that high school students (and teachers) are put back in their temporal, developmental places?

On the surface, this assertion is so commonplace it seems hardly worth contesting. After all, what's the point of having grade levels if they don't correspond with carefully calibrated curricula that move students progressively through set stages of development? Our own educational conditioning inclines us to equate temporal relations with a numeric sequence (grade 11, grade 12, first year, second year, and so on) and to plot and measure progress according to distances between points on a straight line. But the calibration of this "unified progress-time" requires us to ignore or erase quite a lot of complexity and diversity (Tsing "On Scalability").

For instance, to assume that writing in high school is or should be less rigorous than writing in college, we must, to some degree, buy into the promise of standardization and ignore diversity across differently situated, populated, and resourced high schools and colleges. This assumption also requires some homogenization of students and teachers that conflates their values, pursuits, and practices with uniform institutional cultures. In this way, a singular and iconic culture of high school can be imagined as mechanized and structurally determined while an iconic culture of college encourages autonomy, experimentation, and the pursuit of deeper meaning through writing (Sommers and Saltz). In other words, unified progress-time asks us to conceive of high school as an absolute space-time, isolated and pure, from which all students launch their college careers and, likewise, project college (and career) as stable and singular targets. This view of progress also presents a relative uniformity in the ways students develop cognitively and socially and individualizes these processes, focusing on personal rather than collective development.

This correlation of age and grade with level of maturity and ability requires us to ignore diverse histories of experience and participation across contexts in and out of school, as if social maturity and cognitive ability were internal conditions unaffected by bodies, experiences, identities, investments, communities, contexts, resources, and support. These sorts of correlations become more viable across larger distances between grades (hence, current debates around some states granting access to DE as early as the seventh grade). However, the vast majority of students enrolled in DE are high school juniors and seniors (Marken et al.).[4] Based on "what we know about learning and development theory," can we claim these students are significantly different from their college counterparts in terms of cognitive and social development? Not if we follow Lev Vygotsky and the majority of contemporary developmental psychologists who conceive of development as a complex dialectical process rather than an accumulation of changes calibrated to set stages of formal education (73).

Ultimately, to maintain the divide between high school and college writing, we must continue to invent and circulate what Paul Prior terms "tales of school learning." Over the course of two centuries of educational discourse, such tales have insisted that "learning happens inside specific territorial communities, each of which owns its own space of knowledge and discourse" (n.p.). Students must enter these spaces "by moving step-by-step along a sequentially graded curricular path" (n.p.). As we assert above, despite material efforts to realize such tales, experiences and practices of college and high school, including academic writing, remain imbricated and mutually constitutive. Learning has never been contained or containable within slices of time and stable spaces. This is because individuals and groups develop or, rather, *become* "not inside domains, but across the many moments of a life. Becoming happens in spaces that are never pure or settled, where discourses and knowledge are necessarily heterogeneous" (n.p.).

Nonetheless, tales of school learning and the narratives of progress that drive them powerfully shape our expectations, perceptions, and practices in the writing classroom. Anna Lowenhaupt Tsing describes progress as a "forward march, drawing other kinds of time into its rhythms" (*The Mushroom* 21). This unifying march is especially strong in formal education, where the bounding and measuring of individuals and abilities often prevent us from recognizing the heterogeneity, agencies, and resistances that constitute scenes of writing. If students are trained to contain their literacies within particular times and spaces, they (and we) are less likely to notice the agencies and new spatiotemporal formations constantly emerging from their distributed practice. In other words, containerized metaphors of literacy education often prevent students from recognizing the complexity and value of their own intertwined literacies. Moreover, tales of learning that present institutions, disciplines, and courses as singular and stable with clear paths to success encourage students to accommodate apparently preexisting structures rather than challenge and change them. And when spaces and structures turn out to be less predictable than anticipated (as they always do), our sedentaristic logic makes it difficult to see possibilities for remaking paths and places. In other words, students' abilities to perceive and act effectively in heterogeneous, layered, and dynamic spaces are hampered by formal schooling's insistence on a future that unfolds as a series of inevitable encounters with bounded and stable spaces.

Of course, giving up the divide is a risky proposition, as our disciplinary expertise and institutional positions have depended, in large part, on productions and assumptions of difference. We don't mean to minimize this risk or to suggest that deep-seated ideological constructs are easily dismissed or re-imagined. We do, however, recommend acknowledging the economic and political motivations for these boundarying activities and confronting their consequences (Gal and Irvine). For instance, it is possible that the proliferation of DE composition is due in part to our insistence on the existence of a uniform set of practices called "college-level" writing, elemental to an identifiable "college experience." If college writing exists as an ostensive reality, it can be stabilized and scaled to high schools across the globe for tremendous profit. It can be employed as a litmus test for "college readiness." What high school student wouldn't want early access to something/someplace so consequential to their future success, and what teacher or administrator wouldn't want to grant it? As Sara Goldrick-Rab has shown, students and families take on tremendous debt and financial hardship in pursuit of *the* college experience. And they often bypass more affordable and closer-to-home colleges to find it (echoing the words of the nineteenth-century Baltimore school administrator above, they feel compelled to study "elsewhere"). Consequently, we must take great care with how we participate in the construction of college and college writing as a singular experience, with how we locate it in space and time, and with what we promise in terms of its future payoff.

CONSEQUENCES: CONTAINING STUDENTS' EXPECTATIONS, PERCEPTIONS, AND PRACTICES

We believe the prevailing logic that bounds and measures space-time, activities, knowledges, communities, and individuals undergirds many of the most pressing problems in contemporary education—that is, segregation, standardization, militarization, corporatization, and unequal access to resources and opportunities. To take just one example, Casie Moreland has traced the history of segregation in DE composition to the Civil Rights era, identifying racial disparity in the development and application of these programs and attributing it in no small part to what we are identifying as the boundarying technologies of entrance and placement examinations (*White Resistance*). Elsewhere, Moreland links this history to the nineteenth-century context explored here, positing that "advanced standing, advanced placement, and therefore dual enrollment programs that enable students to gain college credit for writing in high school were an almost instantaneous response to the first-year writing requirement that began in 1885" ("Chasing Transparency" 174). From one perspective, the development of these programs merely formalizes what had long been a reality for many students, particularly those who already occupy positions of racial and economic privilege—the overlap and fluidity between high school and college writing practices. Though she doesn't explore the point, Moreland is tapping into the argument we are making here: that programs like DE rely on sedantarist conceptions of educational institutions and practices and that, because of this conception, these programs construct and perpetuate (as much as they address or "bridge") divides between high school and college writing practices. From this perspective, DE composition can be viewed as itself a boundary—an attempt to mask the fluidity of these categories by creating a formal enrollment category to contain them. What this chapter adds to work like Moreland's is an interrogation of the history of DE and segregation as a consequence of the ongoing boundarying and differentiation between the space-time of high school and college. While fully excavating the sedentarist and colonialist (Massey 4) foundations of such educational structures and problems is well beyond the scope of this chapter, we would like to invite readers into an interrogation of how the maintenance of the "high school–college divide" through discourses and pedagogies of containment has shaped (and continues to shape) students' expectations and perceptions of college, of "college-level" writing, and of themselves as students and writers.

NOTES

1. In fact, all educational institutions (such as academies and colleges) had complex, hybrid identities that overlapped with one another. See Geiger; Leslie.
2. See Moreland for additional commentary on the Committee of Ten and its connection to the history of DE composition ("Chasing" 173; *White Resistance* 3).
3. These stages build on the "grading" of larger, primarily urban public schools in the nineteenth century, which organized classes by age and ability. Students were typically promoted annually or biennially based on successful completion of the year's course of study (or by petition to the principal) and thus were often of a similar age to others in their classes. The high school and college, however, were often entered by admission examination and thus included students from a range of ages far wider than modern readers might assume: high schools and academy rosters might include students up to twenty-one years of age, while the average age of eighteen for college matriculation reflects the fact that students into their thirties were entering college alongside those in their very early teens (Association of American Universities 35–36; also see Leslie; Lueck).
4. According to a national survey of dual enrollment programs conducted by the National Center for Education Statistics, 91 percent of high schools offering dual enrollment reported eligibility for grade 11, and 97 percent did so for grade 12. Forty percent of institutions reported eligibility for high school students in grade 10, and 25 percent reported eligibility for high school students in grade 9 (Marken et al. 3).

WORKS CITED

Addison, Joanne, and Sharon James McGee. "Writing in High School/Writing in College: Research Trends and Future Directions." *College Composition and Communication*, vol. 62, no. 1, 2010, pp. 147–179.

Association of American Universities. *Journal of Proceedings and Addresses of the Tenth Annual Conference*. Association of American Universities, 1909.

Brockman, Elizabeth, Marcy Taylor, MaryAnn K. Crawford, and Melinda Kreth. "Helping Students Cross the Threshold: Implications from a University Writing Assessment." *English Journal*, vol. 99, no. 3, 2010, pp. 42–49.

Brown, David W., and Laura L. Aull. "Elaborated Specificity versus Emphatic Generality: A Corpus-Based Comparison of Higher- and Lower-Scoring Advanced Placement Exams in English." *Research in the Teaching of English*, vol. 51, no. 4, 2017, pp. 394–417.

Denecker, Christine. "Transitioning Writers across the Composition Threshold: What We Can Learn from Dual Enrollment Partnerships." *Composition Studies*, vol. 41, no. 1, 2013, pp. 27–50.

DeStigter, Todd. "On the Ascendance of Argument: A Critique of the Assumptions of Academe's Dominant Form." *Research in the Teaching of English*, vol. 50, no. 1, 2015, pp. 11–34.

Edmonds, Gerald S., and Tiffany M. Squires. *Bridging the High School–College Gap: The Role of Concurrent Enrollment Programs.* Syracuse UP, 2016.

Fleming, David. *From Form to Meaning: Freshman Composition and the Long Sixties, 1957–1974.* U of Pittsburgh P, 2011.

Gal, Susan, and Judith T. Irvine. "The Boundaries of Languages and Disciplines: How Ideologies Construct Difference." *Social Research*, vol. 62, no. 4, 1995, pp. 967–1001.

Geiger, Roger L. "The Era of Multipurpose Colleges in American Higher Education, 1850–1890." In *The American College in the Nineteenth Century*, edited by Roger Geiger. Vanderbilt UP, 2000, pp. 127–152.

Goldrick-Rab, Sara. *Paying the Price: College Costs, Financial Aid, and the Betrayal of the American Dream.* U of Chicago P, 2016.

Hannah, Mark A., and Christine Saidy. "Locating the Terms of Engagement: Shared Language Development in Secondary to Postsecondary Writing Transitions." *College Composition and Communication*, vol. 66, no. 1, 2014, pp. 120–144.

Hansen, Kristine. "The Composition Marketplace: Shopping for Credit versus Learning to Write." In *College Credit for Writing in High School: The "Taking Care of" Business*, edited by Kristine Hansen and Christine R. Farris. NCTE, 2010, pp. 1–39.

Hansen, Kristine, and Christine R. Farris, eds. *College Credit for Writing in High School: The "Taking Care of" Business.* NCTE, 2010.

Hoffman, Nancy, Joel Vargas, and Andrea Venezia, eds. *Minding the Gap: Why Integrating High School with College Makes Sense and How to Do It.* Harvard Education P, 2007.

Labaree, David. *Making of an American High School: The Credentials Market and the Central High School of Philadelphia, 1838–1939.* Yale UP, 1992.

Leslie, Bruce W. "Where Have All the Academies Gone?" *History of Education Quarterly*, 41, no. 2, 2001, pp. 262–270.

Lueck, Amy. *A Shared History: Writing in the High School, College, and University, 1856–1886.* Southern Illinois UP, 2019.

Malek, Joyce, and Laura R. Micciche. "A Model of Efficiency: Pre-College Credit and the State Apparatus." *WPA: Writing Program Administration*, vol. 40, no. 2, 2017, pp. 77–97.

Marken, Stephanie, Lucinda Gray, Laurie Lewis, and John Ralph. "Dual Enrollment Programs and Courses for High School Students at Postsecondary Institutions: 2010–11." US Department of Education, National Center for Education Statistics, 2013. http://nces.ed.gov/pubs2013/2013002.pdf. Accessed July 6, 2022.

Massey, Doreen. *For Space.* Sage, 2005.

McCrimmon, Miles. "Bridging the Divide: Dual Enrollment Five Years Later." *Teaching English in the Two-Year College*, vol. 41, no. 4, 2014, pp. 397–400.

McWain, Katie. "Finding Freedom at the Composition Threshold: Learning from the Experiences of Dual Enrollment Teachers." *Teaching English in the Two-Year College*, vol. 45, no. 4, 2018, pp. 406–424.

Moreland, Casie. "Chasing Transparency: Using Disparate Impact Analysis to Assess the (In)Accessibility of Dual Enrollment Composition." In *Writing Assessment, Social Justice, and the Advancement of Opportunity: Perspectives on Writing*, edited by Mya Poe, Asao B. Inoue, and Norbert Elliot. WAC Clearinghouse and UP of Colorado, 2019. https://wac.colostate.edu/books/perspectives/assessment/. Accessed May 12, 2022.

Moreland, Casie. "White Resistance, White Complacency: The Absent-Presence of Race in the Development of Dual Enrollment Programs." 2018. Arizona State University, PhD dissertation.

Nineteenth Annual Report of the Board of Directors of the St. Louis Public Schools, for the Year Ending August 1, 1873. Democrat Litho. and Printing Co., 1874.

Patterson, J. P., and David Duer. "High School Teaching and College Expectations in Writing and Reading." *English Journal*, vol. 95, no. 3, 2006, pp. 81–87.

Prior, Paul. "How Do Moments Add Up to Lives: Trajectories of Semiotic Becoming vs. Tales of School Learning in Four Modes." In *Making Future Matters*, edited by Rick Wysocki and Mary P. Sheridan. Computers in Composition Digital P, 2018. https://ccdigitalpress.org/book/makingfuturematters/prior-intro.html. Accessed May 12, 2022.

Reese, William J. *The Origins of the American High School.* Yale UP, 1995.

Reiff, Mary Jo, and Anis Bawarshi. "Tracing Discursive Resources: How Students Use Prior Genre Knowledge to Negotiate New Writing Contexts in First-Year Composition." *Written Communication*, vol. 28, no. 3, 2011, pp. 312–337.

Report of the Committee of Ten on Secondary School Studies: With the Reports of the Conferences Arranged by the Committee. Committee of Ten on Secondary School Studies. Published for the National Educational Association by the American Book Co., 1894.

Sommers, Nancy, and Laura Saltz. "The Novice as Expert: Writing the Freshman Year." *College Composition and Communication*, vol. 56, no. 1, 2004, pp. 124–149.

Taczak, Kara, and William H. Thelin. "(Re)envisioning the Divide: The Impact of College Courses on High School Students." *Teaching English in the Two-Year College*, vol. 37, no. 1, 2009, pp. 7–23.

Tinberg, Howard, and Jean-Paul Nadeau. "Contesting the Space between High School and College in the Era of Dual-Enrollment." *College Composition and Communication*, vol. 62, no. 4, 2011, pp. 704–725.

Tsing, Anna Lowenhaupt. *The Mushroom at the End of the World: On the Possibility of Life in Capitalist Ruins.* Princeton, NJ: Princeton UP, 2015.

Tsing, Anna Lowenhaupt. "On Nonscalability: The Living World Is Not Amenable to Precision-Nested Scales." *Common Knowledge*, vol. 18, no. 2, 2012, pp. 505–524.

Twenty-Ninth Annual Report of the Commissioners of Public Schools, to the Mayor and City Council of Baltimore. Sherwood and Co., 1858.

VanOverbeke, Marc O. *The Standardization of American Schooling: Linking Secondary and Higher Education, 1870–1910.* Palgrave Macmillan, 2008.

Vygotsky, Lev. *Thought and Language.* MIT, 1986.

Wilder, L., and Robert P. Yagelski. "Describing Cross-Disciplinary Analytic Moves in First-Year College Student Writing." *Research in the Teaching of English*, vol. 52, no. 4, 2018, pp. 382–403.

Wilson, Mary. "Class Discussion." Dual Enrollment Writing, Robinson High School, Apr. 17, 2018.

3

LOCATION, DELIVERY, AND THE HISTORICAL DIVIDE BETWEEN SCHOOL AND COLLEGE ENGLISH

Joseph Jones

Among the more compelling and enduring aspects of the historically troubled relations between high schools and colleges is the way high schools have mostly deferred to the way colleges have defined the discipline of English. At the heart of such deference is the college preparatory function that schools serve. While that preparatory function might be so indelible as to seem beyond scrutiny, the discipline of English, as perceived and practiced by those in college English departments, has rarely concerned itself with the far more diverse curricular undertakings secondary school English has explored and with which it has sometimes been burdened. There were gestures in high school English teaching and curricula throughout the first half of the twentieth century to define the mission of high school English in terms more expansive and visionary than college prep. Reformers issued imperatives for high schools to turn away from organizing curricula by academic disciplines to ones more vocational and concerned with the majority of students who would contribute to society through skills and labor that did not require college degrees. Such gestures and imperatives mostly dissipated as the long, diffuse progressive era of education drew to a close in the late 1950s—and seem to have disappeared entirely since the passage of No Child Left Behind and the disarray of its demise.

Not coincidentally, it was in the 1950s that well-intentioned and well-financed efforts to have high school students earn college credit began in earnest. This chapter interweaves representative historical texts and contemporary accounts to highlight the peculiar curricular space dual enrollment (DE) English courses occupy between and within high school and college. But it is not only curricular space: the material, institutional spaces occupied by dual enrollment courses provoke a politics of location too often not articulated in what may be otherwise

https://doi.org/10.7330/9781646422531.c003

justified critiques. Of particular note is the hushed resentment regarding the encroachment upon "college English" and the whispered doubts regarding the efficacy of high school teachers delivering "college-level" writing. The relations between secondary and postsecondary English studies have a long history of disputation, yet the extension of DE agreements between public, charter, and private schools and postsecondary institutions can make possible new opportunities for cooperation even as they manifest new iterations of the school/college conflict regarding the teaching of writing and the subject positions of those doing the teaching.

FORMATIVE RELATIONS BETWEEN HIGH SCHOOL AND COLLEGE ENGLISH

Considered in broad strokes, the relationship between secondary school English and college English has sometimes been contentious, sometimes cooperative, but mostly unmarked by sustained efforts at shared responsibility—even though calls for collegiality are familiar. A cursory review of history reveals that colleges have persistently found fault with their incoming students, even as they mostly avoid criticizing high school teachers. After a century of decrying the preparation of the students enrolling in college, one might fairly ask: who or what is the reason for the deficiency? Yet from the beginning, what occurs in college English has directly determined the values and practices of secondary school English.

John Brereton's description of the founding of Harvard's composition program in the 1870s, justified as it was by a series of Harvard reports regarding the poor preparation in writing of its incoming students, has especial pertinence because it makes clear where colleges first placed blame: "These reports were part of an attempt to get the secondary schools to improve their writing instruction; in effect, though, they diminished the role of first-year composition and expressed the hope of removing it entirely from the college curriculum and placing it in the schools" (26). Arthur Applebee notes in his comprehensive, essential history of English in American schools, *Tradition and Reform in the Teaching of English: A History*, that the beginnings of English as a major school subject in the 1890s mirrored the development of English as a college subject insofar as instruction in literature supplanted instruction in "grammar" and rhetoric (31–37). Once most American secondary schools at the end of the nineteenth century had finally established "English"—as opposed to rhetoric—as a required course, schools began to consider their charge as broader than only preparing their students for college (Kliebard 87). Given the tremendous growth in high school enrollment around the turn of the twentieth century, most high school students were not destined to continue on to college.

For those who were, Harvard's Adams Sherman Hill aimed his 1879 article "An Answer to the Cry for More English" at their teachers, expressing the sort of criticism not too unlike criticism one might hear today. That is, the inadequate preparation of college students is not necessarily the teachers' fault because teachers work in trying conditions that make the ideal impossible: "The overburdened and underpaid teacher had every inducement to cling to the prescribed routine" (46). The prescribed routine? The one that produces writers who even after graduating "from our best colleges . . . could not write a letter describing their own Commencement without making blunders which would disgrace a boy twelve years old" (46). Hill contended that Harvard was "doing as much for the English of her students as can reasonably be expected while the schools do so little" (56). The dissatisfaction with the preparation of incoming students manifested not only in curricular expectations but in admissions practices as well. Each has legacies with continuing effects on secondary school and higher education.

Because of their distrust of high schools, elite eastern colleges would not accept admission by certificate from accredited high schools—as many colleges in the Midwest and West did—and insisted instead that prospective students pass a series of entrance examinations. Especially troubling for the schools was the fact that each college devised its own entrance examination. The disparity of demands and test dates made preparing students for the exams particularly trying for teachers in preparatory schools. Moreover, the individual college entrance tests often dictated school curricula by specifying the texts students should study. The University of Michigan's Fred Newton Scott, writing in 1901, famously likened the relationship between eastern colleges and secondary schools to feudalism (366). The solution settled on was the creation of a series of achievement tests that all colleges could use as entrance examinations, an effort one commentator described as "an attempt to introduce law and order into an educational anarchy which towards the close of the nineteenth century had become exasperating, indeed almost intolerable, to schoolmasters" (Fuess 3).

The first exams were not without detractors, including some critics from the very colleges that had initiated their development. Hill and others at Harvard presumed the exams would provide the salutary pressure to elevate the performance of incoming students and, by implication, of their teachers. They didn't. The most vociferous opposition to the exams, however, came from secondary schools, many of which not only questioned the design of the exams but also objected to the shift to testing, which they considered tacit repudiation of their efforts. Likewise, some resisted the imposition of college curricular goals on the secondary schools. Applebee observes, however, that because "one function of the high school was preparatory, and because then as now the success of its preparatory courses was more important to a school's prestige than its finishing courses, radical change was forced upon the schools in a remarkably short time" (31).

The power of the colleges to dictate high school curriculum in the nascent discipline of English went largely unchallenged until twenty years or so into the twentieth century, when schools began trying to distinguish their educational mandate as more comprehensive than college preparation. Applebee credits perspectives derived from the progressivism associated with John Dewey for forging attitudes that "contributed directly to the emancipation of the high school from the college program in English" (48). That emancipation from the college program in English, however, was short-lived. The College Board's Frank Bowles notes in his collected papers that secondary education in the late 1940s and early 1950s was heading toward a general education program rather than a continuing adherence to the college program of discipline-specific coursework: "No one at the time foresaw that colleges would be able to reassert themselves and regain control of their entrance requirements. However they did so . . . and the idea of general education in the secondary schools vanished" (38–39).

FIRST EFFORTS AT STARTING COLLEGE EARLY

Criticisms of public education in general, and of progressive initiatives in particular, prompted the initial mid-twentieth-century explorations related to earning college credit while still in high school. Critics charged that progressivism's concerns for the whole child neglected the intellectual training the most able students deserved and, as Cold War fears intensified, that society needed for its brightest students. The concern was ostensibly for the intellectually gifted wasting time in the last two years of high school and first two years of college because of a perceived redundancy in curricula. The remedy imagined was not a more individualized curriculum or more innovative secondary programs but, rather, introductory college courses.

Concern for the "academically talented" gained considerable impetus from experiments sponsored by the Ford Foundation's Fund for the Advancement of Education, known simply as the Fund. With an endowment of $70 million, the Fund's ambitious mandate was "to advance and improve formal or institutionalized education in North America" (Woodring 1). Three projects in the early 1950s—the Program for Early Admission to College, the School and College Study of General Education, and the School and College Study of Admission with Advanced Standing—identified two ways of ameliorating the encumbrance on "the most able students": early college admission and advanced placement through examination. Given their historically persistent though often unwarranted low regard for high school teaching and teachers, America's most elite colleges and universities did not then embrace "dual enrollment." The first dual enrollment program, the University of Connecticut's Cooperative Program for Superior Students begun in 1955 (Estes 332), was not a Fund initiative, although its title suggests at least an initial commitment to the same intended cohort.

The Fund's first experiment, an early admissions program funded and launched to some fanfare in 1951, nevertheless is relevant to considerations of DE. In its report of the early admissions program, *They Went to College Early*, Philip Coombes, secretary and director of the Fund, justifies the program by criticizing the public school system for its insistence on age-level, grade-level grouping and progression: "The most serious victims—the most handicapped under this lock step arrangement—turn out to be our ablest youngsters for whom the pace is too slow and the academic diet too thin" (vii). Eleven colleges opened their doors to "420 freshman who differed from the average college freshman in two striking respects: they were roughly two years younger and only a few of them had finished high school" (*They* v–vii). The Fund supported "preinduction scholarships" for four years for an amount that totaled almost $3.5 million, awarded to "1,350 carefully selected students" between 1951 and 1954 (Woodring 153). The Educational Testing Service was asked to compare the success of the students relative to a control group that enrolled in college in the traditional manner. Despite some initial difficulties, the early admission students generally earned higher academic averages than the control group. Neither colleges nor the secondary schools, however, embraced the program without reservations. The colleges were primarily concerned about the students' social development, so researchers collected data about their "adjustment" to college from faculty members and the students themselves. A team of psychiatrists was engaged to evaluate the students. Data indicated modest differences between the "scholars" and the control group in terms of "shyness," "inhibition," and "dating" that flattened out during their four years of college.

Concern for the social development of students who begin college coursework early is reiterated in some contemporary critiques and assessments of DE. Howard Tinberg and Jean-Paul Nadeau have written thoughtfully about the challenges posed by the widespread adoption of DE, and among their primary concerns are the "students' maturity level, their developmental level as both students and writers" ("Contesting" 713). They ask: "While college faculty treat students as adults matter-of-factly, should dual-enrolled students who are, in fact, not adults, be treated as such" (714)? A second study by Tinberg and Nadeau includes the recommendation that "future studies of dual-enrolled students need to include a consideration of these students' social and psychological adjustments on entering college classrooms" ("What Happens" 40). The fact that such concerns arose and were investigated at the inception of early college programs suggests that affective considerations do indeed merit addressing. Among the compelling findings of one recent qualitative study was that even though the high school DE students generally performed at or above the level of their community college peers, the primary criticism by college faculty about their DE students was that they seemed less emotionally mature and less likely to seek support when they encountered academic problems (Ferguson, Baker, and Burnett 89). With that said, almost half of the community college instructors in the study could not identify former DE students in their classes. The authors recommend that "support services for students who enroll in dual enrollment courses taught at high schools and community colleges may be necessary to nurture the development of students' affective and nonacademic skills and behaviors" (91).

In the mid-1950s, however, the secondary schools involved were more distressed about losing some of their most talented students to college early; some principals even refused to inform students of the availability of Fund scholarships. One principal went so far as to call the early admissions program "an A-bomb dropped on secondary education" (Woodring 153). When funding for the program ended in 1954, largely because of resistance from the high schools involved rather than from the colleges, there were twelve participating colleges—including HBCU's Fisk and Morehouse—and eleven of them established their own early admission programs. By 1956, 29 of the 169 members of the College Board had established early admissions programs. Such programs remained small, and the absence of financial support from the Fund limited their expansion beyond very small numbers of carefully selected students.

Criticism regarding the lack of articulation between high school and college English informed that initial experiment of high school students beginning college work early. Such criticism seemed verified by another 1951 Fund initiative, the School and College Study of General Education, which surveyed alumni from college preparatory schools and discovered that their most common complaint about the first two years of college was "the duplication of course content" from high school (*General Education in School and College* 4). Compare that with Kristine Hansen and colleagues' 2015 report "How Do Dual Credit Students Perform on College Writing Tasks after They Arrive on Campus? Empirical Data from a Large-Scale Study," which sought but was unable to discover evidence demonstrating writing performance differences between DE students and their college peers. Particularly unsettling for the authors of the 2015 report was that students on their campus echoed students from the 1950s: interviews revealed that they saw little difference between first-year composition (FYC) and their high school coursework, despite a thoughtfully designed FYC course that "includes a strong focus on rhetoric, with assignments to write arguments from sources, to analyze rhetoric, and to combine media and modes of presentation" (78). The authors lament that "the different purposes and genres of writing that constitute the focus of our course did not seem to make much of an impression on the students we interviewed. For most of them, writing is writing, and whatever it is about or what form it takes doesn't matter" (78). They speculate that students' attitudes may come from the misguided conception of "general writing skills," a conception categorically rejected by writing studies theorists. Perhaps a more practical explanation for the students' views—in 2015 as well as in 1951—is that writing produced primarily or exclusively for teacher inspection must indeed all seem of a type.

PROBLEM AS OPPORTUNITY

The critique leveled more than sixty years ago by Albert Kitzhaber in his well-known National Council of Teachers of English (NCTE) convention address, "Death—or Transfiguration," still applies to more FYC programs than it should: the course takes on too much (i.e., endeavors in fifteen or thirty weeks to "fix" language patterns formed over fifteen years), lacks the intellectual rigor of other introductory college courses, diverges wildly in content or focus from campus to campus (and often from classroom to classroom on the same campus), and is nearly impossible to assess in a way that validates success. There have, of course, been many thoughtful and successful initiatives addressing such criticisms (e.g., Writing about Writing most recently and effectively), but a panoramic view of the FYC landscape confirms the persistent accuracy of much of Kitzhaber's critique. Kitzhaber attributed the muddled nature of FYC in 1960 to the "widespread failure of college English departments to recognize sufficiently that the teaching of language and writing is one of their inescapable responsibilities, and to include among requirements for future English teachers a selection of courses pertinent to the teaching of these" (372). Can it be averred that this negligence has been sufficiently addressed by most departments of English? Yet if one reads "Death—or Transfiguration" with a spirit of generosity toward DE, one might see in his recommendations pragmatic means for improving high school teaching and enriching high school English curricula while also creating space for reconsidering college disciplinary practices and alliances with secondary school colleagues through DE.

Kitzhaber asserts that "the high school is where much of the present work of Freshman English ought to be taken care of" (369). But this is no mean echo of the previous century's Harvard reports or Adams Sherman Hill's reproach. Rather, in the Portland High School Curriculum Study—a multiyear project that sought to transform high school English through curriculum planning by high school and college faculty that also included summer institutes on college campuses for high school teachers—Kitzhaber locates possibilities for articulation and joint action. The study's reports "urge us college teachers not to rest content with pious lamentations about the high school teacher's thirty-hour class schedule and 160 or 180 students; instead, we should lend our own prestige, influence, and powers of persuasion to a campaign for a reduced work load" (371), which he acknowledges would require "a degree and kind of cooperation between teachers at the two levels that probably is unprecedented, a systematic and continuing endeavor by the college English teachers to concern themselves actively with the high school curriculum and the professional welfare of their high school colleagues" (371). Kitzhaber hastens to add that should such changes occur, that would not free colleges from teaching writing but would make possible "a new Freshman course"—the "transfiguration" announced in his eschatological title.

For Kitzhaber, the problem of FYC is its amorphousness. That problem of FYC, however, is not necessarily the problem with DE. For FYC programs shepherded by writing specialists, the challenge of DE is not the curriculum but where and by whom it is taught. The professionalization of WPA work has created administrators who view FYC not as a burden so much as a calling, not as a problem to be solved so much as an opportunity to enact best practices in writing instruction. Secondary school teacher preparation programs, however, are often deficient in imparting those practices to new teachers (Pasternak et al.; Hillocks; Smagorinsky and Whiting). Moreover, as those within writing studies continually recompose FYC, those in the high schools remain distant and mostly excluded from that conversation. Thus, DE may not summon the historical suspicion that high school teachers are not doing their jobs so much as the suspicion that high school teachers are not capable of teaching writing in the way university faculty deem appropriate. Katie McWain notes sympathetically that high school teachers "often make decisions about when, where, and how students encounter college writing curriculum without a nuanced understanding of the theory and practice behind it" (407).

High school English teachers tend to appropriate those disciplinary lines of inquiry that they perceive have some practical application. The tension between theory and practice tends to conscribe action, for theory often serves as critique rather than support. There is also a sort of hegemony to theory, at least when it is practiced on those to whom the theory has not been explained or those who have had no hand in developing it. It is not that those in the schools resist theory or that they demand practicality above all else. Rather, those who describe theories of composition often position themselves above those who teach composition so that theory seems as far removed from teacher needs as the theorists seem from the classroom. The charge of the typical high school English teacher has remained remarkably stable, accreted from a century of college directives or disinterest: endeavor to engender some appreciation of literature, endeavor to provide instruction in the most basic skills of composition, and endeavor to make less forbidding the prospect of what may await students in college—often done with only the most prescriptive, imperfect sense of what that might be. Yet as Christine Denecker notes, "The real key to ameliorating gaps between secondary and post-secondary writing instruction is open, respectful, and productive dialogue among instructors on both sides of the composition threshold" (41). Dual enrollment makes such dialogue more likely because the DE teacher has a defined curricular mandate provided by the cooperating college.

Compare and contrast the DE teacher with the Advanced Placement (AP) teacher, who is also engaged in delivering "college-level English" in high school to high school students. Both groups of teachers earnestly, dutifully even, try to honor a version of English that has been transmitted to them—from a cooperating college for the DE teacher, from the College Board for the AP teacher. In fundamental ways, though, the college English course offered to the AP English teacher is a fiction, an imagined version of a first-year college English course that the teacher then contrives, influenced utterly by the implicit curriculum of AP (i.e., preparing students for the AP exam). With its emphasis on test performance, AP's implicit curriculum requires that teachers attenuate the writing process. The College Board declares in its description of the AP language course that "the process of composing is the essence of the first-year college writing course, and the AP English Language and Composition course emphasizes this process." Two sentences later, a greater truth emerges: "These extended, revised essays are not part of the AP English Language and Composition Exam, but the experience of writing them will help you become a more self-aware and flexible writer (which may help your performance on the AP Exam)" (College Board).

The DE teacher, by contrast, has the opportunity to teach an explicit FYC curriculum designed by college writing specialists for their students. Yet in most high schools, dual enrollment occupies a space below Advanced Placement English. The imprimatur of the College Board and the Educational Testing Service (ETS) and the AP exams could account for some of DE's continued prestige. The exams have been around for decades (AP Literature first appeared in 1954, AP Language in 1980), and their standardization suggests quality, even if AP curricula bear little resemblance to the kinds of things thoughtful college writing courses may actually do. A less visible factor that appeals to some for whom accepting DE credit is problematic is that the AP exam overrides the course grade and the instructor who determines it. In fact, a student can take an AP exam without having completed an AP course. One-time high school teacher and longtime WPA Irvin Peckham contends: "The dismissal of high school teachers' knowledge is in the air we breathe" (258).

With that said, WPAs rightfully fret about the quality of their writing programs and do all they can to ensure quality by developing thoughtful, pertinent curricula; by mentoring novice, sometimes uninterested instructors; and by assessing program effectiveness. Dual enrollment often reminds those professionalized as composition specialists of the modest status of the first-year course. Despite the often brilliant and nobly tenacious efforts of those in writing studies who have appreciably elevated the teaching of writing on many college campuses, dual enrollment (and AP and International Baccalaureate [IB] and College-Level Examination Program [CLEP] and American College Testing [ACT] and the other means of FYC exemptions those in admissions allow) is a pointed reminder that many parents, students, and college administrators regard FYC as an inconvenience that can be taught by almost anyone anywhere. Kara Taczak and William Thelin's assertion that a poorly conceived DE course "furthers a regressive view of composition in the eye of the public, a view that does not take into consideration the research in the field and that focuses on current-traditional precepts to guide its perceptions" (7), concisely articulates the unease of many WPAs regarding DE.

In the 2015 qualitative study by Colin Ferguson and his colleagues referred to previously, the authors compared "the perceptions of rigor" among high school DE teachers, community college faculty teaching DE students on the college campus, and community college faculty teaching college students on the college campus. The high school teachers thought their course was at least as rigorous as those offered on the college campus, an estimation based on reports from former students as well as from their own work with high school and college colleagues. The authors also acknowledge that variance between instructor expectations and notions of rigor is common and therefore suggest that local school districts and cooperating colleges "form advisory boards to review course content and provide resulting recommendations" (91). Such boards should include faculty and administrators from both sites. The National Alliance of Concurrent Enrollment Partnerships has developed models for such assessment and evaluation, as well as for training and professional development.

The high school teachers also reported having little to no latitude in designing assignments or determining grade calculations. McWain describes the relative absence of teacher autonomy as a lack of academic freedom, arguing that high school DE teachers "are surveilled by and made accountable to public stakeholders, including parents, administrators, voters, and legislators, in ways college faculty traditionally are not" (407). The relative absence of teacher autonomy, however, should be considered contextually. For example, Ferguson and colleagues conclude that college faculty who "had the freedom to design a course that effectively reflects their educational philosophies" created courses that "yielded inconsistency and uncontrolled confounding variables when course-level comparisons are made" (88). For the WPAs endeavoring to establish program consistency to ensure common, coherent student learning experiences, "inconsistency and uncontrolled confounding variables" are less a mark of academic freedom than an indication of curricular and perhaps instructor confusion. Yet McWain's larger point is essential: DE programs "must also include a commitment to helping dual enrollment instructors make informed choices about their curriculum, with an understanding of the expectations and best practices advocated by the colleges for whom they teach" (414). After all, recognizing that "transitioning writers across the composition threshold is not so much about what the *students* do as it is about what the *instructors* know or understand about composition practices on both sides of the divide" (Denecker 31, original emphasis) helps shift college faculty from concern about the possible deficiencies of high school DE teachers and toward the sort of dialogue those on the college side of the divide have been claiming for decades that they want to bridge.

DE's location apart and away from the college also renders it suspect to those inside the college. Because the course is taken in high schools and taught by high school teachers, DE students are rarely appreciated as members of the university community, and their teachers are certainly not considered members of the college faculty. A blurring of the historical separation of high school and college occurs in DE, and it tends to trouble those in college, even as their colleagues in high school welcome it. What many critics of DE seem to take particular umbrage at is that DE teachers presume to teach college writing at a location other than a college. We know that where writing is done is a vital consideration of how writing is done. Yet rather than assuming a priori that DE instruction is inferior because of where it occurs, it is incumbent upon colleges participating in DE programs to investigate if or how the course differs from its counterpart on college campuses. As Hansen and colleagues discovered, though, it might be hard to prove that the college writing classroom is necessarily a better location for college writing instruction if we look only at the written products from both locations. The more compelling argument is that a college classroom provides a qualitatively more intellectual environment. However, the assumption that the desired "habits of mind" or essential "threshold concepts" associated with FYC can only be inculcated or broached by college instructors on college campuses seems less tenable if one considers a first-semester TA or a harried part-time instructor racing among eight sections at five different institutions. To be sure, determining the intellectual richness of a site is no easy task. But without study, we can only imagine what is happening or not happening in high school dual enrollment classes.

OPPORTUNITY FOR STRUCTURAL CHANGE

The sweeping revision advocated by Kitzhaber has not come to pass, and the changes he describes in the Portland school district did not last. However, his recommendation for greater collaboration persists as a refrain. To be sure, nearly every article about DE, including this one, echoes the calls for greater collaboration sounded for decades. But schools and colleges need a reason to cooperate, a reason to meet, a reason to collaborate. DE offers the exigence too often absent from calls for greater collaboration and might indeed signal a structural change that necessitates that all those involved (high school teachers, administrators, and counselors and college faculty, administrators, and advisers) meet regularly to review goals, curricula, and assessment data and to air concerns and grievances. It should not be considered "outreach" but, rather, part of the work we all do.[1]

Keeping in mind the thoughtful cautions directed toward the expansion of DE, much of the current research indicates that despite its disorderly emergence, DE seems to mostly deliver quality instruction that benefits qualified students: "Participating students are more likely to graduate high school, enroll and persist in college, accrue college credits, and complete college than students who do not participate in dual enrollment" (Barnett, Maclutsky, and Wagonlander 39). Such research, however, as Melinda Mechur Karp notes, typically presents "a picture of a static, stand-alone initiative in which discrete partnerships of colleges and high schools work together to meet the needs of their particular students" (103); but DE "should be located in the broader context of national efforts to reform postsecondary education" (103). Her justification for investing in DE transcends the disciplinary concerns by focusing instead on the continuing disparity in college enrollment and graduate rates between upper- and lower-income college students and between white students and Latinx and Black students (McFarland et al.). Karp argues that restructuring the relationship between high school and college can fuse "pieces of the pipeline more closely together, helping students make their way through rather than leaking out at key transition points" (105). In a way reminiscent of Kitzhaber's injunction sixty years ago, Karp challenges those involved in DE to "think big" by contextualizing it with "other college readiness and completion efforts, such as senior year transition courses, early warning assessments, or college bridge programs" and by engaging in "policy-related conversations about how to best structure, incentivize, and administer dual enrollment and other college completion initiatives" (110).

College English has long imposed itself on high school English, and high school teachers are at least as loyal to their notions of what their students are going to need in college as to the mandates of the dreadful state tests that have also been imposed on them. Considered as a national phenomenon, DE is rife with shortcomings. Considered locally by those directly engaged in the enterprise, DE is filled with possibilities for genuine school-college collaboration. Mentoring and monitoring those responsible for teaching the first-year college course provide those directing college writing programs with opportunities to address what Kitzhaber considered a key question: we should not ask whether "they write well enough to get by" but "how much better can they be taught to write" (372). There are certainly dynamic examples of how that occurs (e.g., McClure et al.; Moody and Bonesteel; Post et al.). The enduring challenge is whether those in college writing programs with dual enrollment agreements will find the time, resources, and commitment to realize the possibilities for collaboration with the high school colleagues teaching their courses.

NOTE

1. See Hanson and colleagues for a discussion of how such collaboration might be done consistently in large schools-college DE partnerships.

WORKS CITED

Applebee, Arthur. *Tradition and Reform in the Teaching of English: A History.* NCTE, 1974.

Barnett, Elisabeth, Evelyn Maclutsky, and Chery Wagonlander. "Emerging Early College Models for Traditionally Underserved Students." *New Directions for Community Colleges,* no. 169, 2015, pp. 39–49.

Bowles, Frank. *The Refounding of the College Board, 1948–1963.* College Entrance Examination Board, 1967.

Brereton, John, ed. "Introduction." In *The Origins of Composition Studies in the American College, 1875–1925: A Documentary History.* U of Pittsburgh P, 1995, pp. 3–25.

College Board. "AP English Language and Composition: Course Details." AP Students. apstudent.collegeboard.org/apcourse/ap-english-language-and-composition/course-details. Accessed March 2019.

Coombs, Philip. "Foreword: Talent, Education and Democracy." *They Went to College Early: Evaluation Report Number 2.* The Fund for the Advancement of Education, 1957, pp. v–viii.

Denecker, Christine. "Transitioning Writers across the Composition Threshold: What Can We Learn from Dual Enrollment Partnerships." *Composition Studies,* vol. 4, no. 1, 2013, pp. 21–50.

Estes, Helen J. "College Level English in High School." *English Journal,* vol. 48, no. 6, 1959, pp. 332–334.

Ferguson, Colin, Pete Baker, and Dana Burnett. "Faculty Members' Perceptions of Rigor in Dual Enrollment, Accelerated Programs, and Standard Community College Courses." *New Directions for Community Colleges,* no. 169, 2015, pp. 83–91.

Fuess, Claude M. *The College Board: Its First Fifty Years.* College Entrance Examination Board, 1967.

General Education in School and College: A Committee Report by Members of the Faculties of Andover, Exeter, Lawrenceville, Harvard, Princeton, and Yale. Harvard UP, 1953.

Hansen, Kristine, Brian Jackson, Brett C. McInelly, and Dennis Eggett. "How Do Dual Credit Students Perform on College Writing Tasks after They Arrive on Campus? Empirical Data from a Large-Scale Study." *WPA: Writing Program Administration*, vol. 38, no. 2, 2015, pp. 56–92.

Hanson, Jana M., Todd Prusha, and Cort Iverson. "Principal, Teacher, and Counselor Views on Concurrent Enrollment." *New Directions for Community Colleges*, no. 169, 2015, pp. 71–81.

Hill, Adams Sherman. "An Answer to the Cry for More English." In *The Origins of Composition Studies in the American College, 1875–1925: A Documentary History*, edited by John Brereton. U of Pittsburgh P, 1995, pp. 45–57.

Hillocks, George. "Middle and High School Composition." In *Research on Composition: Multiple Perspectives on Two Decades of Change*, edited by Peter Smagorinsky. Teachers College P, 2006, pp. 48–77.

Karp, Melinda Mechur. "Dual Enrollment, Structural Reform, and the Completion Agenda." *New Directions for Community Colleges*, no. 169, 2015, pp. 103–111.

Kitzhaber, Albert. "Death—or Transfiguration?" *College English*, vol. 21, no. 7, 1960, pp. 367–373.

Kliebard, Herbert. *The Struggle for the American Curriculum: 1893–1958*, 3rd ed. Routledge-Falmer, 2004.

McClure, Randall, Kevin Enerson, Jane Kepple Johnson, Patricia Lipetzky, and Cynthia Pope. "Concurrent Enrollment in Rural Minnesota: Addressing the Needs Caused by Shifting Demographics, Economics, and Academics." In *College Credit for Writing in High School: The "Taking Care of" Business*, edited by Kristine Hansen and Christine Farris. NCTE, 2010, pp. 189–207.

McFarland, Joel, Bill Hussar, Jijun Zhang, Xiaolei Wang, Ke Wang, Sarah Hein, Melissa Diliberti, Emily Forrest Cataldi, Farrah Bullock Mann, Amy Barmer, Thomas Nachazel, Megan Barnett, and Stephen Purcell. *The Condition of Education 2019.* National Center for Education Statistics, 2019.

McWain, Katie. "Finding Freedom at the Composition Threshold: Learning from the Experiences of Dual Enrollment Teachers." *TETYC*, vol. 45, no. 4, 2018, pp. 406–424.

Moody, Patricia, and Margaret Bonesteel. "Syracuse University Project Advance: A Model of Connection and Quality." In *College Credit for Writing in High School: The "Taking Care of" Business*, edited by Kristine Hansen and Christine Farris. NCTE, 2010, pp. 227–244.

Pasternak, Donna L., Samantha Caughlan, Heidi L. Hallman, Laura Renzi, and Leslie S. Rusch, eds. *Secondary English Teacher Education in the United States.* Bloomsbury Academic, 2017.

Peckham, Irvin. "Whispers from the Margin: A Class-Based Interpretation of the Conflict between High School and College Writing Teachers." In *History, Reflection, and Narrative: The Professionalization of Composition, 1963–1983*, edited by Mary Rosner, Beth Boehm, and Debra Journet. Ablex, 1999, pp. 253–268.

Post, Joanna Castner, Vicki Beard Simmons, and Stephanie Vanderslice. "Round up the Horses—the Cards Are Racing Downhill! Programmatic Catch-up to a Quickly Growing Concurrent Enrollment Program." In *College Credit for Writing in High School: The "Taking-Care-of" Business*, edited by Kristine Hansen and Christine Farris. NCTE, 2010, pp. 165–188.

Scott, Fred Newton. "College Entrance Requirements in English." *School Review*, vol. 9, June 1901, pp. 365–378.

Smagorinsky, Peter, and Melissa Whiting. *How English Teachers Get Taught: Methods of Teaching the Methods Class.* NCTE, 1995.

Taczak, Kara, and William Thelin. "(Re)Envisioning the Divide: The Impact of College Courses on High School Students." *TETYC*, vol. 37, no. 1, 2009, pp. 7–23.

They Went to College Early. Evaluation Report. Fund for the Advancement of Education (U.S.), no. 2. New York, 1957.

Tinberg, Howard, and Jean-Paul Nadeau. "Contesting the Space between High School and College in the Era of Dual-Enrollment." *College Composition and Communication*, vol. 62, no. 4, 2011, pp. 704–725.

Tinberg, Howard, and Jean-Paul Nadeau. "What Happens When High School Students Write in a College Course? A Study of Dual Credit." *English Journal*, vol. 2, no. 5, 2013, pp. 35–42.

Woodring, Paul. *Investment in Innovation: An Historical Appraisal of the Fund for the Advancement of Education.* Little, Brown, 1970.

SECTION TWO

Perspectives of Alignment

Building High School–College Partnerships

4

THE OPTICS OF OBSERVATION

Exploring Tensions and Opportunities at the High School–College Composition Threshold

Katie McWain and Jackie Hoermann-Elliott,
with Jennifer Hadley

As dual enrollment (DE) partnerships between high schools and colleges become increasingly more common, many postsecondary institutions have implemented required site visits and classroom observations for secondary instructors, ostensibly as a mechanism for ensuring course quality and alignment (Anson). Our institution recently began requiring all departments to observe DE teachers once a year, a mandate that has generated significant resistance among college faculty. To illustrate how these interactions are often perceived by the high school instructors on the other side of the partnership, we begin with a story from Jennifer, a DE first-year composition (FYC) instructor who kindly agreed to serve as a contributing author on this piece. When we asked Jennifer to reflect on her experiences of being observed by college faculty, she shared an anecdote that resonated with us: "This was not at my school, but another adjunct I know said that her observer told her she 'needed to take a bath' after coming to the high school, 'to wash the high school off of her.' To me, that was bothersome. I love teaching in a high school, and I love that I am able to serve my students. I choose to be in a K–12 setting, so I would think it would be important to make sure high school teachers know that they are valued as much as any other composition instructor."

This quotation emblematizes the tensions inherent in DE observations, including the disconnect between high school and college contexts, the privileging of postsecondary over secondary knowledge, and the attitude of surveillance that often pervades mandatory site visits. Our chapter seeks to explore these tensions and to reflect on how writing program administrators (WPAs) and other DE administrators might better understand and even ameliorate the problematic optics of these partnerships, drawing on our experiences in an institutional climate

https://doi.org/10.7330/9781646422531.c004

where DE FYC is a dynamic force poised to gain additional momentum in the coming years.

The rise of DE in Texas has garnered attention from powerful stakeholders, including the Texas Higher Education Coordinating Board, the Southern Association of Colleges and Schools, and the American Institutes for Research (Miller et al.). In 2007, Texas implemented legislation requiring high schools to offer at least twelve hours of college credit, prompting a "massive increase" in program offerings (Moreland and Miller 186). Today, Texas DE policies are constantly shifting in a gesture toward statewide "accountability," forcing postsecondary institutions to adopt revised standards after each legislative session. As new WPAs at a public state university, we (Katie and Jackie) plunged into the administration of a growing DE partnership in 2018. We are primarily responsible for supporting and supervising nine high school instructors who deliver our institution's FYC curriculum on their campuses, including Jennifer, our contributing author.

As our institution begins the complex process of exploring certification with the National Alliance of Concurrent Enrollment Partnerships (NACEP), an accrediting body with rigorous standards, upper-level administration has also implemented annual site visits for DE faculty. These observations provide opportunities to learn more about the composition "threshold" (Denecker) and for "bridging the space between high school and college" (Dennihy 156). At the same time, we know that required visits from college faculty are often perceived by high school teachers as a challenge to pedagogical autonomy or even a surveillance mechanism (McWain).

With these tensions in mind, we have worked to navigate the careful tightrope walk of DE observations, a process documented in this chapter. We begin by exploring the historical secondary-postsecondary divide in composition studies, focusing on DE as a liminal space where this divide becomes especially salient. Drawing on multiple data sources—including our WPA experiences, a qualitative study of DE instructors, and Jennifer's reflections—we offer suggestions for making classroom visits more formative, dialogic, and relationship-based. Exploring successes as well as failures, we share strategies for facilitating observations that fulfill the requirements of external entities (institutions, states, and accrediting bodies) while also providing meaningful professional development that is program-specific and geared toward formative growth rather than unidirectional evaluation. We argue that given the shifting landscape of DE, in which WPAs are increasingly charged with meeting the demands of stakeholders similar to ours in

Texas, observations grounded in shared goals can be productive tools for supporting cross-level collaboration in DE partnerships and assuaging the isolation DE teachers often feel at their home institutions.

THE VIEW FROM AFAR: EMBEDDED DE TEACHERS IN THE FYC LANDSCAPE

We write from our roles as director and assistant director of FYC at Texas Woman's University (TWU)—a midsized, doctoral-granting, Hispanic-serving public state institution in north-central Texas. TWU utilizes an embedded model of DE, in which credentialed high school teachers deliver college curriculum on high school campuses. This approach (selecting and training credentialed instructors to teach FYC in their home institutions rather than sending college faculty to high schools or bringing high school students to college) has both affordances and constraints as a pedagogical delivery system.

Most notably, embedded partnerships illustrate the "betwixt and between" quality described in Victor Turner's ethnographic work on liminality (95). The nature of this delivery model—conceptualized as neither fully in college nor fully in high school but somewhere in between—creates a complex liminal positionality for teachers that can be productive as well as problematic (McWain 408). Embedded programs also reflect Christine Denecker's contention that the DE classroom is a space in which "tensions and inconsistencies between secondary and post-secondary writing instruction have the potential for becoming more clearly defined" (29). According to Denecker, some of the key differences constraining writing pedagogy in high school include the required content and curriculum, state and national standards, and instructor labor conditions (32). In our work with embedded teachers, we also remain cautious of the long-standing secondary-postsecondary divide in composition studies (Green), as well as Melissa Dennihy's observation that "a chasm exists between high school and college educators that can leave teachers on each side imagining what 'they' do as vastly different from what 'we' do" (156). Experience and research have taught us that DE partnerships can "serve as conduits for collaboration, conversation, and professional development" among teachers (Denecker 42.) Yet we also acknowledge Denecker's qualification that successful partnerships must be grounded in "two-way dialogues" (42), a charge we take seriously as WPAs.

In an attempt to foster such dialogues, Melanie Burdick and Jane Greer recommend that DE teachers receive specialized professional development experiences designed to help them synthesize multiple approaches to college-level writing. Similarly, Michael Stancliff and his colleagues argue that "administrators and faculty of FYW programs should become active collaborators with multiple stakeholders in DC/CE partnerships, primary among them, our colleagues teaching high school English" (5). One compelling example, the Conference on College Composition and Communication's (CCCC's) 2015 "Statement on Preparing Teachers of College Writing," recommends "ongoing formative assessment that incorporates opportunities for professional development and improvement, formal mentoring by more experienced or expert colleagues, and participation in curriculum development and assessment" for composition instructors (n.p.). These guidelines, while supportive and well-intentioned, do not account for the liminal position occupied by embedded DE teachers and the sense of alienation they often feel. Although these instructors are often experts with years of pedagogical experience in their own contexts, they are also novices at delivering college curriculum and may lack effective strategies for extrapolating college-level approaches from disciplinary research or "best practices" in composition studies.

Given this unique role, embedded instructors need more than simply a once-a-year summative evaluation from a "supervisory" college faculty member.[1] They deserve access to specialized resources, communities of practice, and two-way communication with their partner institutions to translate FYC curriculum effectively while also navigating the unique contours of the high school environment. One of the pioneers in this area is Chris Anson, who in 2010 proposed a set of recommendations for DE composition programs that includes "entry-level and ongoing training and development" as well as surveys, interviews, focus groups, and internal and external reviews (261). Yet more than a decade later, these assessment standards remain difficult to implement, especially given the responsibilities WPAs must juggle. Instead of offering a comprehensive professional development program like the one outlined above, DE administrators must often rely on a high-stakes practice for teacher evaluation, one frequently used as a "quality assurance" indicator in high school–college partnerships and required for NACEP certification—the classroom observation.

TAKING THE LONG VIEW ON DE OBSERVATIONS

In our first semester as WPAs, we were immediately confronted with the complexity of required observations, a tool that had been used for instructor assessment in our institution's FYC program for several years. Based on successful past experiences at different universities, we both felt that classroom visits can have significant benefits for instructors at all levels—for the observer as well as the observee. In fact, Dennis R. Waller notes that in DE programs in particular, "opportunities to get into the high school classroom and watch the high school faculty partner teach can be a very rewarding experience when approached in a supportive way. Most of my college academic department mentors find the process as much a learning experience for them as for the high school faculty partner" (56).

As early-career administrators adjusting to a new institutional context, however, we felt overwhelmed by our charge—to observe each embedded high school instructor at least once a year. This meant we needed to contact, schedule visits with, obtain course materials for, drive to campus, debrief with, and write reports for nine instructors across five school districts. Unsure of where to start, we began by researching the use of teaching observations as an assessment practice.

One of the first (and only) pioneers of observation scholarship has been Charlotte Danielson, an educational leadership and policy studies researcher who began codifying the numerous and shifting components of observation processes. As early as 1996, she established the Danielson Framework to better support observers and observees as they engage in conversation and reflection around the classroom visit (Danielson and McGreal). Every few years, the framework has been expanded and revised to respond to paradigmatic shifts in teaching, such as the impact of Common Core Standards on content delivery. The 2013 version of the Danielson Framework, which we utilized, breaks assessment into twenty-two components of pedagogical growth (e.g., Knowledge of Content and Pedagogy, Demonstrating Knowledge of Students) spread across four domains of teaching (e.g., Planning and Preparation, The Classroom Environment). Because we both came from institutions that billed the observation process as an opportunity to grow and learn in a peer-to-peer support format, we felt comfortable with this sort of multifaceted approach to pedagogical growth and development. Neither of us, however, had ever been assessed using such an exhaustive instrument as the one authored by the Danielson Group or even one as developed as the observation form we inherited from past administrators at TWU (see appendix 4.A).

Furthermore, like many new administrators in their first year, we did not want—nor did we have time—to create our own instruments, especially ones that could disrupt the expectations of veteran teachers who might be wary of new supervision. Instead, we adopted a previously used observation protocol that most nearly reflects the one designed by Michael C. Flanigan. Similar to the Danielson Framework, Flanigan assesses writing instruction with the intention of developing each teacher's individual style and chooses to focus on stages of the observation process in terms of three phases: pre-observation interview, observation, and follow-up conference (246–249). Much of this evaluative structure is still in play today, as it is common practice to ask instructors what the observed lesson will entail—a period of discovery, as Flanigan describes—followed by attending a class session and debriefing the instructor after it concludes. Flanigan's model for a follow-up conference offers the instructor an opportunity to comment on how the class went, review notes taken in an observation log, and establish a stratagem for continued pedagogical improvement (249).

With the publication of *Assessing the Teaching of Writing* in 2015, Amy E. Dayton revitalized conversations around pedagogical assessment in composition by attending more carefully to its political and ideological dynamics: "Assessing the teaching of writing is a process fraught with conflict . . . When it comes to assessment, practical realities—including a lack of time, administrative resources, or knowledge about best practices—frequently trump our intentions to do a comprehensive job of evaluating classroom performance. Without clear guidelines for collecting and interpreting data, the outcome can be influenced by individual biases about what counts as evidence of good teaching" (3). Brian Jackson highlights a similar tension in his account of observing a high school faculty member from his position as a college faculty member, describing how he attempted to not call too much attention to himself as an interloper in the classroom. While acknowledging the inherent artificiality of this situation, Jackson notes that he finds meaning in the uncomfortable moments, as he considers the observation to be a kind of "macro teaching" that enables WPAs to experience how curriculum is "felt at the delivery point" (47). He accordingly calls for WPAs to "shrug off their status as bosses" by "observing in the spirit of mutual collaboration and formative evaluation, with the instructor's growth as the primary goal" (50). Despite the earnest efforts of Jackson and other scholars who aim for egalitarian, supportive observation procedures, recent research reminds us that the intellectual characteristics and demographics of any writing classroom—particularly in secondary contexts—may complicate observers' perceptions of instructors' pedagogy (Steinberg and Garrett).

In DE programs in particular, the power divide inherent in classroom observations can play out along predictable secondary-postsecondary lines. As Denecker notes, high school instructors "often view [teaching] advice from those 'in the tower' with suspicion," since "the day-to-day practicalities of secondary writing instruction do not meet neatly with the ideals espoused by college composition instructors" (42). Similarly, Amy M. Penrose highlights the fact that required professional development (such as observations) can feel "coercive" and even "hegemonic" for marginalized teachers (116), while Shari Stenberg and Amy Lee point out that classroom visits are frequently viewed as "surveillance mechanisms" (334). Even CCCC's "Statement on Dual Credit/Concurrent Enrollment Composition" seems to frame observations as potentially punitive. This authoritarian ethos is less prevalent in NACEP's guidelines, which recommend positively focused, descriptive site visit reports as one of several artifacts in a detailed partnership documentation process (Focarile et al.). Yet our institution is not currently accredited with NACEP and thus supports evaluative visits over formative ones. Our initial research and experience have thus convinced us that while classroom observations have the potential to facilitate cross-level dialogue in DE partnerships, they can also function as a source of tension and even resentment for instructors. In the sections that follow, we share insights about these tensions from the experts themselves—embedded DE teachers.

A QUICK STUDY IN SURVEILLANCE

In 2016 and 2017, Katie (hereafter "I" in this section) conducted an Institutional Review Board–approved, qualitative study of FYC teacher development across institutional contexts and curricular delivery models in two midwestern states. Data collected for this project included recorded interviews with six embedded DE teachers and informal conversations with the WPAs or equivalent coordinators in several of the high school–college partnerships. When I returned to these data as a new administrator in 2019, intending to explore what I might learn from my study participants, I found an unsurprising trend: although well-intentioned WPAs may claim to approach classroom observations from a supportive standpoint, the observed teachers did not always find the observation to be a productive or useful experience.

One of the themes that continually surfaced in these interviews was the inadequacy of a single, annual site visit for capturing and providing any kind of meaningful feedback on a teacher's pedagogy. Consider how Sam, a thoughtful and confident instructor, described his perception of the yearly observation process in his DE partnership:

> They send me an email and say, "Hey, I'm gonna observe you sometime in the next three months. Let's set up a day" . . . And we do our thing, and then afterwards we usually debrief for a little bit, although we don't always have time, depending on the class. And then they say, "I'll write up some notes and send them to you" . . . It's kind of just wanting to make sure that you're at the level of rigor, and the expectations in the course are what would correspond to what would happen in college. And I think they observe a class and they see, oh, you're doing these things, and this is cool, and this is cool. And so yeah, I like that, good. *Whatever they can observe of one class period out of the whole year.* (Interview, emphasis added)

What is not captured in this written transcript is Sam's ironic tone, which underscores the perfunctory, almost comical rundown of the many steps involved in these re-certification visits. He laughs and then falls silent for several seconds after his concluding thought: "Whatever they can observe out of one class period out of the whole year." It is clear to Sam that an isolated interaction with a single faculty observer—even when appended to a written report and a debriefing conversation, as Flanigan recommends—is not necessarily a meaningful professional development experience that can translate into improved college-level pedagogy.

Mary, an embedded teacher in another state, offered a similar reflection while describing a challenging classroom visit. She found this observation experience difficult because although she was brand-new to teaching DE for this institution and had received little guidance beforehand, the visiting faculty member had "counted off" on Mary's performance rating for miscommunications, such as using the incorrect textbook. As Mary noted, "If you get observed twice a year, you should at least have conversations about the class that often, too, instead of 'just come in and watch what's going on.' But that's like an isolated snapshot. [You need to] have a conversation about, where was this lesson in the scheme of what was going on" (Interview). Mary described her ideal, ongoing observation partnership as a type of professional development "maintenance"—a form of feedback she would value more if it felt truly authentic to her pedagogy and her context (Interview).

These challenges were further amplified by the administrators in my study. Joseph, a supervisor of DE teachers at a two-year college, noted that "we try really hard to observe our comp instructors every two years, but when you go into their classroom, that's the day that they bring out their ideal lesson" (Interview). I know Joseph to be an equitable and generous WPA, so it was disheartening to learn that his program struggled to conduct site observations regularly or that he felt teachers often play up an "ideal" version of their pedagogy for the high-stakes observation moment—a snapshot of the classroom that does not capture the messy, in-process development of daily teaching work. Joseph also spoke at length about his desire to have a dedicated DE coordinator in the English department, someone who could help him conduct more frequent observations and provide support and resources to embedded high school teachers (Interview).

Sally, an enthusiastic and intrepid instructor, was the only study participant who spoke positively about classroom observations. She noted that her sponsoring university enlisted retired composition faculty—presumably because they had more flexible schedules—to observe local DE teachers. As she described this process in her interview, "They're using retired dual credit teachers to come out and [observe], so that's really cool. They just want to observe something and see what's going on and get a sense of what's happening in the schools. And so a lot of driving, but a really cool job, I think." I obtained several past observation reports from this same program, all submitted by retired college composition faculty to the DE director. What follows is an excerpt from one of these write-ups, which describes an unidentified English teacher who did not participate in my study:

> [Question on the report form]: Please provide a narrative that summarizes your observation and any discussion you had with the [teacher]—to be returned along with this sheet to [the University DE director] following the visit.
>
> [Supervisor's response]: Two sections of 29 and 19 students respectively, based the lesson off Hemingway's idea that a short novel can be done in a 6-word memoir. Each student had created a personal six-word memoir which included some grapics [*sic*]. Each stood in front of the room, read the memoir and explained its relevance to the class. These were very interesting and followed up on one line on a note card of "what most people don't know about me." These had been posted with each student's name on the bulletin board outside the classroom door. This is a culturally diverse community of students so such tasks are excellent in so many respects. ("Classroom Assessment")

While this report is clearly well-intentioned and the observed class period sounds engaging and creative, it does raise some questions. First, leaving aside the fact that this was a literature-focused lesson,[2] the description does not demonstrate evidence of any professional development scaffolding: how did this lesson fit into the context and overall trajectory of the course? What were the teacher's articulated goals and pedagogical approaches? How did the students experience the lesson?

Did the observer plan to provide constructive feedback or even ask questions? Was there any opportunity for dialogue?

I am also interested in the subtext behind this observer's pronouncement that the six-word memoir assignment is "excellent in so many respects" for a "culturally diverse community." Why? Did this activity seem well-aligned because it focused on personal identity, thus providing an opportunity for writers to bridge the connection between a canonical white male author and their own lives? How did the observer actually perceive this class population and their learning needs—and why were they unable to say so explicitly? Was this a missed opportunity to address culturally responsive pedagogies in a debriefing conversation? Did such a conversation even take place? While the visit outlined above may well have been a positive experience for both teacher and observer, the report's vagueness underscores the inherent tensions of using classroom observations as a singular mechanism for teacher assessment and development—a theme echoed throughout my interviews with embedded teachers.

AN EYE TOWARD RELATIONSHIP BUILDING

Katie's study provided a kind of productive distance for analyzing teacher accounts, as she was not in a supervisory role over any of her participating instructors. The promise of anonymity and the study's IRB approval gave interviewees license to speak freely about their experiences being observed. In contrast, when Jackie reached out to contributing author Jennifer, a DE FYC instructor she had observed in her position as assistant WPA, we knew there was an inherent power dynamic in this request to contribute. We both had established working relationships with Jennifer; Katie knew her as a thoughtful teacher-scholar from serving as her instructor in a graduate composition pedagogy seminar, while Jackie and Jennifer had developed a relationship through the observation process. It was important to us to feature a DE teacher's voice in this chapter, and as a strong instructor and impressive graduate student who taught *us* key lessons during our first year as WPAs, Jennifer seemed like the ideal choice. We were excited when she agreed to contribute, and we offer in this section a miniature case study drawn from both Jennifer's and Jackie's reflections on the observation experience they shared. Jennifer contributed her written notes and provided feedback on our multiple drafts of this chapter, so we feel confident that it at least partially represents her experience. At the same time, we acknowledge the inherent potential for coercion and misrepresentation in writing alongside any of our high school teaching partners, over whom we have an inherently supervisory role.

Notably, this particular account represents a learning experience on both sides of the partnership. The exchange took place during Jennifer's first semester teaching DE FYC and was also the first site visit Jackie conducted, so both parties were new to the process of DE observations as well as to their own positions. A seasoned classroom teacher herself, Jennifer serves as the DE FYC instructor for juniors on her high school campus. Her fifteen years of teaching experience include twelve years teaching English language arts and reading in a Title I school, with the last three on her current public high school campus.

In accordance with Flanigan's model, Jackie reached out to Jennifer with the initial observation request. After they selected a mutually agreed-upon date and time, Jackie asked Jennifer to email her with context about her day-of-the-visit lesson plan to frame her observation.[3] On the day of the visit, Jackie positioned herself among the students, taking notes on a laptop for the duration of the fifty-minute class period. Later, Jackie emailed Jennifer with her observation write-up and scheduled a phone call for the two of them to debrief.

While Jackie was impressed with Jennifer, she still found the observation report difficult to write. Based on preliminary research and conversations with a colleague who teaches at the secondary level, Jackie decided to take an ethnographic approach to the write-up, framing her note-taking process as a transcription. She attempted to capture as much thick description as possible by recording time stamps, listing concrete actions and dialogue, and using neutral language. Although Jackie viewed this new rhetorical situation as a learning experience, her challenges underscore yet another source of tension in DE observations: the observer's unavoidable subjectivity. Bearing this in mind, we invited Jennifer to contribute her perspective to our chapter, for the same reason that we ask all instructors to read and respond to our observation reports: we want to underscore how much we value them as equal partners in the sometimes prismatic process that is DE observation. Once this chapter proposal was accepted, we invited Jennifer to recount and reflect on her experience in whatever format she found most useful.

In Jennifer's words, the observation experience "could have been a stressful thing, but I did not feel stressed. I think it was made clear that the intent of the observation was for growth." This theme resurfaced throughout her reflection and offers a promising counterpoint to the experiences of the teachers in Katie's study. We are happy to hear

Jennifer describe the feedback she received from Jackie as "positive, encouraging, and helpful in building [her] confidence in the classroom," and we appreciate that she remembers much of her observation experience as an opportunity to grow rather than to be policed. Similarly, from our perspective as observers, we find that focusing on growth—rather than checking vague boxes to identify what a teacher did or didn't do "correctly" during a class visit—allows both parties to feel comfortable engaging in dialogue after the observation had ended.

Jennifer also noted that she valued Jackie's appraisal of her strengths as a teacher, along with areas identified for continuing development. As Jennifer explains in her reflection, "In the spirit of growth . . . Good leaders always look for the good first, so it is very necessary to have that mutual openness and understanding that it is not a 'Gotcha!' [moment] or meant to nitpick." Harking back to the "wash-the-high-school-off" comment shared by her colleague, Jennifer suggests that observers should communicate to DE faculty that they are valued as much as any other composition instructor. Jackie took care to make a respectful, open-minded entrance into Jennifer's classroom and to assure her from the outset that she was more interested in having a conversation about teaching than in furnishing a one-sided lecture on pedagogical best practices. This cross-level observation pedagogy was similarly illustrated through an assignment Jennifer completed in Katie's graduate course, which asked teacher-learners to observe and write a reflection letter about another instructor's FYC class—an activity that affirmed, in Jennifer's mind, much of what she was already doing in her own course.

Worth noting, also, is the importance of our close working relationship with Jennifer in making this observation experience a successful one. In her reflection, Jennifer points out that meeting Katie and Jackie prior to teaching her first DE FYC course allowed her to feel more comfortable reaching out when she had questions or needed support during the semester. Jennifer's experience in Katie's graduate seminar further strengthened this relationship, providing them with weekly opportunities for pedagogical dialogue and face-to-face contact. As a result, the professional connection the three of us built was unusually strong, and we do not intend to posit this relationship as some sort of ideal for all DE partnerships. In fact, Katie and Jackie have struggled to establish a similar level of collegial closeness and communication with some of the other embedded DE teachers in the program, an effort that is ongoing. Instead, we offer our collaboration with Jennifer as a model for what observer-observee interactions can potentially become: a mutually respectful relationship grounded in dialogue, transparency, and a shared commitment to growth across the secondary-postsecondary composition threshold.

A PRISM OF POSSIBILITIES

After listening to Katie's study participants and reading Jennifer's thoughts, we remain acutely aware of both the affordances and the constraints of teaching observations as an assessment tool. We recognize that the solitary nature of embedded instruction—as well as the inherent power dynamics that shape the DE classroom—come to bear on the relationships we seek to establish with our partners in secondary education. The three of us agree that more can and should be done to nurture meaningful relationships across partnerships, especially when considering that the labor of high school instructors accounts for approximately one-third of our FYC course sections offered at TWU. Improving our observation process is a necessary first step, one that requires ongoing dialogue and relationship building in combination with constructive, transparent feedback from our embedded teaching partners. While we cannot offer an easy formula for DE observations, we have gleaned recommendations for practices that can either hinder or facilitate the type of dialogic, generative experiences we hope DE observations can be.

First, instructors repeatedly expressed that a lack of consistency, transparency, and respect from college teaching partners was one of their biggest challenges in navigating the observation process. Whether it was Mary fielding critiques for circumstances out of her control or Jennifer's unnamed colleague saying she needed to "wash the high school off," we heard accounts illustrating the deleterious effects of sporadic, inequitable, and unsupportive observation practices that were all too common in teachers' experiences. We also know from our review of the literature that a single annual observation should never serve as the sole instrument for evaluating a teacher's progress, let alone dictate employment, promotion, or program accreditation. Similarly, observations should not be the only opportunity for sharing face-to-face conversation and meaningful feedback with instructors. We are concerned that too often in our field, a onetime classroom visit from a reluctant college faculty member serves as sufficient "teacher development" in DE partnerships. Joyce Malek and Laura Micciche make a recommendation along these lines: "Given the proliferation of DE policies rolling out across the country, another option for writing faculty is to influence as much as possible what is taught in DE high school composition courses, how, and by whom" (92). We appreciate Malek and Micciche's investment in contributing to quality FYC instruction across contexts, but the fact that this "influence" is described as unidirectional seems like a missed opportunity for collaboration that is truly dialogic and cross-level.

In addition, if college faculty are required to rate, report, and/or distribute observation feedback to upper-level administrators after visiting a teacher's classroom, we can work to make this process more collaborative, providing instructors with the opportunity to respond to and reflect on our narratives of the observation while contributing their own. For example, Jackie avoids making value judgments about a teacher's pedagogy until the end of her observation write-up, when she provides formative feedback on strengths and areas for growth. This tactic helps her refrain from making decisions about an instructor's performance before watching the entire class period unfold and taking a few days to reflect and process what she sees. In the same way, when observers have questions or concerns emerging from a classroom visit, we can use these moments as starting points for professional enrichment and conversation with teachers, administrators, or other stakeholders in a partnership rather than viewing them as opportunities to chastise or "remediate" instructors for what we observe.

Instead, we offer practices that both we and our DE colleagues found useful, extending beyond an obligatory annual observation. First, though we may not currently have the resources to implement the type of rigorous DE assessment and teacher development program outlined in a heuristic such as Anson's, we can informally survey teachers about their contexts and the kinds of resources they need. We can, whenever possible, take a page from Anson's book and offer opportunities for "formative cross-observations" (252) between high school *and* college instructors. Katie recently piloted an assignment along these lines in her graduate composition theory and pedagogy seminar, asking students (graduate teaching assistants and DE teachers alike) to observe an on-campus FYC instructor and then invite that same faculty member into their own classrooms. Rather than providing a rating or a performance evaluation, teachers in this exchange wrote reflective letters about what they learned from the experience and shared them with one another, creating more of an authentic pedagogical dialogue. Crafting descriptive reflections also aligns with recommendations in NACEP's issue brief on classroom visits, in which Denecker suggests that faculty liaisons note the students' "body language, to see when they are engaged, when they are confused, and when they lose interest" (Focarile et al. 4). It requires little time and energy to invite a high school teacher into our classrooms, and this gesture, in turn, might make them feel more comfortable when we repay the visit in a supervisory role, as in Jennifer's experience.

In addition, if college faculty are required to rate, report, and/or distribute observation feedback to upper-level administrators after visiting a teacher's classroom, we can work to make this process more collaborative, providing instructors with the opportunity to respond to and reflect on our narratives of the observation while contributing their own. For example, Jackie avoids making value judgments about a teacher's pedagogy until the end of her observation write-up, when she provides formative feedback on strengths and areas for growth. This tactic helps her refrain from making decisions about an instructor's performance before watching the entire class period unfold and taking a few days to reflect and process what she sees. In the same way, when observers have questions or concerns emerging from a classroom visit, we can use these moments as starting points for professional enrichment and conversation with teachers, administrators, or other stakeholders in a partnership rather than viewing them as opportunities to chastise or "remediate" instructors for what we observe.

Finally, we acknowledge that by asking Jennifer to contribute to this chapter, we have offered her a unique privilege (and at the same time, a unique responsibility) that we are not able to offer every DE instructor. We are fortunate to have a colleague with whom we can facilitate this kind of professional dialogue—a two-way exchange that further enriches our existing relationship. Of course, we realize that not every instructor has the time, the resources, or even the interest in doing such work, but the formation of this chapter and Jennifer's help in writing it has further strengthened our partnership. In closing, we offer a final comment gleaned from her reflection: "More than anything, I appreciate being asked for feedback. Thank you for the opportunity to share my thoughts." We acknowledge that we can never eliminate the tensions facing DE instructors and observers throughout the observation process, an undertaking that is inherently pan-optical and politically charged. However, to the extent that it is possible, we urge other administrators to maintain open lines of communication about the observation process as an opportunity for fostering dialogue, growth, and relationship building with DE instructors.

APPENDIX 4.A

FYC OBSERVATION INSTRUMENT

First-Year Composition Observation Form

Instructor: __________

Course and section: __________

Designation:

_____ Online	_____ Evening
_____ Honors	_____ Dual Credit

Term: __________

Date: __________

Time: __________

Room: __________

Part 1: To be filled out by the instructor prior to the class session:

Briefly describe your objectives for this class session in relation to the overall course plan:

Describe the method of instruction to achieve these objectives:

How will the students participate?

Part 2: To be filled out by the observer after the class session:

Please provide comments on the instructor's strengths and areas of improvement.

How would you rate the overall performance of the instructor?

_____ Superior	_____ Effective
_____ Needs Improvement	_____ Unacceptable

Please add any additional comments here:

Part 3: To be filled out by the instructor after the follow-up conference:

Date of follow-up conference: __________

Mentor name: __________

NOTES

1. This recommendation is also outlined in the NACEP Issue Brief focused on classroom visits (Focarile et al.).
2. In this particular partnership, high school students receive credit for Advanced Placement English and the sponsoring university's FYC course simultaneously, which means they also have to fulfill requirements for AP literature and composition or AP language and composition during the semester(s) they take FYC. Regional accreditors such as the Southern Association of Colleges and Schools are currently debating whether to make high schools disambiguate their AP

curriculum from their DE curriculum, which would eliminate arrangements such as this one.

3. See appendix 4.A for the observation instrument we use, including questions for instructors to answer ahead of time. In the spirit of transparency, we should note that we inherited this instrument from previous program leadership and have since revised and updated the instrument.

WORKS CITED

Anson, Chris. "Absentee Landlord or Owner-Tenants? Formulating Standards for Dual-Credit Composition Programs." In *College Credit for Writing in High School: The "Taking Care of" Business*, edited by Kristine Hansen and Christine R. Farris. NCTE, 2010, pp. 245–271.

Burdick, Melanie, and Jane Greer. "Paths to Productive Partnerships: Surveying High School Teachers about Professional Development and 'College-Level' Writing." *WPA: Writing Program Administration*, vol. 41, no. 1, 2017, pp. 82–101.

"Classroom Assessment." [Instructor Redacted], Aug. 23, 2016, [University].

Conference on College Composition and Communication. "CCCC Position Statement on Preparing Teachers of College Writing." CCCC, 2015. www.ncte.org/cccc/resources/positions/statementonprep. Accessed May 12, 2022.

Conference on College Composition and Communication. "Statement on Dual Credit/Concurrent Enrollment Composition: Policy and Best Practices." CCCC, 2012. https://cccc.ncte.org/cccc/resources/positions/dualcredit. Accessed May 12, 2022.

Danielson, Charlotte. *The Framework for Teaching: Evaluation Instrument.* Danielson Group, 2013.

Danielson, Charlotte, and Thomas L. McGreal. *Teacher Evaluation to Enhance Professional Practice.* Association for Supervision and Curriculum Development, 2000.

Dayton, Amy E. *Assessing the Teaching of Writing: Twenty-First Century Trends and Technologies.* U of Colorado P, 2015.

Denecker, Christine. "Transitioning Writers across the Composition Threshold: What We Can Learn from Dual Enrollment Partnerships." *Composition Studies*, vol. 41, no. 1, 2013, pp. 27–50.

Dennihy, Melissa. "'Forget What You Learned in High School': Bridging the Space between High School and College." *Teaching English in the Two-Year College*, vol. 43, no. 2, 2015, pp. 156–169.

Flanigan, Michael C. "From Discomfort, Isolation, and Fear to Comfort, Community, and Confidence." In *Preparing College Teachers of Writing: Histories, Theories, Programs, Practices*, edited by Betty P. Pytlik and Sarah Liggett. Oxford UP, 2002, pp. 242–253.

Focarile, Teresa, Christine Denecker, and Kimberly Guenther. "NACEP Issue Brief: The Classroom Visit." *NACEP*, 2019, pp. 1–10.

Green, Nicole. "Branching Out, Growing Together: Toward Creating a New Secondary/Postsecondary Collaborative Branch on the NCTE/CCCC Family Tree." Conference on College Composition and Communication, 2017, Portland, OR. Conference Presentation.

Jackson, Brian. "Watching Other People Teach: The Challenge of Classroom Observations." In *Assessing the Teaching of Writing: Twenty-First Century Trends and Technologies*, edited by Amy E. Dayton. U of Colorado P, 2015, pp. 45–60.

Joseph. Personal Interview. Aug. 9, 2016.

Malek, Joyce, and Laura R. Micciche. "A Model of Efficiency: Pre-College Credit and the State Apparatus." *WPA: Writing Program Administration*, vol. 40, no. 2, 2017, pp. 77–97.

Mary. Personal Interview. Sept. 17, 2016.

McWain, Katie. "Finding Freedom at the Composition Threshold: Learning from the Experiences of Dual Enrollment Teachers." *Teaching English in the Two-Year College*, vol. 45, no. 1, 2018, pp. 406–424.

Miller, Trey, Holly Kosiewicz, Courtney Tanenbaum, Drew Atchison, David Knight, Beth Ratway, Scott Delhommer, and Jesse Levin. "Dual Credit Education Programs in Texas, Phase II." *American Institutes for Research*, Dec. 2018. http://www.60x30tx.com/media/1428/dual-credit-education-programs-in-texas.pdf. Accessed May 11, 2022.

Moreland, Casie, and Keith D. Miller. "The Triumph of Whiteness: Dual Credit Courses and Hierarchical Racism in Texas." In *Rhetorics of Whiteness: Postracial Hauntings in Popular Culture, Social Media, and Education*, edited by Tammie Kennedy, Joyce Middleton, and Krista Ratcliffe. Southern Illinois UP, 2016, pp. 182–194.

Penrose, Amy M. "Professional Identity in a Contingent-Labor Profession: Expertise, Autonomy, and Community in Composition Teaching." *WPA: Writing Program Administration*, vol. 35, no. 2, 2012, pp. 108–126.

Sally. Personal Interview. Oct. 31, 2016.

Sam. Personal Interview. Nov. 10, 2016.

Stancliff, Michael, Erin Whittig, Lisa McIntyre, Shirley Rose, and Duane Roen. "Collaborative Assessment of Dual Enrollment: The View from Arizona." *Journal of Writing Assessment*, vol. 10, no. 1, 2017, pp. 1–13. journalofwritingassessment.org/article.php?article=117. Accessed July 20, 2019.

Steinberg, Matthew P., and Rachel Garrett. "Classroom Composition and Measured Teacher Performance: What Do Teacher Observation Scores Really Measure?" *Educational Evaluation and Policy Analysis*, vol. 38, no. 2, June 2016, pp. 293–317.

Stenberg, Shari, and Amy Lee. "Developing Pedagogies: Learning the Teaching of English." *College English*, vol. 64, no. 3, 2002, pp. 326–347.

Turner, Victor. *The Ritual Process: Structure and Anti-Structure*. Routledge, 1995.

Waller, Dennis R. "A Quality Concurrent Enrollment Program: Five Considerations." In *Bridging the High School–College Gap: The Role of Concurrent Enrollment Programs*, edited by Gerald S. Edmonds and Tiffany M. Squires. Syracuse UP, 2016, pp. 41–58.

5

NAVIGATING THE LANDSCAPE OF PROFESSIONAL DEVELOPMENT

Dual Enrollment Teachers Map College Composition into the High School Classroom

Melanie Burdick and Jane Greer

The development and support of teachers is a critical component of any dual enrollment (DE) program. The accreditation standards set by the National Alliance of Current Enrollment Partnerships (NACEP) stipulate that "faculty liaisons at the college/university provide all new concurrent enrollment instructors with course-specific training in course philosophy, curriculum, pedagogy, and assessment prior to the instructor teaching the course" and that "concurrent enrollment instructors participate in college/university provided annual discipline-specific professional development and ongoing collegial interaction to further enhance instructors' pedagogy and breadth of knowledge in the discipline" (NACEP). Within writing studies, the Conference on College Composition and Communication's (CCCC's) "Joint Position Statement on Dual Enrollment in Composition" similarly articulates that high school teachers assigned to teach college-level writing in a secondary school setting should "receive initial training in course delivery as well as ongoing pedagogical and professional support from the sponsoring institution." Like the NACEP accreditation standards, the CCCC "Joint Position Statement on Dual Enrollment in Composition" emphasizes the importance of ongoing staff development for secondary teachers and the critical role played by on-campus faculty liaisons and mentors.

Beyond such policy statements, researchers in writing studies who study DE programs have underscored the importance of faculty development for teachers delivering college writing classes to high school students. As the growth of DE courses was accelerating in the late 1980s and early 1990s, David E. Schwalm and Michael J. Vivion debated how writing program administrators (WPAs) should respond. While Schwalm characterized DE courses as a "potential threat to our students' chances

https://doi.org/10.7330/9781646422531.c005

of developing college-level literacy" (51) and urged WPAs to "resist dual enrollment arrangements" (54), Vivion accepted "the reality of the pressures to offer college credit on the high school campus" (57). Vivion then listed four characteristics of his institution's DE program that helped ensure quality experiences for high school DE students by focusing on the selection and supervision of the secondary teachers involved in the program, "their opportunities for professional development," and the ongoing "collaboration between on-campus and high school faculty" (57). More recently, Chris M. Anson has argued for the importance of faculty development for secondary teachers in the preliminary rubric he offers for assessing DE programs. He notes that it is "insufficient for . . . program administrators simply to 'align' dual-credit high school teachers to the pedagogical demands and routines of the college course" (262). He urges faculty development programs to afford DE writing teachers meaningful interactions with other DE writing teachers as well as with campus-based writing teachers, and he notes that all faculty development "must undergo continuous evaluation" (263).

Despite the recognition that DE programs must offer meaningful, substantive professional development to secondary teachers who are charged with delivering college composition in the high school classroom, there has been a dearth of research that specifically seeks to understand how DE teachers take up the professional development opportunities available to them. Kristine Hansen and Christine R. Farris's foundational text, *College Credit for Writing in High School: The "Taking Care of" Business*, contains personal accounts of DE teachers, including their professional development as well as program descriptions that highlight the training offered to teachers (Post et al.; Farris; McClure et al.; Moody and Bonesteel; Thalheimer). Similarly, qualitative research studies of DE programs have tended to focus on how such programs impact students and have taken a broad view of teachers' experiences, including how they understand their roles and define college-level writing and how they deal with academic freedom and the Family Educational Rights and Privacy Act in secondary schools. For example, Christine Denecker's insightful research focuses on how high school and college teachers define key elements of writing instruction and how varying definitions can shape the transitions writers must make as they move from secondary to postsecondary institutions. More recently, Katie McWain has used her research on DE teachers to ask "how might we . . . support the development of high school instructors who are invested in the academic freedoms and political possibilities of college writing" (407). McWain interviewed high school teachers as well as secondary and postsecondary administrators responsible for writing programs and/or DE programs. She concluded that despite the challenges high school teachers encounter in delivering college-level courses in a secondary school context, they "often found ways to question, adapt to, and intervene in their teaching situations from the unique positionality they inhabit" (419). By interviewing and working with DE teachers, both McWain and Denecker highlight the complex, critical work high school teachers must do in delivering college-level writing instruction in a secondary school context. We hope to contribute to this conversation by exploring the varied sources of high school teachers' understandings of college-level writing. More specifically, this research question provided focus for our study: how do DE teachers respond to the professional development opportunities available to them as they map college-level writing into the high school classroom?

For this chapter, we offer a discussion of the qualitative results of a mixed method study that involved surveying and conducting focus groups with high school teachers with DE experience. Conducted in 2014–2015, our research leads us to the argument that secondary teachers navigate a complex landscape of professional development opportunities (e.g., workshops provided by postsecondary institutions that sponsor DE programs, Advanced Placement [AP] training, International Baccalaureate [IB] curricula, national and regional conferences, professional journals) as they map college-level writing into the secondary classroom. Offered only in high schools, programs such as AP and IB are, of course, quite distinct from DE classes. High school students enrolled in AP or IB courses must perform well on standardized exams to earn college credit, and postsecondary institutions determine the minimum exam scores they will accept as an equivalent for entry-level college courses. In contrast, DE courses allow students to complete college courses in their high school classrooms. When a high school student completes a DE course, their grade is transcripted by the sponsoring postsecondary institution, and the credits they have earned can be transferred to other postsecondary institutions. The teachers in our study were keenly aware of these differences among AP, IB, and DE; and over the course of their careers, they had encountered a wide range of such approaches that purported to bridge the chasm between high school English and college composition courses. These teachers drew on their experiences with diverse curricular structures and professional development opportunities in a variety of ways as they represented college writing to their high school students rather than merely adhering to or implementing a model syllabus or pedagogies prescribed by the postsecondary institutions that sponsored DE at their high schools.

METHODS AND PARTICIPANTS

Our Institutional Review Board-approved study included a quantitative collection of survey data followed by a qualitative, narrative-based series of focus group interviews. The research began with the survey sent to 455 teachers in 85 schools and 55 school districts. To select survey participants, we used publicly available staff directories on high school and district websites. The school districts were located in the thirteen contiguous counties that surround the midwestern universities where we work in western Missouri and eastern Kansas. Multiple focus groups were then organized based on volunteers from the survey participants.

Survey Background

A summary of the survey data, which we have previously reported on, provides a background to the qualitative data that are discussed in detail in this chapter (Burdick and Greer). While eighty-one teachers completed the survey, this only provided an 18 percent response rate. Kim Bartel Sheehan has identified "churn" (the act of users changing email addresses) as one way email survey response rates can be unreliable. We attribute this lower than ideal response rate in part to "churn" and an unavoidable coverage error. We could not determine how recently a school/district had updated its online staff directory. In addition, many school websites do not designate teachers' course assignments, in which case we emailed the survey invitation to all English/language arts teachers at a school knowing that many would disregard it because they were not teaching courses applicable to our study.

The survey results provided a broad overview of who was teaching DE writing courses in our region, how these teachers envisioned college-level writing, and which professional development resources they were using to provide college-level writing instruction. From the survey, three results emerged:

1. DE teachers in our area are experienced, even expert teachers.
2. They have encountered a range of professional development resources that inform their work in the DE classroom.
3. Their definitions of college-level writing are generally aligned with those of postsecondary, on-campus writing instructors. (Burdick and Greer)

Our survey data showed that DE teachers view college-level writing as a broad series of thinking abilities and activities. Survey participants defined college-level writing as the ability to skillfully communicate across a variety of genres, topics, and audiences. Definitions of college-level writing also included writing across disciplines (see also Burdick and Greer).

While we gathered quantitative survey data on several points in the first phase of the project, including DE teachers' definitions of college writing, for the purposes of this chapter we focus on analysis of the qualitative data that was designed to answer these three questions: what features might mark a professional development opportunity as particularly useful to high school teachers? How do teachers evaluate the value of particular pedagogical approaches they encounter at workshops and conferences or in journals? How do teachers bridge the distance between widely disparate mandates from various stakeholders who encroach on their classrooms?

Focus Groups

To begin to answer our questions, we elicited volunteers from our survey respondents to participate in focus group interviews. We held five focus group interviews with between one and three participants at each session and began each interview by asking the participants to write for approximately five minutes in response to a prompt (see appendix 5.A). The prompt invited participants to think about their experiences as teachers and the sources of their professional knowledge. Our goal with this pre-writing activity was to provide each participant with an independent, central focus before beginning the discussion.

The interview itself consisted of a protocol of seven main questions and a number of follow-up questions (see appendix 5.B). We asked probing questions only when participants did not share detailed information. Interviews were video and audio recorded, and the audio was transcribed. Following the interview, the participants were prompted to look back at their original writing response and to add anything to what they had provided from the first writing prompt or in the interview. With this post-interview writing activity (see appendix 5.A), we hoped to ensure that if there had been a change in their perspective throughout the conversation, the change would be identified. This activity also enabled participants to provide feedback they may have felt uncomfortable sharing with the group.

Data and Analysis

Our data set thus consisted of two writing responses from each participant as well as focus group interview transcripts. Participants in the focus group interviews included high school teachers who taught a variety of college-level writing courses, ranging from IB to AP to DE programs. For the analysis, we identified a narrower data set that included a group of four teachers: Penelope, Allison, Ava, and Charlie. (The teachers chose pseudonyms, which we use throughout this chapter.) These teachers were selected because they all taught in a DE program through their high schools. They also all taught additional classes ranging from freshman English to IB classes for seniors. In addition, two teachers worked as adjunct instructors at postsecondary institutions, which we believe also informed their understanding of college-level writing in their high school instruction. In line with qualitative research methodologies, the selection of participants was not based on an aspiration to be representative of all DE writing teachers. Indeed, we stand firmly on the position that all qualitative research by definition is interpretive and contextual (Denzin and Lincoln; Creswell and Miller; Marshall and Rossman), and both our selection of participants and analysis of the data are based on an interpretive and naturalistic stance exploring a range of DE teachers' experiences in our region.

Our data analysis included both deductive and inductive coding. We understood from the survey data that teachers were navigating among a variety of professional development opportunities. Therefore, in looking at the interview transcripts and pre-/post-writing done by participants, we first individually coded the data, identifying instances when teachers described professional development opportunities and articulated why and how they found these opportunities useful in their teaching. We compared and synthesized our individual coding results and then, from these combined codes, composed participant narratives to portray the themes, actions, and experiences of each individual teacher.

In composing participant narratives, we align ourselves with theoretical commitments common among educational researchers who embrace qualitative methodologies. Jean Clandinin and Michael Connelly see narrative as an analytic structure, but more important, they identify narrative as a cognitive phenomenon connected to John Dewey's theories of experiential learning. David Schaafsma and Ruth Vinz promote narrative in literacy research, focusing on how stories can portray multiple layers of language and learning. And Jeong-Hee Kim identifies narrative's importance in educational research because it places teachers' lived experiences at the forefront of understanding questions regarding curriculum and school policy. Broadly speaking, our commitment as qualitative researchers was "to gather accounts as completely as possible and to represent our data and our data research participants fairly" (Charmaz 87).

NARRATIVES OF NAVIGATION

Drawing from the data set described above, we offer narratives describing how four participants navigated the professional development landscape as they mapped college composition into their high school classrooms. These teachers all had significant experience as DE instructors, and they reflect the larger pool of survey respondents in terms of their academic training, the length of time they have been teaching, the range of courses they teach in their high schools, and the average number of students enrolled in their classes.

In our analysis of the focus group transcripts, we came to see that these four teachers described a range of practices and relationships critical to their professional development as DE instructors. More specifically, we recognized that the practices and relationships described could be organized along two continuums of professional development experience. The first continuum ranges from influential to un-influential experiences. The second continuum ranges from informal to formal experiences. For example, while one teacher experienced formal practices, such as professional development workshops, as un-influential, another may have experienced them as extremely influential and helpful to her professional growth. Important to note is the finding that most participants had experience teaching DE as well as other college-level or college preparatory English classes (AP, IB). Teachers described using trainings interchangeably, seeing training from different programs not as distinct areas of professional knowledge applicable only to the delivery of a particular curriculum but rather as a range of information from which they could select what would work best for their varied teaching contexts. For example, one participant identified AP scoring sessions as especially influential across all the classes she taught because it provided her with a formal space to talk with other teachers about student writing. The following narratives portray the range of these relationships and how they played out in teachers' lived experiences.

PENELOPE

Penelope teaches at Troy High School (THS), a suburban high school in the Midwest that serves 1,700 students in grades 9–12. Penelope describes herself as a white woman and the student population at THS as "somewhat diverse." She pointed out that Troy is the only high school, among three in her school district, that is currently experiencing enrollment growth, noting that THS "draws a lot of people because of its athletic teams as well as academic offerings." As a master teacher who has been in the classroom for over a decade, she has taught DE courses sponsored by a local community college as well as AP classes. At the time of the focus group interviews, Penelope was teaching two sections of senior Honors English for students enrolled in the IB program at THS as well as four sections of Advanced Honors English (pre-IB) for sophomores.

Because of the diversity of her teaching experiences and the length of her career, Penelope draws on a wide range of resources in crafting her understanding of what it means to deliver a DE course. She described her work as an AP teacher as the most important opportunity she had to understand "college-level" writing: "I used to teach Advanced Placement English, and I still read the AP exams. The AP exams are [the] coming together [of] the college teachers and the high school teachers. I have felt that was the best professional development ever. We would sit around and talk about writing and what writing looked like in each of our classes. That's something I miss with IB, that we do not get enough opportunity to discuss with the college people."

Unfortunately, Penelope did not find the professional development opportunities available through the community college that sponsored the DE courses she taught to be particularly helpful: "It kind of consisted of teaching from a text. There wasn't a great deal of anything from the school. Here it is. You teach it as best you know." She turned to professional publications for support: "When I taught the 110 class, I did subscribe to *CCC*." But she also noted that "I think it always seems like I would get—I get more ideas out of *English Journal*. I turn down more page corners there than I did with that one [*CCC*] . . . I like reading about teaching in English." Penelope is keenly attuned to the differences in *CCC*, which purports to circulate the "most current scholarship and theory in the field" as it "supports college teachers in reflecting on and improving their practices in teaching writing" (College Composition and Communication), and *English Journal*, which positions itself as a "journal of ideas" for middle and high school teachers and emphasizes its power to circulate information about how secondary teachers are "applying practices, research, and multimodal literacies in their classrooms" (*English Journal*). Although she welcomes formal opportunities to learn with and from college teachers, she finds her professional development needs are best met by professional publications targeted toward high school teachers.

CHARLIE

Charlie identifies himself as a white man. He described the school where he teaches as "a large suburban high school serving mostly high SES [socioeconomic status] students." At his high school, he teaches DE classes sponsored by a local community college, but his understanding of how to deliver college writing instruction comes from an array of sources—the professional development workshops offered by the community college partnering with his school for their DE program, his interactions and debriefing with his students to assess what they find helpful in his instruction, and his own experiences as an undergraduate and as a graduate teaching assistant (GTA) while he pursued an MA in English literature.

Although Charlie regularly participated in the workshops offered by the postsecondary institution that sponsored his DE classes, he did not describe these workshops as pertaining to curriculum or pedagogy. He describes them as "less about understanding what we're supposed to be helping our students learn with respect to writing and thinking and reading and more about the . . . interesting things . . . on campus," such as library resources and upcoming events and guest speakers. Charlie described the college's professional development offerings as "interesting stuff, but none of which really translates to [how] I'm going to be a better teacher of writing. If the target is to help me be a better teacher of writing, they're missing that mark."

Instead, Charlie reflected during the interview on his own experiences as a college student, explaining how it informed his teaching of college writing. As an undergraduate, he was successful in composition courses, and he carried those lessons and a sense of writerly expertise into writing for graduate school. He now works to pass that feeling of success and transfer along to his high school students. He stated that "even though it's twenty-years-old information, some of it is still pretty relevant."

He also uses the training and oversight he learned when he taught composition as a graduate student in English literature to help him understand what college-level writing instruction looks like. Finally, his current DE courses are modeled after his own experiences as a graduate student: "I teach [them] in a way that is as faithful to a graduate university seminar in literature as is possible within the context of a high school classroom for twelfth graders." Charlie understands the context he is working within; however, he sees the experiences of college writing as those that require a very different pedagogy wherein the students take more responsibility for their learning.

Accordingly, Charlie describes the best professional development as coming from his students or other teachers. Regarding his students, he learns from them by checking in about every two weeks: "We take part of a class day, as students have finished up a unit of work, I ask them what sorts of things did they find useful or useless, engaging or not engaging; what sorts of things helped them increase their skills; what sorts of things were a waste of time. Sometimes I find that what seemed like it was useless or wasted to them was because I didn't highlight why we were doing it well enough."

Other than learning from his students or reflecting upon his own successes as a student, Charlie suggested that the most valuable professional development he had experienced occurred "when teachers who actually teach writing get an opportunity to sit down with each other and discuss what their struggles and successes are, tricks they've found to make their work better." Classes, workshops, and trainings where he has been able to talk with other writing teachers have made him think more carefully about his instruction. For him, these have been infrequent and have mostly surrounded AP training or scoring.

AVA

Ava describes herself as a multiracial woman, and she teaches at Jefferson High School where students of color make up 90 percent of the school's population. Ava is the only DE instructor at her high school, and she also teaches composition as an adjunct for a community college.

It was clear that Ava found most of her resources for teaching college writing in conversations and relationships with other teachers, both high school and college instructors. She has actively searched out mentors and collaborators to help her think more carefully about her teaching. For example, she attends meetings and workshops at the university that sponsors her DE courses. She met a college instructor at one such meeting and has kept in touch with her to obtain ideas and feedback regarding how to best structure her DE course.

Even while working to create relationships with other teachers of college writing, Ava believes she could do more. This feeling is what prompted her to participate in the study: "With regard to college writing, I am very limited. I was excited to become a part of this so I could listen and learn from others." Ava's concern about her "limited" resources for teaching college writing is linked to her feelings of isolation at her adjunct position. She describes a lack of affiliation with the community college where she teaches in the evenings: "I feel very disconnected in the sense that I'm at a satellite campus, and it's at night, and I'm always the last one to leave . . . This is my third semester. When I can juggle my schedule and when there are meetings or adjunct workshops or whatever to attend on that campus, I try to take the time to be a part of that . . . I should try to get in there and make some more connections."

Ava sees herself as responsible for creating the connections she needs. She knows she can benefit from "juggling her schedule" and putting forth the effort to "get in there and make some more connections." For the time being, she does what she can with the resources she has. In her interview she stated that she learns more from listening to her students than she does from other teachers: "They tell me what works for them, what doesn't."

ALLISON

Allison teaches at a suburban high school and identifies as a white woman. She teaches high school DE courses for a local four-year university as well as AP composition and literature courses. Beyond her high school work, she also teaches college composition as an adjunct at a private university and methods classes in an English education program at a public university. Allison identifies what many postsecondary faculty would see as common sources of professional development: attending academic conferences. But for Allison, attending both regional and national conferences seemed to be less about presenting her own work and more about an opportunity to form relationships with other teachers. In describing her experiences, Allison never spoke about making presentations; instead, she talked about her excitement as she attended sessions, listening to and meeting well-known scholars and authors as well as learning from other classroom teachers.

Allison's focus on learning from other teachers at professional conferences is perhaps not surprising given how she describes her earliest experiences as a DE teacher: "When I started teaching dual credit in 1998, I had two strong mentor teachers that I was able to teach with them for one year, and then they both retired, and then I had all the sections. At least for that one year, they really helped me with practices and instruction and how to work with the dual credit to know my audience. That really helped me, with mentoring, with working closely with those two teachers."

She also describes taking personal days off work to go and observe her friends who are teachers because she learns so much by watching them teach. Like Ava, Allison said she was motivated to participate in the study because she thought it would be another place where she could learn more about college writing. She also recently participated in her local National Writing Project site events and through these events found mentors at the university to whom she turns for teaching advice and suggestions: "I feel conversations with colleagues help me but not necessarily in . . . my high school building, I hate to say. It's more relationships I have at [the local university] or personal relationships with other teachers . . . I love that when you have somebody who's like-minded and you can bounce ideas off of them . . . if you want to do something different or new."

In contrast, she described her experiences with professional development at the state and school district levels as extremely inconsistent. When she assisted in her state's curriculum design, she felt she learned a lot working with other teachers from across the state. However, at two different school districts, the professional development experiences were vastly different: "I worked at a district where professional development was a source of, I don't know, anger I guess . . . the teachers felt resentful because we weren't being trained in what we needed . . . Now I work in a district where my mentor is in charge of professional development. She's a visionary." As an experienced teacher who has taught DE courses since the late 1990s, Allison has been able to identify, search out, and use what is constructive.

ANALYSIS AND IMPLICATIONS

As these narratives make clear, Penelope, Charlie, Ava, and Allison are all eager to learn more about how to be better teachers of college writing in their secondary classrooms. They also personify the survey data in our study that showed how secondary teachers charged with delivering college-level writing to high school students made use of just under six (5.97) different professional development resources as they constructed their curricula and designed their pedagogical strategies (Burdick and Greer 92). AP training, professional journals, conferences, textbooks, and workshops organized by postsecondary institutions emerge as sources of knowledge about teaching college-level writing for these teachers.

Furthermore, these narratives demonstrate how critical relationships are in shaping the ways teachers map the expectations and norms of college-level writing into the high school classroom, particularly relationships with respected, trusted colleagues. The conversations among college and high school teachers at AP scoring sessions, the influence of mentors on developing teachers, even the memory of impactful teachers from a teacher's own past can play powerful roles in shaping how DE classes are taught. Some of these relationships are highly structured, while others are more informal. And some relationships are highly satisfying and others are not, thus driving teachers to find alternative sources of professional knowledge.

Indeed, the relationships that emerge in the narratives of Penelope, Charlie, Ava, and Allison might be plotted along intersecting axes of how the level of formality of a relationship relates to the influence of that relationship. Our findings suggests that the more formal the relationship, the less influential it is; the more informal the relationship, the more influential.

In Penelope's case, the community college that sponsored the DE courses at her high school provided little professional development or support for her. Instead, she found most satisfying her experiences with the highly structured AP scoring sessions in which she participated. She described them as "the best professional development ever," and she valued the fact that college teachers and high school teachers came together to talk about student writing. This structured relationship with fellow teachers was highly influential for Penelope as she taught college-level writing to high school students.

Charlie similarly participated in structured opportunities to form relationships and have conversations with fellow teachers; in the focus group interview, he stated a strong preference for organized occasions when "teachers who actually teach writing get an opportunity to sit down with each other and discuss what their struggles and successes are, tricks they've found to make their work better." For Charlie, though, such occasions were rare. Instead, he expressed frustration with the formal opportunities for expanding his professional knowledge about college-level writing that were available to him. He described the workshops offered by the community college with which his school district partners for DE courses as focusing on upcoming campus events and library resources rather than being about "helping our students learn with respect to writing and thinking and reading." Dissatisfied with the structured opportunities for professional development available to him, Charlie relies instead on his own experiences as an undergraduate writer and his training to be a GTA when he was pursuing an MA in English literature.

For Ava and Allison, relationships were also critical as they navigated the professional development experiences available to them; however, their relationships were far more informal than the structured interactions that unfold at organized workshops or AP scoring sessions. Allison described the informal mentoring she received from more experienced teachers who coached her during the early years of her career, particularly in terms of her DE course assignment. She also continues to build strong relationships with teachers throughout the area. She described using her personal days to visit other schools and postsecondary institutions, seeking to observe fellow teachers. Her participation in the local National Writing Project has helped her build a network of informal but influential professional relationships.

Ava, the only DE teacher in our data set who is working in an urban high school, was eloquent about her desire to have stronger relationships with fellow teachers who might support her professionally. When she attends formal meetings and workshops organized by the university that sponsors DE courses at her high school, her primary goal is to identify potential mentors and collaborators with whom she might have a reciprocal and ongoing professional relationship. Ava blamed herself for not already having stronger informal connections with colleagues who might further support her professional development. Indeed, Ava was self-critical in describing her role as an adjunct instructor at a community college where she had been teaching an evening section of first-year writing for the past three semesters. She stated in the focus group interview that she should do a better job of "juggling her schedule" and working harder to "get in there and make some connections." We found Ava's desire for deeper professional relationships and her self-criticism particularly significant, given recent critiques of DE programs that bolster the upper classes and work "mightily against the goal of providing greater opportunities to all students" (Moreland and Miller 190). If teachers working in urban high schools, like Ava, feel isolated, it is no surprise that DE programs are not functioning as engines of opportunity.

These four narratives identify varied ways DE instructors navigate among the resources available to them and underscore the significant role relationships play in their professional development. As WPAs and campus leaders charged with ensuring quality writing instruction for all students enrolled in first-year writing, whether they are on postsecondary campus or in a high school classroom, we draw from our research three significant lessons.

First, we recognize with new urgency the importance of acknowledging the breadth and diversity of high school teachers' experiences. Indeed, we note that three of our participants had experience teaching college writing as adjuncts or as a graduate instructor. Christine Farris has urged us to see high school DE teachers as equal to those teaching on the college campus: "As concurrent enrollment moves from trend to business-as-usual, we must acknowledge that a growing number of high school teachers are now college teachers as well" (281). Our research makes us wonder how many DE teachers are teaching part-time on college campuses and are in fact college faculty, regardless of whether we also acknowledge them to be college teachers in their high school classrooms.

Professional development workshops hosted by our postsecondary institutions for DE teachers might thus be seen as occasions for teachers to put curricular philosophies and pedagogical tactics in conversation with each other. Designing workshops for DE teachers that simply seek to introduce them to a writing program's philosophy or to explicate a model syllabus for a first-year writing course may not have the desired impact on what actually happens in DE classrooms. Moreover, professional development workshops hosted by postsecondary institutions that sponsor DE courses should provide ample opportunities for relationship building. Whether formal or informal, relationships were critical as teachers in our study navigated among the many professional development opportunities available to them.

Beyond offering formal workshops for professional development for DE teachers, WPAs and other institutional leaders should also seek to foster other occasions for relationship building and knowledge exchange. In each of the narratives shared here, the high school teachers actively sought out opportunities for professional growth, and in some cases, they castigated themselves when they did not build strong relationships with their college counterparts. Electronic formats, such as listservs, discussion boards, and wikis, are means by which such professional exchange can be fostered. Local and regional conferences that address the needs of both high school and college can promote connection and common cause among teachers at all levels. Even a decision by a WPA to hold office hours in the evening or on a weekend, when a teacher like Allison might be on campus to teach as a contingent faculty member, can provide a critical avenue for ensuring that DE teachers can meet their professional development needs.

Second, WPAs might do well to emphasize their own work in the classroom as they plan professional development workshops for DE teachers. In describing opportunities for conversation and their valued, long-standing relationships, none of the teachers in this study spoke about school principals, curriculum specialists, literacy coaches, or other non-classroom-based personnel. Repeatedly, the teachers spoke of being highly satisfied when they had opportunities to talk with other teachers about their classroom experiences. So rather than make a PowerPoint presentation that summarizes research and scholarship on helping students develop strong peer response skills or elucidates a program-wide rubric for evaluating students' efforts at peer response, a WPA might instead lead a discussion based on artifacts from their own classroom—prompts or guidelines for peer response they distribute to their students and examples of student work (with permission).

Finally, we have developed a heightened sense of the importance of moving into the circles where DE teachers are finding the most professionally rewarding conversations, including AP scoring sessions; the important institutes and workshops offered by local affiliates of the National Writing Project; professional publications, such as *English Journal*, that more specifically address secondary teachers; and the annual NCTE convention. Based on the experiences Penelope, Charlie, Allison, and Ava shared, these are the spaces where they are forging, or trying to forge, formal and informal professional relationships.

CONCLUSION

Both NACEP and researchers in composition have offered powerful arguments about the importance of professional development for DE teachers (Vivion; Anson). Indeed, NACEP's May 2015 Issue Brief, focused on the importance of "Discipline-Specific Professional Development for Continuing Instructors" (Allen et al.), offers inventive examples of professional development that teachers are likely to find influential, including author visits, research presentations, collaborative course content development, electronic communication forums, and classroom observations. We certainly concur with the brief's call for ongoing, discipline-specific professional development and increased collaboration among faculty at secondary and postsecondary institutions, and we have been inspired by the examples it offers.

Excellent models for such professional development exist elsewhere as well. Patricia J. Sehulster has offered one such model for building productive professional relationships. In her 2012 *TETYC* contribution, she describes "Writing Forums" held at SUNY-Westchester Community College. Originally targeted for DE teachers, the forums have expanded to include any interested high school teachers in the area as well as participants from a range of postsecondary institutions (343). Working first in small groups and then coming together as a collective at each meeting, participants have over the years compared high school writing assignments, college English writing assignments, and college writing assignments from across various disciplines; discussed technology in the writing classroom; and taken up issues related to assessment and assignment design. As Sehulster notes, the college-level faculty who organized the forums worked to avoid hierarchical attitudes about the relationships between secondary and postsecondary teachers and a top-down model of professional development, promoting instead collaborative "inquiry and dialogue" (343).

Our study stands as a reminder, though, that such formally organized professional development opportunities designed to promote the delivery of high-quality DE classes may not be universally available. Even when secondary teachers do participate in formal training to deliver DE courses, they might not find some of the professional development experiences particularly impactful. Instead, the secondary teachers in our study were navigating a varied professional development landscape that included formal experiences, such as scoring AP essays, and informal experiences, such as connecting with like-minded colleagues at conferences or drawing on role models from their own educational experiences. The experiences of the teachers in our study suggest that both formal and informal professional development experiences can be significant for teachers. As Miles McCrimmon has eloquently observed:

> Those who prosper teaching dual enrollment manage to transform their comfortable notions of territory and professional identity into more complicated, productive, and provocative realms of territoriality and bicultural identification. They develop a liminal conception of territoriality that opens more pedagogical avenues to them. Like a hybrid species they must learn to adapt to the new environment in order to survive and ultimately thrive in it. High school dual-enrollment teachers can be particularly adept at this technique (220).

The DE teachers in our study wisely recognized that "in order to survive and thrive," they need a range of relationships with fellow educators who can help them navigate the territory of professional development opportunities and then successfully map college writing for and with their high school students.

APPENDIX 5.A

Pre-Interview Writing Prompt:

Before we talk about your experiences teaching college level and college preparatory writing, please spend a little time free writing to reflect upon your experiences and professional knowledge.

- Please describe how you envision the goals of a first year college composition course.
- Where do you think your ideas originated?
- How do you think you put these ideas into practice in your high school (college credit or college prep) English class?

Post Interview Writing Prompt:

Please read through the writing that you did at the beginning of our focus group. On this separate piece of paper, please make any additional responses that you think could help us understand the ways you have learned about how to teach high school students college level or college preparatory writing.

- Is there anything new you thought of that you want to add?
- Is there anything that you wrote that needs clarification?

APPENDIX 5.B

Interview Protocol

Primary Questions	*Probing Questions*
Can you describe in a few words what you think some goals of a first-year college composition class are?	
What specific professional development or formal training have you had in the teaching of college composition?	A. Please describe what that training consisted of. B. If not—why do you think you haven't had such training? 1. Do you think it wasn't necessary? 2. Was it just not available? 3. Were you not offered any such training? 4. Were you not interested? 5. Unable to attend?

What other informal ways have you learned about the teaching of college composition?	
What things do you do in your classroom to prepare your kids to write in college?	A. Writing assignments? B. Activities? C. Readings?
Where did you learn to do these things? How did you come up with the idea to teach in these ways?	A. From your formal training? B. Other informal sources? C. Other experiences?
How do you assess for yourself whether or not you have prepared your students for college composition?	
Is there anything else that you'd like to share that would help us with our study?	

WORKS CITED

Allen, Linda, Christine Denecker, Deanna Jessup, and Tim Stetter. "Discipline-Specific Professional Development for Continuing Instructors." *NACEP Concurrent Enrollment Issue Brief*, May 2015. www.NACEP.org. Accessed May 12, 2022.

Anson, Chris M. "Absentee Landlords or Owner-Tenants? Formulating Standards for Dual-Credit Composition Programs." In *College Credit for Writing in High School: The "Taking Care of" Business*, edited by Kristine Hansen and Christine R. Farris. NCTE, 2010, pp. 245–269.

Burdick, Melanie, and Jane Greer. "Paths to Productive Partnerships: Surveying High School Teachers about Professional Development Opportunities and 'College-Level' Writing." *WPA: Journal of the Council of Writing Program Administrators*, vol. 41, no. 1, 2017, pp. 82–101.

Charmaz, Kathy. *Constructing Grounded Theory*, 2nd ed. Sage, 2014.

Clandinin, D. Jean, and F. Michael Connelly. *Narrative Inquiry: Experience and Story in Qualitative Research.* Jossey Bass, 2000.

College Composition and Communication. NCTE.org, https://cccc.ncte.org/cccc/ccc. Accessed Feb. 5, 2021.

Conference on College Composition and Communication (CCCC). "Joint Position Statement on Dual Enrollment in Composition." Nov. 2019. https://cccc.ncte.org/cccc/resources/positions/dualcredit. Accessed Feb. 5, 2021.

Creswell, John W., and Dana L. Miller. "Determining Validity in Qualitative Inquiry." *Theory into Practice*, vol. 39, no. 3, 2000, pp. 124–130.

Denecker, Christine. "Transitioning Writers across the Composition Threshold: What We Can Learn from Dual Enrollment Partnerships." *Composition Studies*, vol. 41, no. 3, 2013, pp. 27–50.

Denzin, Norman K., and Yvonna S. Lincoln. "Introduction: The Discipline and Practice of Qualitative Research." In *Strategies of Qualitative Inquiry*, edited by Norman K. Denzin and Yvonna S. Lincoln. Sage, 2008, pp. 1–43.

Dewey, John. "Experience and Education." *Educational Forum*, vol. 50, no. 3. Taylor and Francis Group, 1986.

English Journal. NCTE.org. https://ncte.org/resources/journals/english-journal/. Accessed Dec. 31, 2019.

Farris, Christine. "Minding the Gap and Learning the Game: Differences That Matter between High School and College Writing." In *College Credit for Writing in High School: The "Taking Care of" Business*, edited by Kristine Hansen and Christine R. Farris. NCTE, 2010, pp. 272–282.

Hansen, Kristine, and Christine R. Farris, eds. *College Credit for Writing in High School: The "Taking Care of" Business.* NCTE, 2010.

Kim, Jeong-Hee. *Understanding Narrative Inquiry: The Crafting and Analysis of Stories as Research.* Sage, 2015.

Marshall, Catherine, and Gretchen B. Rossman. *Designing Qualitative Research.* Sage, 2014.

McClure, Randall, Kevin Enerson, Jane Kepple Johnson, Patricia Lipetzky, and Cynthia Pope. "Concurrent Enrollment in Rural Minnesota: Addressing the Needs Caused by Shifting Demographics, Economics, and Academics." In *College Credit for Writing in High School: The "Taking Care of" Business,* edited by Kristine Hansen and Christine R. Farris. NCTE, 2010, pp. 189–207.

McCrimmon, Miles. "Contesting the Territoriality of 'Freshman English': The Political Ecology of Dual Enrollment." In *College Credit for Writing in High School: The "Taking Care of" Business,* edited by Kristine Hansen and Christine R. Farris. NCTE, 2010, pp. 208–226.

McWain, Katie. "Finding Freedom at the Composition Threshold: Learning from the Experiences of Dual Enrollment Teachers." *Teaching English in the Two-Year College,* vol. 45, no. 4, 2018, pp. 406–424.

Moody, Patricia A., and Margaret D. Bonesteel. "Syracuse University Project Advance: A Model of Connection and Quality." In *College Credit for Writing in High School: The "Taking Care of" Business,* edited by Kristine Hansen and Christine R. Farris. NCTE, 2010, pp. 227–244.

Moreland, Casie, and Keith D. Miller. "The Triumph of Whiteness: Dual Credit Courses and Hierarchical Racism in Texas." In *Rhetorics of Whiteness: Postracial Hauntings in Popular Culture, Social Media, and Education,* edited by Tammie M. Kennedy, Joyce Irene Middleton, and Krista Ratcliffe. Southern Illinois UP, 2017, pp. 182–194.

National Alliance of Concurrent Enrollment Partnerships (NACEP). "2017 National Concurrent Enrollment Partnership Standards." www.nacep.org/accreditation/standards/. Accessed April 26, 2019.

Post, Joanna Castner, Vicki Beard Simmons, and Stephanie Vanderslice. "Round Up the Horses—the Carts Are Racing Downhill! Programmatic Catch-Up to a Quickly Growing Concurrent Enrollment Program." In *College Credit for Writing in High School: The "Taking Care of" Business,* edited by Kristine Hansen and Christine R. Farris. NCTE, 2010, pp. 165–188.

Schaafsma, David, and Ruth Vinz. *On Narrative Inquiry: Approaches to Language and Literacy (an NCRLL Volume).* Language and Literacy Series, NCRLL Series. Teachers College P, 2011.

Schwalm, David E. "High School–College Dual Enrollment." *Journal of the Council of Writing Program Administrators,* vol. 15, no. 1–2, 1991, pp. 51–54.

Sehulster, Patricia J. "Forums: Bridging the Gap between High School and College Writing." *Teaching English in the Two-Year College,* vol. 39, no. 4, May 2012, pp. 343–354.

Sheehan, Kim Bartel. "E-mail Survey Response Rates: A Review." *Journal of Computer-Mediated Communication,* vol. 6, no. 2, 2006, n.p.

Thalheimer, Steve. "From Advanced Placement Student to Concurrent Enrollment Teachers: A Personal and Professional Evolution." In *College Credit for Writing in High School: The "Taking Care of" Business,* edited by Kristine Hansen and Christine R. Farris. NCTE, 2010, pp. 119–137.

Vivion, Michael J. "High School–College Dual Enrollment and the Composition Program." *Journal of the Council of Writing Program Administrators,* vol. 15, no. 1–2, 1991, pp. 55–60.

6

HIGH SCHOOL TEACHERS IN THE FYC ECOLOGY

Revising the Terms of Contingency

Scott Campbell

On occasion, famous chemists felt the need to apologise when speaking to an audience of scholarly professors, because their subject was not mathematical, and because their laboratories were filled with strange smells, potentially poisonous airs, caustic liquids, fire, and smoke.

—Manuel DeLanda, *Assemblage Theory*

This chapter calls attention, albeit somewhat obliquely, to a wariness sometimes felt by those who practice academic work that does not readily present itself as systematic and fully legible. In his discussion of apologetic eighteenth-century chemists, Manuel DeLanda draws on and adapts the concepts of Gilles Deleuze and Felix Guattari to describe "minor science" as a productive knowledge-making community whose consensus practices (and associated textbook knowledge) remain relatively open when compared with those in "major" fields because of a domain knowledge that resists idealization. According to DeLanda, "Minor fields allow phenomena in their domain to pose problems, and indeed, are forced by changes in the domain to constantly face new problems" (91). To DeLanda, minor does not connote lesser; minor fields, as with the chemistry example, can be in the process of "becoming major" if the conditions are right. One such example is how the Periodic Table emerged as a more complete coding of what had been experienced as a breakdown of the classical ordering of elementary substances. But minor science, variously called "nomad," "ambulant," or even "eccentric" science by Deleuze and Guattari, is artisanal in character and has wider variation. It operates in a more heterogeneous, local manner, committed to following the grain of the wood it is working with rather than reproducing a more centralized, abstracted field of knowledge.

https://doi.org/10.7330/9781646422531.c006

I begin here not to analogize composition as a minor field, tempting as this is, but to call attention to a comparable set of forces that is especially visible in what is still composition's most active and contested site—first-year composition (FYC). For many years FYC has been a primary site for the development of the discipline of rhetoric and composition (what I'll just call "composition" here) through the extensive reach of its teaching mission. But if FYC acts as the face of composition, a point of first contact for most who teach or practice composition at the university level, its still profoundly heterogeneous makeup and often heavy reliance on the teaching of contingent faculty and graduate students expose it to criticism that poses its disparities as markers of immaturity or lack of seriousness. FYC, in part because of its labor model, can seem remote from the content of the field of composition, less vitally engaged with field-defining research. The fact that more and more FYC courses happen at high school dual enrollment (DE) sites, geographically remote from college campuses, would only seem to exacerbate this uncertainty. But we can test assumptions that uncertainty necessarily indicates weakness or failure by exploring DE activity, which introduces its own set of complicating factors and additional material constraints. DE FYC, in fact, seems an especially appropriate place to consider the implications of seeing composition as shared work across multiple domains and as in important ways productively undisciplined.[1]

In this chapter, I offer a framework for the conversation about DE FYC by positing dual enrollment as an important but neglected example of academic contingency and also a catalyst for remaking our understanding of the relationship between teaching and the field of composition. Specifically, I look at FYC's long-standing and seemingly inextricable positioning within its vast, ambitious teaching commitments and its authorization of this work from an increasingly more defined disciplinary identity. By engaging with focus groups of currently active DE teachers, I document perspectives of those encountering FYC and composition work from high school spaces. Despite what is often construed as a plain contest between the field's circulating ideas (especially its scholarship) and its material constraints, my work tells a story distinct from the familiar laments about declining power and compromise, with their hints—both implicit and explicit—that contingency connotes something broken and incomplete, perhaps even shameful.

In posing the DE kaleidoscope in terms of assemblage theory, I argue here that academic contingency in FYC is as much a factor of curricular drift and de-territorialization as of simple economics and that DE activity, as a powerful amplification of contingency, can provide a working laboratory for FYC that, once engaged, can help to describe and inform FYC work, not just deliver it. The health and productivity of FYC, as well as its relationship to the composition field, may depend less on achieving a unified vision built on traditional academic hierarchy and replicable courses than on animating connections with and between those who are doing this work.

ACADEMIC CONTINGENCY AND DUAL ENROLLMENT

Debates about contingency often present the "adjunctification" of the academy as the inevitable product of an age of academic austerity—a labor problem, through and through (Bousquet). Surely at least a part of the movement toward DE, and probably the greatest factor in its development and rise, is the compression of time and space that DE enables. One can be *both* a high school and college student simultaneously, and in this way DE can be presented as an efficiency by its proponents or even a timely commodification of college credit (Hansen 5). But the labor equivalent of this efficiency, that instructors, too, are simultaneously high school and college faculty, may sit less easily. Viewed as an "outsourcing" of college work to high school faculty (Hansen and Farris xxv), DE operates in parallel to or as a subset of the familiar lament that reliance on adjunct labor dilutes and weakens curricula that should be coming through tenure-line faculty whenever possible. A consequence of this common public articulation of FYC DE as a course one can check off while still in high school is that FYC requirements become ever more recognizable to students as obstacles to be overcome rather than as integral components of a college education. As Kristine Hansen and Christine R. Farris put it, FYC DE has become part of the "taking care of" business, something for students to accomplish *before* attending college (xxxii). Even at the university level, the proliferation of high school credit for FYC courses is often championed by admissions staff, deans, and some faculty who may have little interest in teaching or even understanding the work of lower-level writing courses. The diminishing investment in teaching FYC often has an economic motive, but there is disinvestment, too, of a more substantive kind.

Some of the scholarship of DE supports a move away from using high school teachers as college faculty when possible. David Schwalm, one of the first to publish on this topic in the early 1990s, argued more recently that DE has potential as a "disruptive" innovation (225), redrawing the boundaries between high school and college by offering advanced coursework for some high school students. But in what he views as an overreach, DE tends to seek, instead, *equivalence* between high school and college courses rather than wholesale rethinking of FYC.[2] Today's DE programs offer college credit as a mainstreamed component of high school coursework and as a free pass from college composition. To Schwalm, the maturing of the digital culture and online teaching make DE arrangements unnecessary, a solution to a problem that no longer exists. Why not simply ask the students to take a college course *online* with college faculty? "An online [DE] course *is* the college course taught by a college instructor. The problem of course integrity disappears. Online courses simply eliminate the need for the [DE] model and the complex solutions we have come up with to address the problems it raised" (227–228). Schwalm's desire to shore up "integrity" intrigues; surely, we cannot prefer that FYC move to high schools, whatever its contribution to the high school experience, if the result is a subtraction of the impact of college faculty on these courses.

Schwalm's confidence in the on-campus version of FYC, however, overlooks problems of equity and access with online courses and does not attend to the growing pessimism about the labor practices for FYC at on-campus sites and higher education more broadly, with its continued dependence on contingent faculty. Nancy Welch and Tony Scott's, *Composition in the Age of Austerity* provides a good example of doleful prospecting about this material reality in its repeated turns toward metaphors of finality and failure. If we think Ann Larson's suggestion in her piece, "Composition's Dead," offers the worst-case scenario, we are soon told by one of the book's editors, Scott, that, in fact, composition may even be *un*-dead:

> There is a recurring moment in contemporary stories in the now established genre of zombie apocalypse in which characters, bitten by a zombie, understand their coming deaths and the ghostly resurrection of their bodies and minds that will follow. They often make some last "human" statement or act before they die, and then they come back to a new type of "life" driven by reaction, ceaseless movement, and the urgent, itchy desire to pursue and consume with no memory or distinguishing identity. If composition is to be more fully animated by entrepreneurialism, we are already seeing its last living acts. (217)

The threat in these accounts is often characterized as an untenable separation of the field's further development and elaboration as research and its deep reliance on the labor of teachers who do not have access to or time for such research. The fear expressed is that insurmountable material constraints lead composition into an unthinking, "zombie" simulacrum. Undoubtedly, FYC programs that rely heavily on under-supported instructors are responsible for the effects of doing so. Even a cursory review of the literature on the use of part-time and graduate student instructors at universities paints a bleak portrait of things as they are, in terms of both the teaching/scholarship bond and the economic precarity of the individuals doing the teaching. Instructors in this environment are subject to what Gary Hall calls the "Uberfication of the University," a state in which academic laborers must act as "microentrepreneurs," grouped together by circumstances but always in competition for higher scores on evaluations and, from this, more (but always temporary and conditional) opportunities. Citing the archly named "sharing economy" as a model for these developments of a "socially weakened form of capitalism" (16), Hall describes the stress and isolation of so many higher education faculty whose contingent status does not even rise to the level of "employee."

But the economic argument takes on a very different character in DE spaces. High school teachers in FYC, while technically adjunct faculty, *are* usually full-time employees, albeit of high schools, not universities. They are also in environments that posit professional development almost entirely in terms of teaching, not research. In an instant, what is perceived on campus as only a labor issue affecting academic quality becomes much more a debate about disciplinary identity, membership, and mission.[3] When the university or college provides the earned credits but the high school, in fact, pays the teacher, the impetus for the high school teacher to go through the trouble of DE certification and teaching is more ambiguous. Although DE FYC often happens within contexts and guidelines presented by organizations such as the National Alliance of Concurrent Enrollment Partnerships (NACEP), Council of Writing Program Administrators (CWPA), and the National Council of Teachers of English (NCTE), regional accrediting bodies, and local departmental oversight, one must wonder what, in fact, holds all this work together. Can one be a faculty member, teaching courses for a university, and not be a funded student or employee of the overseeing institution? Clearly, the predominant models of professional expertise and authority within the academy—models that have always been at least implicitly challenged by the work of composition—are even more exposed as inadequate today, when so many teachers even on campus operate at least partially beyond the constraining factors of higher education hierarchies.

A DE FYC component of a writing program makes visible a problem in the disciplining of composition that has been with us from the start, namely, FYC's function as a preparation for generalized academic work rather than an introduction to a discipline. As general education offerings often delinked from departmental missions or majors, FYC courses must meet the needs of students seeking business, science, and social science degrees and more. The development of "Writing about Writing" courses at some institutions could be said to address this unmooring by recapturing writing studies as an informing body of scholarship, and, surely, some universities do better than others in communicating the relationships between FYC and potential work in writing studies or composition, including often robust minors or majors. Nonetheless, the vast majority of those charged with teaching FYC courses nationally, at both college and high school sites, do not actively contribute to the field's disciplinary knowledge within the recognized parameters of academic research. With adjunctification and the use of graduate students at on-campus sites, this liminality takes on an understandably negative character, a drift from an ideal.[4]

But how little we know about the desires, motivations, and qualities even of on-campus adjunct faculty when we constantly weigh them against a standard of scholarly and professional achievement that may provide only a negative image. David Bartholomae notes a remarkable statistic from an Association of Departments of English staffing survey indicating that only about 50 percent of part-time faculty members "would prefer a full-time position," a number that in its ambivalence nicely registers the limitations in accounting for the "typical" part-time faculty member (21). Contingent faculty trouble the professional and disciplinary boundaries within the academy, but posing this trouble as a problem to be solved may only reproduce the faulty logic of remediation that for so long bedeviled our conception of students. Adjunct faculty often come to and participate in teaching for reasons other than a commitment to the academy or its disciplines. Composition has become adept at accounting for the multiplicity of needs of and potential in nontraditional students. Much of our work points to these complexities, once understood as merely problems needing remediation, as by now a crucial source of vitality in our work and mission. Can we see the same opportunity in revising how we address and work alongside our "nontraditional" faculty, especially those who work almost wholly outside the college spaces?

In my time as the coordinator of one of the oldest and largest DE English programs, with over 100 participating high schools across the state, I have come to recognize the extraordinary complexity and variation of high school–college partnerships. Even within my conventionally structured program, where all DE courses happen at high school sites, the list of potential variations can include: geography (e.g., urban and rural schools or proximity from the university campus), socioeconomic factors (e.g., the makeup of the school or its instructors), district or school requirements (e.g., Common Core adherence or shared syllabi), type of school (e.g., technical school or arts academy), daily schedule (e.g., forty-five minutes every day or twice weekly at eighty minutes), calendar (e.g., semester or full year), available course materials (e.g., books or technology), as well as a blizzard of unforeseen, emergent factors that can involve parents, politics, and pretty much anything else. Add to this the many DE models that alter or diverge from the model of delivering a college course at a high school site, and it is fair to say that there is no summing up or categorizing "general" DE programs without tremendous loss. Even the most well-considered curriculum, effectively communicated and supported by ample interaction with college faculty, cannot simply iron out the wrinkles of the DE fabric but must account for and when possible draw from these differences.

What I propose, then, is a model for engaging with the sometimes radical heterogeneity of these partnerships, one that accounts for the active, ongoing relationships in effect without deferring to an idealism not practicable in the current climate. Taking contingency (if not contingent labor per se) as a given rather than noise in the system means understanding the work of FYC as inherently situated and emergent, as open-ended and heterodox. And it in effect joins WPA work, which often adopts traditional academic forms, to our field's more animated interactions with polyvalent forces, particularly in what gets called ecological or post-human composition. In what follows I bring together the flexible, supportive terms of assemblage theory with accounts from several DE FYC instructors of their work within this assemblage, with the goal of seeking better ways to acknowledge and learn from the academic work of contingent faculty.

DE TEACHERS IN THE FYC ASSEMBLAGE

The assemblage concept circulates within the composition field as a term used to designate the dynamic and layered complexity of writing itself. Writing is described *as assemblage*, an emergent organized whole so complex as to resist codification. Kristopher M. Lotier uses this language to critique teaching models that would seek to reverse engineer "good writing" into something stable and teachable, a simplifying reification that must over time be replaced by what he describes as "the postprocess mantra that writing cannot be taught but can be learned—each time, anew" (372). Likewise, much of Kathleen Blake Yancey and Stephen J. McElroy's *Assembling Composition* primarily addresses assemblage as a term of art applied to writing. The book's contributors often use the term loosely to suggest a broad category of collected materials, something akin to collage. Although some contributors take on a more specific engagement with the assemblage theory derived from Deleuze and Guattari that I use here, there is little use of assemblage theory to explore the rich mix of materials and expressions—the ever-shifting bodies, objects, codes, and statements—of a writing program.[5] In this section, I outline some of the key features of this more sharply defined assemblage theory to provide a conceptual resource that can help better describe the relationships and agencies operating in DE FYC programs.

Any combination of heterogeneous parts in an organized (if still heterogeneous) functional relationship can be called an assemblage. The term itself suggests *assembly*, of course, but its originating French term, *agencement*, indicates a more active role of the components within an assemblage, an agency associated within its assembly attributable to the co-functioning of elements, not merely as a synthesis or product of a larger design. It is this latter quality, the *co-functioning* of elements, that is so valuable for understanding the contingency of DE FYC instructors, whose role as members of an FYC assemblage requires continuous contact with "concurrent" or "dual" roles as high school teachers. In the terms of Deleuze and Guattari, an assemblage is "what holds heterogeneities together without their ceasing to be heterogeneous" (329).

Crucially, an assemblage is singular—it may have similarities with other assemblages but is never an exact duplication—and it is dynamic. It continues to mutate and transform through constant remaking. What this means is that an assemblage has an individual quality, a unique historical presence without exact equivalence. An assemblage is also always attached to and made up of other assemblages (Bryant). Calling something an assemblage, then, does not in itself solve any problems, and, to an extent, it risks positing a defining term—a category that, if used with sloppiness, can look like a stabilizing abstraction rather than a tool for improving our understanding of how things work. But the strength of assemblage theory is its challenge to theoretical constructs that assert unifying, ordering behaviors that simplify complexity. Assemblage theory seeks a more true-to-events accounting of capacities and manifestations that neither subordinates local forms and activity to an overarching articulation or structure (top-down idealisms) nor limits causation to classic materialist preference for solely bottom-up development (a base and superstructure logic). DeLanda's somewhat contested term, *realism*, prioritizes the activity of the assemblage over whatever terms are used to conceptualize or describe them. And to the extent that an FYC program makes use of components such as adjunct faculty and high school teachers, a similar realism must counter narratives of stabilizing unity provided by shared disciplinarity.

DeLanda poses assemblage as a "concept with knobs," providing a way to grasp and understand assemblages without attributing their properties and activity to single, unidirectional causes. Rather, we can attend to the relative strength of the bonds between associated components along two parameters: territory and coding. In effect, assemblage theory offers concepts to help us resist positing an essence or a structure that stands apart from each individual instance, although the constant shaping and reshaping that happens when territories or codes are contested can reveal relative strengths and weaknesses. In the example of composition, we can see what's at stake. Turn the knobs of disciplinarity up—emphasize PhDs and scholarship—and we might pose composition as a recognizable academic discipline, with all the familiar hierarchies. Members of such a composition assemblage are coded by a regulated institutional order, the conferring of degrees and promotions, driven largely by the approval granted by the most influential members of the field. The letters associated with tenure-line positions, both at the moment of first hire and at various points of promotion, are powerful examples of the field remaking itself along a model maintained by a self-regulating elite. There are tremendous benefits from shared, tightly coded disciplinarity, and were FYC to function more as an introduction to composition's relatively stable field knowledge, it would have a more codifiable curricular presence. As one of the teachers I spoke with put it, "My colleagues teaching a [DE] Biology 101 course use the exact same textbook, lecture notes, and exams as their on-campus counterparts." The possibilities for alignment and consistency are much higher.

But prioritizing alignment and consistency neglects the diverse contributions of those who teach FYC, many of whom are expert teachers and innovators. To better describe and engage with FYC realities, we turn the "knobs" back toward de-territorialization and less coding, giving attention to the complex relations that emerge with the greater variability necessitated by contingency and what we might call "concurrency," a responsibility to additional and sometimes competing organizational forces. Contingent faculty, here, do not present as failed or in-training professors but as actors with varying motivations and agenda. They enter the assemblage only to the extent that it helps them meet their own goals, and it is productive for them in the ways they measure productivity. Like students, who may be on any number of paths but who converge for this course, faculty engage in FYC work while performing additional, often equally demanding roles. Concurrency, in this way, describes the state of doing composition while also doing something else. That is, concurrency is the experience of the overwhelming majority of the teachers and students of FYC courses.

De-territorialization, within assemblage theory, describes the movement of things out from and beyond their supposed "intended" paths, a movement that often suggests a disarticulation of a known form or practice, a dissolving of what had been a primary relationship. But it is also a sign of life and new purpose, an exploration of capacities that have been dormant or neglected. Mark Bonta and John Protevi describe de-territorialization as "the process of leaving home, of altering your habits, of learning new tricks" (78). To imagine DE FYC as a de-territorialization of FYC is not to say that either is decaying or dying. But it does require a willingness to attend to the ways composition work can open to new uses and new combinations without relying on sharply codified and stabilized field knowledge. It depends, too, on releasing ourselves from notions that would suggest equivalence and full compatibility between DE and adjunct faculty work and the more tightly coded, supervised teaching of graduate students and those more fully within the academic departmental structure. And it means taking more interest in how high school DE sites are themselves de-territorialized and transformed by partnerships with colleges. If FYC is designed to draw student writers into habits of mind and practices beyond those provided by high school curricula, its place *within* these high schools seems especially worth considering.

DE scholarship often explores DE arrangements with similar terms of turf or territory. Miles McCrimmon, for example, notes the "merging of contexts" (222) in DE partnerships, calling for dialogue and understanding of mutual interests—practices that might foster the creation of a "shared territoriality" (224). McCrimmon describes the resulting, wider understanding of both high school and college realms as a "bicultural identification": "Those who prosper teaching dual enrollment manage to transform their comfortable notions of territory and professional identity into more complicated, productive, and provocative realms of territory and bicultural identification. They develop a liminal conception of territoriality that opens more pedagogical avenues to them" (220). Likewise, Christine Denecker sees DE sites as places to openly share information about important differences: "It is in this space that the tensions and inconsistencies between secondary and postsecondary writing instruction have the potential for becoming more clearly defined" (29). Meaningful collaboration and dialogue between instructors and program coordinators may not solve or remove differences, but it can foster awareness of the multiple, sometimes competing forces that flow through a writing program. As Denecker writes, "It is about what the *instructors* know or understand about composition practices on both sides of the divide" (31, original emphasis).

Using territory, or assemblage more specifically, I posit a notion of composition work that challenges the negative valence of contingency in DE work without quite accepting the premise that a fully operative "biculturalism" can be developed.

OFF CAMPUS BUT IN THE CONVERSATION

To learn more from teachers, I convened focus groups totaling seventeen DE FYC instructors from across the state, and we worked together in groups of differing sizes for about seventy-five minutes per session. In these conversations, I asked teachers to describe their place within the FYC ecology.[6] My goal was to explore DE teachers' sense of their own disciplinary (and departmental) identity, especially along three contested pairings or partnerships: high school and college settings, English and composition (as fields), and composition (or writing) and literature (as curriculum). I asked about their motivations for seeking a role in a DE program, what they see as their sources of disciplinary knowledge for this work, and how they see their placement within the university structures set up to support or enable that work. Although these initial discussions serve as just an early, partial engagement with DE teacher expectations and experience within a specific program, the responses suggest the importance of affective affiliation with a perceived college mission and a desire to make use of the partnerships to support and advance one's work. But most also indicated little awareness of departmental or disciplinary goings-on at the on-campus institution, other than familiarity with FYC practices and requirements. The teachers spoke in terms that underscore the urgency of seeing and supporting the co-functioning relations of this particular assemblage rather than prioritizing disciplinary authority over their work. These teachers, comfortable in their professional roles at the high schools, expressed no great anxiety or concern about being perceived as partial or incomplete disciplinary members. Some are engaged in graduate work, and the group included at least one doctoral candidate. But the FYC mission—the work they are charged to do—is perceived as one of practical engagement with students and not an activity informed by a sharply defined set of shared disciplinary characteristics. This light register of the texts and questions that infuse FYC program development is common, too, with on-campus FYC instructors and is surely an ongoing challenge for program administrators.

If the concern in many DE discussions at the administrative or curricular level is one of turf or of disciplinary rigor, however, these self-selected groups of teachers came into the conversation with enthusiasm for the high school–college partnership and, quite often, an excitement about what they decided was the *space* provided by the college course in the high school setting. Many used positive terms of personal or professional satisfaction (*stimulation, freedom, challenge, desire*) and posed FYC teaching against what was described as more formulaic or rigid requirements in their other courses. Most saw their DE courses as much closer to their preferred mode of teaching and as a desirable option for future work. As one teacher put it, "I feel we get to do what every English teacher wishes they could do." The DE course, in these focus groups but also in my ongoing work with DE instructors, is often posed by teachers as a relief from arbitrary and often intrusive regimentation. More than anything else, these teachers expressed appreciation for the greater responsibility they felt as college faculty in choosing the direction and content of their courses.

But despite this generally shared understanding of DE FYC as a *freedom from*, these same teachers expressed uncertainty about the positive, recognizable characteristics of the college courses themselves other than a shared commitment to *doing writing* within contexts that provide structure, feedback, and opportunities for revision. These effective process-era practices are in widespread use but are not often tied to exact or specific sources or arguments. In Neal Lerner's terms, the teachers experience a situation where a common writing pedagogy circulates but official curriculum, often distant from instructor and student experience, is left aside or unofficially revised (62). Asked to describe their own understanding of the specific disciplinary knowledge informing the FYC courses or to note recent developments in the field, many declined or described their contact with the field as happening "years ago" or "in grad school." Marking the difference of working within a high school setting, those with teaching experience at both the high school and college levels expressed satisfaction with the largely pedagogical knowledge circulating in on-campus FYC programs in contrast to high school "PD," which they almost universally described as unhelpful. As one put it, "While I was teaching [on campus] there was always rich information about teaching English." Others described gleaning information from college bookstores or hearing from returning students about what they do in their college classes.

There was some agreement that the site visits, workshops, and conferences provided by the DE program—such as a recent one-day workshop dedicated to responding to Linda Adler-Kassner and Elizabeth Wardle's collection *Naming What We Know: Threshold Concepts of Writing Studies*—offer needed input and opportunity for discussion. However, most waved off any request to define a specific field knowledge unique to these college courses. Said one teacher, "I feel like I'm less in touch with the field of English and more in touch with the field of education." Describing the discipline as "fuzzier" or without a sharply defined set of traits—"we're all kind of figuring this out for ourselves"—teachers often posed the DE FYC course as (again) an alternative to something they see as negative rather than a defined something.

The range and uncertainty of the discussion of what FYC is suggests something more than just the seeking of membership within terms ascribed by the high school or college. In this uncertainty is a movement away from content (often literature) and toward activity (writing) and, at least to this group of teachers, a movement away from prescribed forms of "school writing." One teacher sought ways to mark these differences with terminology, saying to students, "Get this word, *English*, out of your head!" Another described the literary mandarins in her high school English department as "Keepers of the Sacred Flame." Such teachers, who feature exposure to a literary content, present English as an entry into a closed society of knowers with teacher at the top of the hierarchy, someone who says to students, "I can show [the Sacred Flame] to you." We might see FYC here as enabling critique of notions of "English," especially those that prioritize literary analysis or inert content coverage.

In contrast, DE FYC was described as student-centered and productively open-ended. Key terms from the FYC program itself—*inquiry, student-driven, project-based*—bubbled up alongside fresh thinking about how to describe this work. One teacher described herself as a "metacognitive Sherpa," and the laughing, affirmative response to this statement underscored the sense these teachers have that their role is more one of facilitator and guide than repository of disciplinary knowledge—an attitude not far from Lotier's description of post-process pedagogy. Teachers with experience in this DE program seemed comfortable inventing provisional terms like these for what they described as less a content knowledge or expertise than an activity, a motion. And while familiar terms of secondary education, such as "skills," came up in our conversations, they figured more as words to capture this motion than an inert set of defined practices. In this way, the teachers showed an artisanal tendency toward seeing composition as what DeLanda might describe as a nomad or minor science, "following the flow of matter" rather than working toward axioms.[7]

When asked directly about their own sense of disciplinary identity, responses again illustrated distance from an on-campus sensibility. Notes of one group's multi-voice response to the question of whether they see themselves as members of a university English department read as follows: "No. No. No. No. Very, very tangential. Adjunct at best. Not even. I am a teacher at my own school first." One teacher described the limitation of even the word *adjunct*: "Even with being an adjunct, I don't feel linked. I'm somewhere out floating." When adjunct means tangential or seemingly tacked on rather than adjoining (a part of), the intended bond between the individual's work and the college context breaks down and co-functioning can become covert functioning, a masking of high school pedagogy in the guise of a college course. This same teacher expressed this gap as an artifact of coolness coming from on-campus counterparts: "I did not feel respected when I started." Composition as a field brought only puzzled looks or misrecognition. If teachers took on the term *compositionist*, it was as an equivalent of *writer* and usually creative writer: "I've never seen that word. I am a language artist and scientist. I study language." Or, from another teacher: "You always have another new word (a redefining) for things we've been doing." Clearly, our shared vocabulary is a work in progress.

Such comments from within this one DE program might not translate to other settings. And the often weak bond with disciplinary or departmental knowledge from this group surely raises concerns about the consistency of the work. My goal is not to shrug off the seriousness of this potential miscommunication. Nevertheless, this system of contingent instructors often proves to be more agile and flexible than a traditional department, taking on, for example, a recent initiative in multimodal composition in diverse and creative ways and transitioning to COVID-necessitated online teaching more smoothly than on-campus faculty. This teacher assemblage is always adding, subtracting, replenishing, and remaking with an intricacy that cannot be captured. It also constantly struggles with the negative effects of such porosity and openness. This ever-reconstituting collection of instructors enacts the paradox of defining success outside of the terms established by traditional departments. Should we commend these achievements or question the loss of so much that is essential to conventional academic success? When DE FYC has worked in this setting, when it has been interesting and productive, the connections between teachers and the program discourse are stronger and the spell of isolation and silence around the work is broken. But this strengthening of ties must be more than mere oversight or scrutiny of individuals. It can't be a one-way implementation of program design *onto* these teachers. As I learn more through my interactions with DE FYC instructors, my appreciation for what they and their students accomplish grows, and my administrative role is increasingly one of listening, collecting, and circulating.

A common element in successful DE FYC programs is non-evaluative participation that often includes a great deal of speaking and writing, a description of one's work, and the articulation of values tied to this work. DE programs can provide more context, smarter environments, for instructors without "unbundling" the labor with mandatory syllabi, preformed pedagogies, or reified processes. And these contributions to program ecology surely include ongoing engagement with and circulation of research in composition studies. I'm not denying that some level of oversight weaves its way into this ultimately unequal relationship. It is fundamental that programs review and respond to work that happens within them. But building in more opportunities to describe one's work in exchange for more materials from the program's other instructors, for example, or asking DE teachers to lead or co-lead sessions at workshops and conferences can establish an emphasis on emergent links and relationships over DIY self-reliance or compliance with what is perceived as a prescribed curriculum. Assessment can provide an especially significant role in developing this communication when it diverges from its often-used role of program verification or measurement. Models abound for using assessment as research into a program's work (rather than simply a measuring of it). Jeff Rice, for example, has offered "networked assessment" as a tracing of connections "to teach us about the relationships circulating in our own program that we have yet to see as being part of a given network" (38). Essential to his practice is a "lack of dependence on a conclusion."

CONCLUSION

To see a DE program in terms of assemblage, we might map FYC activity that does not impose an unhelpful and unrealistic hierarchy that always leads back to tenure-line WPA positions and settled disciplinarily identity. Assemblage theory, which stresses heterogeneity and opportunistic but often nested temporary relationships, helps us grasp a complex labor question without resorting to binaries, and it offers a challenge to academic disciplinarity in its resistance to unity or even, really, structure. Too often, the lament over de-territorialization in the academy exposes a will toward centralization that seems already in conflict with the mission and practices of many or most compositionists. Since its emergence in the 1960s, composition has *always* operated with a more flattened hierarchy than traditional disciplines, and, often because of its deep involvement with first-year students and vast teaching obligations, composition has tended to prioritize teaching and engagement. High school faculty, who self-identify as teachers more than scholars and who seek to contribute to the program knowledge, animate the debates about composition's pedagogical mission in fresh, exciting ways.

With that said, assemblage does not preclude disciplinarity. I have tried to show that it is not an antidote or an alternative but, rather, a way to describe the bonds and relationships that establish the whole. Writing programs are always re-territorializing by recoding through documents (new syllabus guidelines or revised learning outcomes) and domain enforcement (required on-campus workshops and orientations, site visits). And they depend on research and more tightly codified disciplinary activity, including peer review and publication, at least in some sectors. But prioritizing a strict disciplinarity comes at a cost to the range of activity and experiment of the assemblage.

Although his work takes him in a considerably different direction, Bruce Horner's recent exploration of disciplinarity in composition shares my optimism for a field that acknowledges the labor of its members as much more than the production of the academy's commodified categories: "Arguments to improve the labor situation of composition through achievement of professional academic disciplinarity accede to commodification's elision of the necessity of labor to the realization of knowledge (its 'production' and also its 'reproduction'), and hence they accept terms of exchange that exclude questions of labor altogether. Insofar as the knowledge commodified is 'English,' over which compositionists have difficulty claiming either exclusive ownership or esoteric knowledge, such tactics are even more unpromising" (167).

Some caution is in order. Posing FYC as an entity that holds together in ways that differ from conventional disciplinary organization raises a number of questions about potential accommodation to a continued erosion of faculty and disciplinary authority (Gunner). Surely at least part of what is at issue in the expansion of DE programs has to do with a collapse of support even for the relatively low-level investment of traditional FYC models. We cannot prefer that circumstances necessitate a limited field knowledge from so many of our instructors. But where full staffing of FYC courses without reliance on contingent faculty has not happened, the responsible options are to withdraw/contract or approach contingency complexly, as a potentially fruitful but necessarily different arrangement.

DE programs thrive in ways that often escape notice and belie claims that things must necessarily be getting worse. At a high school site, an FYC course provides a coveted space where many of the most engaged students work with instructors who are themselves among the school's best. Teachers and students at these sites contend with pressures that are unfamiliar to on-campus faculty. At high schools, FYC provides a platform for experimenting with college writing and, in doing so, revising how writing functions in those spaces. Such courses can never be the same as on-campus versions, but composition, with its long history of finding energies in neglected and marginalized spaces, asks us to move beyond a top-down program architecture into productive engagement with these situated, complex, and indeed contingent sites.

NOTES

1. I have in mind Adam Banks's celebration of the "funkiness" of composition—the "ways in which our field has arrived at disciplinary maturity and yet remains undisciplined, unable to be disciplined" (270).
2. Although 2017 revisions to NACEP standards softened the emphasis on equivalence to include language such as "aligns with" or "has ongoing collaboration with," the previous standards spoke of DE courses and curricula as needing to be "the same" as on-campus versions (NACEP).
3. The factors of pay and workload do not, of course, magically disappear, but I want to underscore the ways that DE teachers take on "contingency" as an experience of disciplinary identity, not (for the most part) an economic condition.
4. Liminality is taken up in much DE scholarship as well (e.g., Hofmann and Voloch; Denecker; McWain).
5. Alex Reid frequently writes about academic work and spaces with assemblage theory, as do, to a lesser extent, Byron Hawk and Thomas Rickert. But none of these scholars follows through on an examination of either FYC or DE spaces.
6. This study was approved by the University of Connecticut's IRB (UConn IRB PROTOCOL X18–117 APPROVED 9/19/18). I have left names off as a condition of this approval. The questions used in the conversations are provided as appendix 6.A.
7. DeLanda, too, notes the workshop practices of minor sciences: "The relatively flat hierarchy of the workshop, its reliance on flexible skills, and its ability to work with heterogeneous raw materials indicate an assemblage with low values for the territorialisation and coding parameters" (82).

APPENDIX 6.A

HIGH SCHOOL TEACHERS IN THE FYC ECOLOGY

Revising the Terms of Contingency//Questions for Focus Group//IRB Protocol: X18–117

This study explores the disciplinary identity of those who teach college English courses in high school settings. Specifically, I am interested in hearing more about your sense of the relationships (and the differences) between college and high school English, and, as well, how you see yourself as positioned within or between those two worlds. I am also interested in your understanding of the distinctions between literary studies and composition and what these two elements contribute (if anything) to your work as a teacher in a concurrent enrollment English program.

Impetus

1. What motivates you to be a teacher of college-level English?

Disciplinary Identity: English

2. What do you see as your primary sources of information about the field of English? (This could be coursework, the reading of books or journals, engagement with other faculty, etc.) Describe as specifically as you can your contact with these sources.
3. How would you define the specialized knowledge of the field of English? What does it mean to have expertise in this field?
4. Do you see yourself as a member of a university English department? How would you describe what we might call your "disciplinary identity," your felt sense of membership within a specific university discipline?
5. Do you feel you have full access to the field knowledge expected of an active college instructor? What barriers or obstacles do you see to achieving or maintaining this expertise?
6. How does your training in secondary education (and your ongoing professional development in secondary education) inform your work as a college instructor?

Disciplinary Identity: Composition

In what follows, I use the term "composition" to describe the field or discipline that is also commonly known as "rhetoric and composition," "composition studies," or "writing studies."

7. What do you see as the relationship between literary studies and composition? How would you describe the shared features as well as the distinctions between these two groupings or points of emphasis?
8. How would you define the specialized knowledge of the field of composition? What does it mean to have expertise in this field?

9. Do you see yourself as a compositionist, as someone who practices within the discipline of composition? Explain. What other terms might you use to describe your role as a writing instructor?

Conclusion

If there is time, we will spend the remainder of the session on attending to potential omissions or unfinished details.

10. What would you like to add to our conversation that you have not yet had a chance to say?

WORKS CITED

Adler-Kassner, Linda, and Elizabeth Wardle. *Naming What We Know: Threshold Concepts of Writing Studies.* Utah State UP, 2015.

Banks, Adam. "2015 Chair's Address: Ain't No Walls behind the Sky, Baby! Funk, Flight, Freedom." *College Composition and Communication*, vol. 67, no. 2, 2015, pp. 267–279.

Bartholomae, David. "Teaching on and off the Tenure Track: Highlights from the ADE Survey of Staffing Patterns in English." *Pedagogy: Critical Approaches to Teaching Literature, Language, Composition, and Culture*, vol. 11, no. 1, 2010, pp. 7–32.

Bonta, Mark, and John Protevi. *Deleuze and Geophilosophy: A Guide and Glossary.* Edinburgh UP, 2004.

Bousquet, Marc. *How the University Works: Higher Education and the Low-Wage Nation.* New York UP, 2008.

Bryant, Levi. "DRG: 'Assemblages against Totalities.'" *Larval Subjects*, Sept. 8, 2010. larvalsubjects.wordpress.com/2010/09/08/drg-assemblages-against-totalities/. Accessed May 16, 2022.

DeLanda, Manuel. *Assemblage Theory.* Edinburgh UP, 2016.

Deleuze, Gilles, and Felix Guattari. *A Thousand Plateaus: Capitalism and Schizophrenia.* Translated by Brian Massumi. U of Minnesota P, 1987.

Denecker, Christine. "Transitioning Writers across the Composition Threshold: What We Can Learn from Dual Enrollment Partnerships." *Composition Studies*, vol. 41, no. 1, 2013, pp. 27–50.

Gunner, Jeanne. "Disciplinary Purification: The Writing Program as Institutional Brand." *JAC*, vol. 32, no. 3–4, 2012, pp. 614–643.

Hall, Gary. *The Uberfication of the University.* Minneapolis: U of Minnesota P, 2016.

Hansen, Kristine. "The Composition Marketplace: Shopping for Credit versus Learning to Write." In *College Credit for Writing in High School: The "Taking Care of" Business*, edited by Kristine Hansen and Christine R. Farris. NCTE, 2010, pp. 1–39.

Hansen, Kristine, and Christine R. Farris, eds. *College Credit for Writing in High School: The "Taking Care of" Business.* NCTE, 2010.

Hofmann, Eric, and Daniel Voloch. "Dual Enrollment as a Liminal Space." *New Directions for Higher Education*, vol. 158, Summer 2012, pp. 101–107.

Horner, Bruce. *Rewriting Composition: Terms of Exchange.* Southern Illinois UP, 2016.

Larson, Ann. "Composition's Dead." In *Composition in the Age of Austerity*, edited by Nancy Welch and Tony Scott. Utah State UP, 2016, pp. 163–176.

Lerner, Neal. *Reformers, Teachers, Writers: Curricular and Pedagogical Inquiries.* Utah State UP, 2019.

Lotier, Kristopher M. "Around 1986: The Externalization of Cognition and the Emergence of Postprocess Invention." *Conference on College Composition and Communication*, vol. 67, no. 3, 2016, pp. 360–384.

McCrimmon, Miles. "Contesting the Territoriality of 'Freshman English': The Political Ecology of Dual Enrollment." In *College Credit for Writing in High School: The "Taking Care of" Business*, edited by Kristine Hansen and Christine R. Farris. NCTE, 2010, pp. 208–226.

McWain, Katie. "Finding Freedom at the Composition Threshold: Learning from the Experiences of Dual Enrollment Teachers." *TETYC*, vol. 45, no. 4, May 2018, pp. 406–424.

National Alliance of Concurrent Enrollment Partnerships (NACEP). *Program Standards and Required Evidence for Accreditation*. 2011. http://nacep.org/docs/standards/NACEP-Standards-2011-and-Required-Evidence.pdf. Accessed May 12, 2022.

Rice, Jeff. "Networked Assessment." *Computers and Composition*, vol. 28, 2011, pp. 28–39.

Schwalm, David. " 'Taking Care of' Writing." *WPA: Writing Program Administration*, vol. 36, no. 1, 2012, pp. 220–229.

Scott, Tony. "Animated by the Entrepreneurial Spirit: Austerity, Disposession, and Composition's Last Living Act." In *Composition in the Age of Austerity*, edited by Nancy Welcome and Tony Scott, Utah State UP, 2016, pp. 205–219.

Welch, Nancy, and Tony Scott, eds. *Composition in the Age of Austerity*. Utah State UP, 2016.

Yancey, Kathleen Blake, and Stephen J. McElroy, eds. *Assembling Composition*. NCTE, 2017.

7

WHEN COLLEGE FACULTY GO TO HIGH SCHOOL

Dual Enrollment and the Changing Scenes of "First-Year" Composition

Annie S. Mendenhall and David Gehler

Several years ago, a dean asked our department to teach dual enrollment (DE) first-year composition (FYC) at local high schools. Newly appointed as director of composition, Annie, armed herself with position statements and scholarship, prepared to argue that high school students would benefit from taking FYC on our college campus. Not persuaded by these arguments, the dean suggested that if the department could not staff DE courses, he would need to "revisit" the course caps in FYC, which had recently been reduced to twenty-two students. Left with few alternatives, Annie and the chair worked with David, a recently hired instructor with high school and college teaching experience, to develop this new DE partnership. Such is the origins story of our current DE program. We bartered to maintain our course cap victory in FYC but in doing so began a new DE program with little planning or investment from the department. This story illustrates how DE often operates at the sidelines of the already fraught instructional space of FYC, exposing the ways FYC programs are simultaneously desirable and dismissed, institutionally important but frequently outsourced.

Teaching DE courses at high schools compounds the interrelated curricular and labor challenges of FYC, raising questions about the role of the instructor and location in pedagogy. Does FYC cover content that nearly any English instructor can teach, anywhere, to any student? What is the relationship among course learning outcomes, disciplinary best practices, and the plethora of delivery models for FYC? And how do program policies, including those related to assessment and course caps, operate across FYC spaces subject to different power dynamics? Answering these questions is complicated by the rapid yet precarious growth of DE, which has led to inconsistent staffing, curriculum, and

https://doi.org/10.7330/9781646422531.c007

location practices. Emerging data, as we will show here, are only beginning to present a picture of the range of DE faculty, institutional affiliations, and site locations. Published research on college faculty teaching DE on high school campuses, whom we refer to as *traveling DE faculty*, has been minimal; but their experiences of transience, we argue, have much to add to research on DE and FYC as a whole.

In this chapter, we analyze how precarity in DE staffing and David's experiences as a traveling DE faculty reveal limitations in the disciplinary guidelines for FYC outlined for writing program administrators (WPA), known as the WPA Outcomes Statement ("Outcomes"). Since its first iteration in 2000, the Outcomes Statement has provided a framework defining "the writing knowledge, practices, and attitudes that undergraduate students develop in first-year composition." We argue that DE courses taught in high schools face structural limitations in achieving the three major student learning outcomes (SLOs) in the Outcomes Statement ("critical thinking, reading, and writing"; "writing processes"; and "rhetorical knowledge"). However, those structural limitations raise larger questions about the extent to which FYC outcomes—both local and disciplinary—are contingent on the environmental and social resources of college campuses. While we argue that WPAs and faculty need to know about the constraints we describe when developing DE FYC partnerships, we also call for further research and storytelling to explore the effects of site and labor structures on student learning.

THE SPACE OF DUAL ENROLLMENT IN NATIONAL AND LOCAL CONTEXTS

Traveling DE faculty constitute one small but significant kind of DE program. According to the National Center for Education Statistics, 66 percent of DE programs at high schools have some postsecondary instructors teaching in their programs, and 19 percent employ college instructors exclusively (Shivji and Wilson 8). Readers may wonder, though, how many students take DE classes at a high school. In fact, the majority of DE students (86%) take at least one DE course at a high school location (2). Traveling DE faculty thus constitute one of many forms DE delivery may take—a variety in delivery that may be due to DE's rapid growth. In our state, Georgia, appropriations for DE have increased by 350 percent since 2014 and now involve at least 35,000 students (Griffin and McGuire 13). Consistent with national trends, 17 percent of Georgia's DE courses are delivered at high schools, and these courses may be taught by college or certified high school faculty

(10). When taught on college campuses, DE courses are more common in the Technical College System of Georgia, which covers 50 percent of DE courses, than in the University System of Georgia (USG) (36%) (n.p.). However, our university, a USG institution, had over 700 students enrolled in all types of DE courses in fall 2019, up nearly 150 students from the prior year ("Fall 2019"). The variety in delivery makes it challenging to gather statewide data on who is teaching DE FYC and whether these programs have any kind of consistent content or outcomes.

Consequently, some stakeholders express concerns about DE's efficacy, concerns that appear to be warranted. Existing research suggests that DE has "no discernible effects on general academic achievement" in college, although it does increase students' likelihood of enrolling in college and graduating (US Department of Education 1–2). Kristine Hansen and colleagues found that students who took DE FYC did not perform significantly better or worse on writing tasks than other kinds of first-year students. And yet, while most DE students pass the courses (in Georgia, pass rate for general education English[1] DE courses is nearly 94%), we know anecdotally that DE FYC instructors feel pressure (sometimes explicitly from administrators) to pass DE students when both high school graduation and college credit are contingent on the course (Griffin and McGuire 41). These findings raise serious concerns about the ability of high school DE programs to meet the SLOs of FYC. If DE has little value beyond acclimating students to college, then high school DE courses may provide little benefit without the "high expectations and peer models that the college environment provides" (Berger et al. 52).

Some skeptics have called for proof that DE programs meet SLOs before further investment by the state. A recent report by Georgia's state legislature notes that DE courses lack consistent or clear learning objectives, stating that "without clearly defined goals and objectives, it is difficult to measure program success and assess its cost-effectiveness" (Griffin and McGuire n.p.). In response, the state house of representatives has drafted a bill[2] to place "guardrails" on DE programs, limiting enrollment to high school juniors and seniors[3] and limiting the college credit hours a student can earn (Tagami). This mixed political support creates programmatic instability, making it challenging for WPAs to plan the staffing, spaces, and curricula for such programs. When institutions demand DE FYC absent evidence of its effectiveness, they reinforce the perception that FYC requires little training and few resources to deliver. This misconception already undermines FYC, but given the variety of DE models, such programs further the belief that space and instructor are only tangential to student learning.

THE SITUATED KNOWLEDGE OF DE INSTRUCTORS

In fact, research shows that location is central to instructors' understanding of pedagogy and students' learning, particularly in courses like FYC that help students transfer from high school to college writing. Christine Denecker explains that this transition "is not so much about what the *students* do as it is about what the *instructors* know or understand about composition practices on both sides of the divide" (31, original emphasis). Denecker and other scholars show that the differences between college and high school instructors' knowledge of college-level writing are shaped by their roles. Readers might wonder, then, whether providing FYC training for high school DE instructors or staffing DE FYC with college faculty would influence the success of these courses. Our review of existing research here (and David's experiences described below) suggests, however, that the high school location constrains the way DE faculty apply their knowledge in a high school setting.

Scholars agree that DE instructors' knowledge of composition theory is important, but knowledge alone does not always alter pedagogy. Melanie Burdick and Jane Greer found that most high school DE instructors are experienced and knowledgeable teachers, but the majority (78% of their sample) are unaware of core FYC texts that explain SLOs, such as the "Framework for Success in Postsecondary Writing," a corollary text to the WPA Outcomes Statement that describes the habits of mind and kinds of writing that help students achieve FYC outcomes (91). Of course, this unfamiliarity with postsecondary statements may only reflect differences in high school English instructors' career preparation, since some have degrees focused on literature or were trained during a different era of composition theory. However, only *half* of the high school DE instructors who were familiar with the "Framework for Success" considered it useful for teaching (91). Furthermore, a majority of high school DE instructors (72%) reported that they considered Advanced Placement (AP) training and Common Core standards more useful than professional interactions with college faculty (91–92). Even when high school instructors are familiar with composition terminology, they may, according to Denecker, understand those terms very differently than their college counterparts (41). Why, then, do high school DE instructors find FYC knowledge and practice less helpful than high school resources, particularly when those documents explain and support FYC SLOs?

One answer may be that high school instructors' pedagogies are shaped by teaching in high schools, where they identify their role as someone preparing students to write for "tougher" and "less merciful" college professors (Farris 110). Merely explaining FYC learning outcomes may not alter high school instructors' understanding of this role, especially if they are teaching DE students they had in high school English classes. In contrast, college faculty view writing through their experiences of writing as academic inquiry (110). Denecker argues that college faculty define writing as "creating meaning" as opposed to reporting, in line with their roles (38). And a survey of DE FYC instructors by Jamie L. Erford found that high school instructors represent their responsibility in terms of developing a more challenging course, while college instructors identify with roles of research, professional development, and service to the community (59). In short, instructors' situated identities shape their understanding of writing and FYC pedagogy.

Given these findings, one might assume that staffing DE with college instructors would resolve any incongruities in knowledge. However, ownership of the DE space complicates this in practice. Drawing from her survey data and personal experiences as a traveling DE faculty, Erford argues that the physical location of DE changes high school students' class interactions, communication with faculty, and students' "sense of place"—that is, their perceptions of themselves, the course, and the content (15). Specifically, high school DE students had more familiarity with one another, made less use of college communication resources, and perceived themselves as high-achieving students in contrast to college FYC students' view of FYC as a "normal" class for all students. While Erford argues that aligning high school policies with college policies can mitigate differences, others report anecdotally that high school administrators still intervene in the content—especially when parental concern attracts public attention—regardless of prior negotiated arrangements (Bodmer). Given the competing ownership of the high school DE space, college administrators seem to prefer high school DE instructors, familiar with high school logistics and students (McCrimmon 215). DE staffing thus creates numerous professional development and student learning challenges that are complicated by the power dynamics inherent in the DE relationship. In David's experience, these differences in location, content, and student interaction affect the learning in the class.

TRAVELING TO MEET FYC OUTCOMES IN HIGH SCHOOLS

Equipped with the department's SLOs, the traveling DE instructor faces challenges when visiting an unfamiliar landscape. Our FYC SLOs are based on the WPA Outcomes Statement, and they are directly linked to a "common assignment," which all students must complete and which we use for program assessment. For example, in our second semester of FYC, we ask students to "synthesize a variety of sources to participate in a scholarly conversation" ("First-Year Writing"). In our common assignment, we ask students to demonstrate this learning by documenting their process of finding and evaluating sources and by incorporating "credible sources that represent diverse perspectives." In addition, all students must "revise in response to instructor and/or peer review." Thus, the ability to incorporate sources in a writing assignment depends on research technologies and a community of feedback in the classroom. Like our SLOs, the WPA Outcomes Statement implies that student learning is contingent on technology and people. Its three meta-SLOs for FYC—rhetorical knowledge, critical thinking, and writing processes—suggest that students need experiences with composing technologies, engagement with readers and critics, practice working through drafts, and exposure to diverse genres and audiences. Yet neither our SLOs nor the Outcomes Statement describes whether it is critical that FYC provide students with experience engaging with other *college students and faculty* or writing in other *college courses*. As our chapter's introduction notes, Annie instinctually preferred that DE students attend on-campus courses—a preference which assumed that "the collaborative and social aspects of the writing process" are linked to our campus community and resources (as described in the Outcomes Statement and implied in our program SLOs). When David was assigned to teach these courses and assignments off campus, he questioned whether a class of high school students required him to adjust his instruction and expectations.

For the past three years, David has confronted this question teaching FYC at "Charter High," a charter high school that enrolls students from rural southeast Georgia and focuses on preparing them for careers in science, technology, engineering, and mathematics (STEM). David has twenty-five years' experience teaching in high schools and eight years teaching FYC, including three at our current university. Charter High students are selected from two rural county high schools based on grades and SAT scores. The county is 82.1 percent white; in contrast, our university's campus is 65 percent white.[4] Charter High offers a STEM-focused education, providing students with opportunities for industry partnerships and professional certifications. Most students taking DE courses are also enrolled in multiyear, research-intensive courses and thus have strong research experience. These activities result in unusual schedules, with high school classes (including on-site DE FYC) running between 7:30 a.m. and 2:25 p.m., after which students commute to their district high school for extracurricular activities (e.g., band, sports, clubs). While a unique DE program in some ways, in other ways Charter High mirrors the challenges of high school location that are familiar to David from his years of teaching at other high schools: school activities include non-academic use of class time; college preparatory activities, such as PSAT testing; less flexibility in class scheduling; sports schedules and field trips; and so forth. Most important, instruction is separated from a college campus in ways that shape student learning.

Writing Processes

The WPA Outcomes Statement lists writing process knowledge as a meta-outcome, stating that students should be able to use composing processes, writing technologies, and peer interaction to develop writing. Our program guidelines require multiple drafts developed using different invention strategies, feedback from instructor and peers, and revision. Instruction in writing processes challenges students to collaborate with and critique their own and others' work. Teaching writing processes can be challenging for all FYC instructors. Many students prefer to write improvisational single drafts, something often familiar to them from their high school writing experiences where they tend to write more final essays with fewer revisions. David's experience as a traveling DE faculty affirms Erford's finding that high school DE FYC poses specific challenges to "student interaction through process work and peer feedback," given students' familiarity with both one another and the site of instruction (68).

Differences in high schools' infrastructure make technology use, revision activities, and collaboration difficult. Traveling DE faculty cannot expect an uninterrupted class or a (mostly) working suite of technological conveniences, including projection capability, an (usually) expeditious IT team, and compatibility with the university's software. Although some colleges also lack technology resources, traveling DE faculty must negotiate differing site resources for teaching the same class at both the high school and the college, which in David's experience meant a different preparation at times. Lesson planning is also challenged by frequent interruptions in high school classes, a fact that high school teachers accept and plan for in their curriculum. At Charter High, David's morning class was delayed daily by intercom announcements, a minute of standing silence, and the pledge of allegiance. In addition, there were frequent interruptions for filling out counselor forms, ring ceremonies, school photographs, rehearsal schedules, and field trip departures, to name a few. In one case, administrators used David's class time to deliver PSAT testing. Because traveling DE instructors do not meet daily with students and therefore may be unaware of the high school's schedule, they cannot always plan around these interruptions. The interruptions break the momentum of instruction or suspend collaboration in the room by removing one or more students from a planned group activity.

Although DE students at Charter High were equipped with school laptops and had reliable wifi and IT support, there were complications with accessing the university's learning management software (LMS) to work in real time on assignments and drafts. As a result, instead of synchronous collaboration through the LMS, which keeps retrievable drafts and a record of revisions, many students used pen and paper to complete tasks that were designed to teach "flexible strategies" for revision ("Framework"). These complications impeded David's ability to evaluate the feedback students gave each other, given the impracticality of collecting the physical notes another student makes on a student's essay. In contrast, reliable online work allows the instructor to comment on the efficacy of critical feedback. It also allows students to read layers of constructive criticism from different readers, including David, and learn to model useful critiques, moving beyond "I like your essay" commentary. In short, the technology infrastructure affects the ability to teach critical reading and constructive feedback.

Other infrastructure concerns challenge writing process development in a high school setting. Unlike college students, Charter High students lack a library and a writing center. More than aiding in research or writing, these resources provide another invested audience in the ongoing conversation of a project. Instructors, therefore, must prepare to deliver those services on their own, which means students are exposed to fewer audiences in developing their writing in a semester. This becomes even more problematic when other resources college students need are missing from the site. What is the protocol, for example, for working with students with disabilities or students who need mediation in cases of plagiarism? These students may be more inclined to work with the high school counselor. Does a traveling DE instructor work with the high school's learning counselor prior to the beginning of the term or insist that the student use the university's disability resources off-site for accommodation? If a non-academic problem arises, does the instructor contact the high school? The off-site resources on instructors' syllabi may discourage students from using them. Students may have less control over how to disclose to faculty (when, for example, a parent emails the instructor about a student's needs), or they may be uncertain whether the counselor has already contacted their instructor regarding accommodations. Should students need these resources for their writing processes, both site and procedure remain unclear.

To encourage students to develop their writing processes, instructors often meet individually with students to work on drafting and revision. Traveling DE faculty face the challenges of a commuter—in David's case, an hour's drive in sometimes heavy traffic—away from one's desk, bookshelf, computer, and files. Moreover, one cannot expect a consistent workspace when traveling off campus. Although provided with a computer lab at Charter High to "make himself at home" before class, David frequently moved to allow for testing or makeup work for students. With constant movement and lack of physical office space, it has been difficult for students to find David and for David to maintain regular office hours. Even when physical space is available, high school students' and traveling DE faculty's complicated schedules make it challenging to find reliable office hours for meetings. For example, one semester, David had to leave after teaching three DE sections in the mornings to teach an afternoon course at the college. In another case, David had his courses scheduled back to back, with only a three-minute break between classes. Consequently, face-to-face feedback with students about the writing process took place infrequently. While some may argue that instructors should simply adapt to this different location's demands, consistent adaptations are nearly impossible with varying semester schedules and the uncertain and frequently changing nature of DE partnerships. The reality that DE programs may operate at high schools without appropriate resources demonstrates the extent to which external stakeholders dismiss the importance of process as a critical facet of FYC.

Rhetorical Knowledge

The WPA Outcomes Statement recommends that FYC students develop rhetorical knowledge, including awareness of multiple audiences, genres, and purposes for writing. Our program asks faculty to give students experience evaluating multiple genres, incorporating diverse perspectives, and writing for different audiences. FYC seeks to broaden students' exposure to diverse audiences and to familiarize students with different registers and rhetorical strategies. High school DE courses may struggle to highlight different rhetorical situations for students, regardless of who is teaching the course. Even in school districts with a diverse student body (not always a given with public school districting and charter school admissions), students share geographic and schooling experiences that narrow their exposure to different audiences. The conversations that take place (and may broaden audience awareness) on a college campus between students of varying backgrounds cannot be replicated reliably in the high school setting.

As Burdick and Greer explain, FYC faculty develop "socio-constructivist" pedagogies that build shared rhetorical knowledge through student and faculty interactions with texts. Having diverse interactions is essential to socio-constructivist pedagogy (90). However, certain subjects and attitudes that students may feel free to explore in college classrooms are approached with trepidation or avoided by high school students. Traveling DE faculty encounter different cultures of classroom management and discipline as defined by the schools' codes of conduct, hostility toward certain discussion topics, and degree of parental involvement. On many occasions, students asked David for permission to explore certain topics and then asked whether a parent or administrator would have to know about the topic. Regardless of the instructor's presentation of content, students' location within the high school affects their rhetorical choices about reading and writing. High school instructors teaching DE may have learned to navigate these obstacles, but this may contribute to the problem of exploring varying rhetorical situations and audiences. In college, students expand to fill the new space created by immersion in the college experience. In contrast, traveling DE faculty must fill the space of the hosting institution.

One way they fill this space is by working within the school's culture while encouraging students to step outside their ways of seeing rhetorical situations. For example, Charter High students frequently discussed their former English teacher's assignments and teaching, and what occurred in DE FYC was often measured against this yardstick. Naturally, students measure writing against what they already know. But given that all of the students "knew" the same things from the same English teacher, it was challenging for David to get students to rethink their rhetorical knowledge without responding to the teacher's advice directly. This tendency was exacerbated when, in a few cases, students asked that previous English teacher to help with revision. Once, a student wanted to challenge a grade of "B" based on what that high school teacher discussed. Typically, a college FYC course will have students with sufficiently different writing instruction experiences to share different rhetorical knowledge; however, the students and power dynamics a traveling DE faculty encounters on a high school campus make it difficult to engage different viewpoints to construct writing knowledge. Faced with these challenges, instructors may be more likely to *explain to* rather than *discuss with* students, thus shortcutting the socio-construction of rhetorical knowledge about writing.

Critical Thinking, Reading, and Writing

To teach "Critical Thinking, Reading, and Writing" in our FYC program, students engage in source-based inquiry that requires them to read, critique, and synthesize sources to participate in meaningful conversations. Critical inquiry is challenged when the high school defines different expectations for how students should engage with sources. In the high school space, students remain acutely aware that the high school retains power. Traveling DE faculty must also be aware that their instruction reaches high school administrators and parents. David received only one or two emails from parents per semester, and most of those fell into two categories: parents who asked for clarification of syllabus policies (especially regarding absences) and parents who wanted to convey their child's emotional distress. Just the potential involvement of these stakeholders informs students' critical reading and writing activities.

David's DE students exercised the maturity to take on most discussion topics. But in some instances, the high school placed restrictions, direct and indirect, on communications. For example, all YouTube sites were blocked by default. Even the short videos on research David posted on the LMS met firewalls and were inaccessible to students during class, though the students could watch them from home. (Interestingly, tech-savvy students knew a way around the digital roadblocks, though this often generated ethical discussion.) Practically, this meant they could not search YouTube during in-class activities. While YouTube was universally blocked, filters frequently prevented the viewing of other sites, including many of our university's research resources, which local IT could not help access. When David asked an administrator about this policy, he was told he could ask for clearance of blocked material, but these matters were handled by people David had never met, and students told him it was a lengthy process. This made in-class, guided exercises asking students to find and evaluate sources so onerous as to be impossible.

Students' perception about the high school's involvement had a more insidious effect on student inquiry. Within the space of the high school, David's DE students had a sense of being watched and adjusted accordingly. Their online activity was monitored, a fact that reminded them that they were still in high school. Once, two students argued as to whether they were "allowed" to use their phones in class, with one student claiming college privileges and the other fearing discipline. Even after David granted permission, the students still requested clarification and permission from an administrator. More seriously, another student expressed her reluctance to research depression (as related to cell phone use) because she knew the school sent an automatic warning to the counselor when such sites were accessed. She knew it was a precautionary measure and "not a big deal," but she didn't want to be asked to see the counselor to explain. Traveling DE faculty want to establish a college course with college expectations, but the students get mixed messages that shape their writing activities.

High school principals, counselors, and teachers, of course, are invested in the lives of their "college" students and interested in the life of the "whole child." They will look to bring the traveling DE faculty into conversations about a particular student and will offer to discipline a student who is not performing in the course. Any time David had a student who was failing or who (rarely) was a discipline problem in class, he faced the dilemma of handling it the way he would at the university or communicating with administrators at the high school. The administrators he encountered understood the challenge and were willing to discuss students of concern without acting, but only perhaps because the particular issues he experienced did not warrant it. One time a principal offered to discipline a student who had failed to turn in the first major assignment—a conversation David immediately felt remiss for having started. It took some persuasion to convince the high school administrator that nothing needed to be done on the high school's part and that David only wanted to see if there were extenuating circumstances to consider. A number of times, David faced the dilemma of how to report chronic absenteeism. DE students struggling in the course (or outside of it) rarely considered dropping the course. David encountered one student who stopped coming to class and again felt compelled to inform the high school in addition to the college. College administrators stress that DE faculty should report potential failures, as they may impact a student's high school schedule.

High school administrators play a significant part in communicating with traveling DE faculty, which affects student inquiry tangentially. Although necessary, communication between traveling DE faculty and high school administration frames the learning environment. Students are excited and proud to be taking a college course, and the administrators are proud of their students' success, but both are also keenly aware that the high school still holds power. The Outcomes Statement recommends that faculty teach students to understand the relationships among "language, knowledge, and power," and yet that outcome is ironically challenging to meet with the explicit and implicit restrictions on student inquiry in high school settings.

GOING BACK TO COLLEGE: DE PARTNERSHIPS, FYC, AND PLANNING FOR THE FUTURE

Far from a rote administrative concern, FYC's location shapes the way faculty and students understand and take up SLOs. In turn, WPAs should consider how location and resources might explicitly factor into SLOs, avoiding assuming a placeless classroom and identity-less students. In examining our program's SLOs and our common assignments, which borrow heavily from the language of the Outcomes Statement, it is clear that we need to revise ambiguous phrases, such as "develop flexible composing strategies to achieve a defined purpose for writing" ("First-Year Writing"). What do we mean by this kind of statement? We want students to be able to draft and revise in and outside of the classroom, collaboratively and individually, experimenting with word processors and other software. Students unable to access an LMS and restricted web resources during class may be unable to meet this SLO. Similarly, when we require students to revise in response to peer revisions and to use "credible sources that represent diverse perspectives," we are implying, but not fully stating, that students need to discuss and engage with feedback and consider different perspectives—particularly perspectives that may be marginalized or historically underrepresented. As stated, however, the SLO does little to empower WPAs who observe that DE students are not researching and revising in a classroom where they can fully find sources or where the students are homogeneous as a result of districting policies.

Perhaps the WPA Outcomes Statement, local program SLOs, or other documents might explain what constitutes a college-equivalent FYC experience. This policy work might be accompanied by additional research into whether DE FYC meets SLOs, especially studies that attend to the complexity of instructional site as physical location and participants' experience with a space. To date, holistic rating of student writing has given mixed evidence of DE's impact on students (Hansen et al.). Perhaps portfolio assessment based on the meta-SLOs of FYC might provide a better picture of student learning in DE. Indeed, other kinds of writing outcomes documents, such as the American Association of Colleges and Universities (AAC&U) "Written Communication Value

Rubric," address students' developmental level more than the WPA SLOs do. The AAC&U document shows that a first-year student must transition from thinking of the instructor as the sole audience for writing to learning that an audience brings different "perceptions and assumptions" that should shape their writing process. This kind of language signals the transitional nature of FYC in ways that could be useful for programs.

Our program's experience with traveling DE faculty reveals that faculty knowledge is an important component of program delivery, but the site of instruction informs how that knowledge is transformed into pedagogy. WPAs and DE faculty must plan for technology needs, room assignments, disability accommodations, office space, disciplinary expectations, and parental and administrator involvement. Adam Finkelstein and colleagues' "Research-Informed Principles for (Re)Designing Teaching and Learning Spaces" lists space resources, such as the ability to control classroom technologies away from the podium; access to infrastructure like the internet, learning management software, and databases; and flexible furniture for active learning activities. If a workspace "dramatically shapes labor practice and reinforces a sense of institutional values" (LaFrance and Cox 281), then spaces of instruction matter for writing programs. While college FYC classrooms may sometimes fail to live up to these ideals, such failures reflect the liminality FYC programs experience, of which DE is also a symptom. DE initiatives can thus highlight avenues for programmatic and disciplinary change, exposing the site-labor relationship that WPAs need to consider more broadly in FYC. As Michelle LaFrance and Annica Cox argue, "When public institutions are under fire, economic limitations and spatial relations shape instructional moments as much as any teacher might" (298). Labor and space are often the first to be dismissed when FYC adopts a political function. WPAs need to ensure that traveling DE faculty have the knowledge, resources, and support they need in those spaces and that their experiences contribute not only to program development but also to scholarship.

NOTES

1. "General education English" is the term used by the source, and we repeat it here instead of FYC in case it includes other English courses in the core curriculum (the report is unclear).
2. HB 444 is sponsored by five Republican members of the Georgia House of Representatives. The bill did pass in 2020, limiting dual enrollment to 30 credit hour per student and limiting access to juniors and seniors as well as sophomores with qualifying ACT and SAT scores (Georgia General Assembly).

3. Since 2004, DE has been open to students from ninth through twelfth grades (Lee).
4. Data on county demographics are taken from the US Bureau of the Census. We do not have specific racial demographics for the school.

WORKS CITED

Berger, Andrea, Lori Turk-Bicakci, Michael Garet, Mengli Song, Joel Knudson, Clarisse Haxton, Kristina Zeiser, Gur Hoshen, Jennifer Ford, Jennifer Stephan, Kaeli Keating, and Lauren Cassidy. "Early College, Early Success: Early College High School Initiative Impact Study." *American Institutes for Research*, September 2013. https://www.air.org/sites/default/files/downloads/report/ECHSI_Impact_Study_Report_Final1_0.pdf. Accessed May 13, 2022.

Bodmer, Paul. "Is It Pedagogical or Administrative? Administering Distance Delivery to High Schools." In *Delivering College Composition: The Fifth Canon*, edited by Kathleen Blake Yancey. Boynton/Cook, 2006, pp. 115–126.

Burdick, Melanie, and Jane Greer. "Paths to Productive Partnerships: Surveying High School Teachers about Professional Development Opportunities and 'College-Level' Writing." *WPA: Writing Program Administration*, vol. 41, no. 1, 2017, pp. 82–101.

Denecker, Christine. "Transitioning Writers across the Composition Threshold: What We Can Learn from Dual Enrollment Partnerships." *Composition Studies*, vol. 41, no. 1, 2013, pp. 27–50.

Erford, Jamie L. "Sense of Place and Concurrent Enrollment: Creating College Places in High School Settings." Electronic thesis, University of Findlay, 2017. *OhioLINK Electronic Theses and Dissertations Center.*

"Fall 2019 Enrollment Numbers Finalized for Georgia Southern, University System of Georgia." Georgia Southern University, November 12, 2019. https://news.georgiasouthern.edu/2019/11/12/fall-2019-enrollment-numbers-finalized-for-georgia-southern-university-system-of-georgia/. Accessed May 13, 2022.

Farris, Christine. "The Space Between: Dual-Credit Programs as Brokering, Community Building, and Professionalization." In *Delivering College Composition: The Fifth Canon*, edited by Kathleen Blake Yancey. Boynton/Cook, 2006, pp. 104–114.

Finklestein, Adam, Jennie Ferris, Cynthia Weston, and Laura Winer. "Research-Informed Principles for (Re)Designing Teaching and Learning Spaces." *Journal of Learning Spaces*, vol. 5, no. 1, 2016. pp. 26–40.

"First-Year Writing (for Faculty)." Georgia Southern University, March 11, 2020. https://cah.georgiasouthern.edu/writling/first-year-writing-for-faculty/. Accessed July 13, 2020.

"Framework for Success in Postsecondary Writing." Council of Writing Program Administrators, National Council of Teachers of English, and the National Writing Project, January 2011. http://wpacouncil.org/files/framework-for-success-postsecondary-writing.pdf. Accessed May 13, 2022.

Georgia General Assembly. "Dual Enrollment Act." 2020. HB 444. Introduced in House on February 2, 2019. https://www.legis.ga.gov/api/legislation/document/20192020/192065. Accessed May 13, 2022.

Griffin, Greg S., and Leslie McGuire. *Dual Enrollment: Participation Has Significantly Increased, though Program Lacks Clear Goals.* Report no. 17-09. Georgia Department of Audits and Accounts, Performance Audit Division, 2018.

Hansen, Kristine, Brian Jackson, Brett C. McInelly, and Dennis Eggett. "How Do Dual Credit Students Perform on College Writing Tasks after They Arrive on Campus? Empirical Data from a Large-Scale Study." *WPA: Writing Program Administration*, vol. 38, no. 2, 2015, pp. 56–92.

LaFrance, Michelle, and Annica Cox. "Brutal(its) Meditations: Space and Labor-Movement in a Writing Program." In *Contingency, Exploitation, and Solidarity: Labor and Action in English Composition*, edited by Seth Kahn, William Lalicker, and Amy Lynch-Biniek. WAC Clearinghouse and UP of Colorado, 2017, pp. 279–301.

Lee, Jennifer. "Dual Enrollment Explained." *Georgia Budget and Policy Institute*, February 26, 2019. https://gbpi.org/2019/dual-enrollment-explained/. Accessed May 13, 2022.

McCrimmon, Miles. "Contesting the Territoriality of 'Freshman English': The Political Ecology of Dual Enrollment." In *College Credit for Writing in High School: The "Taking Care of" Business*, edited by Kristine Hansen and Christine R. Farris. NCTE, 2010, pp. 208–226.

"Outcomes Statement for First-Year Composition (3.0)." Council of Writing Program Administrators, National Council of Teachers of English, and the National Writing Project, July 7, 2014. http://wpacouncil.org/files/framework-for-success-postsecondary-writing.pdf. Accessed May 13, 2022.

Shivji, Azim, and Sandra Wilson. "Dual Enrollment: Participation and Characteristics." US Department of Education, Washington, DC. NCES, 2019.

https://www.ajc.com/news/state--regional-education/legislation-affects-valedictorians-who-don-their-high-school/yUqP45r6fnMYklSd1oIm6N/. Accessed May 13, 2022.

US Department of Education, Institute of Education Sciences, What Works Clearinghouse. *Transition to College Intervention Report: Dual Enrollment Programs*. February 2017. https://whatworks.ed.gov. Accessed May 13, 2022.

"Written Communication VALUE Rubric." American Association of Colleges and Universities, 2022. https://www.aacu.org/value/rubrics/written-communication. Accessed May 13, 2022.

SECTION THREE

Perspectives of Legitimacy

Is DE FYC Really FYC?

8

BUT IT'S (NOT) THE SAME

A Data-Driven Look at Equivalency Bias in Dual Enrollment Composition

Dominic Ashby and Jill Parrott

As dual enrollment (DE) composition programs become more popular, a sense of unease and tension among college-level writing instructors grows in parallel. Questions about quality and rigor of instruction, labor issues, academic freedom, and equitable opportunities for students make up the forefront of this discussion, with the rising cost of higher education, retention, and time to degree bearing on the conversation as well. Questions about ethics, logistics, practicality, and benefits of dual enrollment must engage each incredibly complicated variable (and more).

At Eastern Kentucky University (EKU), we know, and on other campuses, we suspect, that the question that pulls at the minds and hearts of the educators most deeply concerned with student writing has been, very simply: can students possibly meet the same intellectual goals in DE classes as they can in traditional first-year composition (FYC) courses? The resounding assumption has often been "no! They cannot possibly." In short, this is what we call the equivalency bias: it's the deeply held belief, based perhaps on experience but often not on evidence, that DE experiences cannot be the same as standard enrollment (SE) experiences. And if they are not the same, the argument goes, they are not as good; they are not equivalent. However, in such conversations about DE programs, equivalency and identicality are often conflated. In evaluating the successes of DE composition instruction at our institution, we focus on equivalency as distinct from identicality: while DE courses may not provide an *identical* experience to that of a college student on campus, they could provide an *equivalent* educational experience based on quality instruction, rigor, and outcomes.[1] In this project, we set out to provide our colleagues and ourselves with carefully gathered data from ethically designed research that can guide our conversations beyond the

https://doi.org/10.7330/9781646422531.c008

bias and into real-world solutions for the actual challenges that, through data, we can confirm in our dual enrollment FYC courses.

Reasons for resistance to DE have been articulated passionately and early on by scholars, such as David E. Schwalm in his 1991 contribution to *WPA*, where he urges writing program administrators not to accept DE courses as equivalent with college-level writing. Many of Schwalm's concerns continue to resonate three decades later: he interprets lawmaker and administrative enthusiasm for DE as driven by financial incentives at the expense of students' learning and objects to the assumption "that writing is a finite skill . . . that can be mastered once and for all" (53). While we share many of his concerns, we diverge from his criteria for measuring what a successful college writing class should be. He argues, "College writing courses are, by definition, taught in the general context of college—a context impossible to replicate in a high school senior English class" (53); in short, Schwalm's measure for equivalency is that the courses be identical in content and space.

Thankfully, today more options for ensuring quality of instruction exist. While some would still like to halt the expansion of or perhaps even reduce DE programs (e.g., Thomson; Evenbeck and Johnson), others argue that a more productive response is greater collaboration between secondary and postsecondary partners. Miles McCrimmon commends the serious work being done to improve DE programs, acknowledging "recent substantive calls for better oversight, communication, accreditation, and peer review across the educational cultures," which shows programs committed to increasing quality, rigor, and collaboration (208). The National Alliance of Concurrent Enrollment Partnerships (NACEP) program accreditation guidelines and Chris M. Anson's suggestions for program assessment aim at ensuring that students have access to materials that would address several of the concerns Schwalm raises. In keeping with McCrimmon, Anson, and NACEP, we recognize systematic, consistent program assessment as an essential step in ensuring equivalency of DE writing courses.

Our assessment methodology involves the application of an assessment rubric to 74 essays from standard FYC courses and 76 essays from dual enrollment courses. We present aggregated assessment data from these 150 essays as a means of reviewing equivalency of goals and outcomes in the course and to question stereotypically held perceptions and biases about dual enrollment (such as too much focus on surface-level features and lower-level concerns, or watered-down assignments), and we find that some of these fears may be well-founded. Our results show a statistically significant discrepancy between the quality of student work in DE courses versus that in standard enrollment courses when measured against our rubric. Echoing Christine Denecker, our conclusions come from the perspective that "transitioning writers [between high school and college] is not so much about what the students do as it is about what the *instructors* know or understand about composition practices" (31, original emphasis); the conclusions we draw are not about what high school–age students are capable of but rather about how the courses are taught and supported.

INSTITUTIONAL CONTEXT

The location in which our study takes place shapes our findings. EKU is a comprehensive regional school with a student population of approximately 17,000, including those in bachelors' and graduate programs. The vast majority of our students are from Kentucky, and 75 percent of EKU alumni are employed in the state after graduation (Kentucky Center). Most relevant to this research, however, is the fact that our service region includes twenty-two counties in southeastern, Appalachian Kentucky, including seven of the thirty most poverty-stricken counties in America: Owsley, Clay, McCreary, Knox, Lee, Bell, and Harlan Counties (Estip). Because of the racial and ethnic demographics of our service region, our student population more closely reflects the region than the greater diversity of the larger United States; for example, students identifying as white made up 85 percent of our student population in the academic year 2019–2020 (Kelley). While data from our study may not speak as acutely to the *very important* national conversations about race and education, they find relevance at the center of another important national conversation about poverty and education, particularly in a region left economically devastated by the fluctuations of the coal industry.

We teach in a state considered hostile to education, evidenced by drastic budget cuts for state institutions over the last decade (Watkins; Wyllie). As Constance Elam discusses in her 2002 article "Culture, Poverty and Education in Appalachian Kentucky," support for public education in Kentucky has historically been "postponed or delayed," in addition to a history of "nonparticipation" resulting from various elements of the "complex socioeconomic situation" that include "staunch individualism," an existence/subsistence orientation, fatalism, fundamentalism, the harshness of the land, poverty, and "physical isolation" (10). Not surprisingly then, a large percentage of our university students—more than 40 percent—are first-generation students ("Graduation Rate"). These socioeconomic and cultural factors play a major role in the ways students and parents as well as K–12 teachers and administrators view DE, most often as a way to save money and to move the students as quickly as possible toward the credential they desire to get a better-paying job.

In several reports, Kentucky appears as having particularly high participation rates in DE programs (Fink, Jenkins, and Yanigiura; Lochmiller et al.). However, unlike some regions with more structured or organized systems in place for assessing DE programs—such as CUNY's College Now Program (Allen and Dadgar) or Iowa's DE program (Crouse and Allen), which is accredited by the NACEP—Kentucky has a less stringent set of requirements, meaning that programs vary significantly across the commonwealth. While Kentucky's Council on Postsecondary Education (CPE) encourages partnerships with NACEP, as of 2019, only two higher education institutions had completed accreditation, both of which are two-year institutions ("NACEP Accredited Programs 2019"). A 2016 report for the Institute of Education Sciences (IES) in the US Department of Education and for the Regional Education Laboratory (REL) in Appalachia reaffirms the positive impact of DE programs on college readiness in the six non-urban Kentucky school districts studied. However, the report also identifies several challenges, including "limited availability of high school teachers with appropriate credentials [to teach DE] . . . inconsistent standards for ensuring course quality, and lack of dedicated staff to manage dual credit programs" (Piontek et al. ii). While the goal of increased access to college courses is commendable, implementation of quality DE programs in Kentucky has been uneven.

METHODOLOGY

At Eastern Kentucky University, first-year composition involves two main courses, English 101 and English 102, which are intended to be experienced in sequence—moving from a focus on critical reading of and writing about shared primary sources in 101 to more independent learning with a focus on critical reading of student-selected texts as part of a longer research project in 102. During this second course, most on-campus faculty collaborate extensively with librarians and the writing studio, supporting students through a series of increasingly difficult projects to build the habits of mind of effective college readers, researchers, and writers.

FYC on our campus is part of a broader General Education program and is assessed every two years. During assessment semesters, we collect an electronic copy of the final research project of this two-course sequence from all SE and DE sections. For this study, we went back to files collected for assessment from spring 2015 and spring 2017 and randomly pulled a total of 150 essays: 76 from dual enrollment sections and 74 from standard enrollment sections spread evenly between 2015 and 2017. We anonymized these 150 essays and created a randomly organized database for review.

To review these essays, we employed the rubric used for our General Education assessment, which was designed by faculty committee to reflect EKU's Quality Enhancement Plan (QEP) focused on critical reading (see appendix 8.A). We feel that this rubric is appropriate and in keeping with our focus: if our research questions are centered around the equivalency of dual and standard enrollment sections of the same course, consistency requires that we use the same tool that we use for programmatic assessment of this course to explore these questions. Finally, the rubric has been reviewed and revised by EKU's First Year Writing, Quality Enhancement Program, and General Education Committees and is informed by three influential educational frameworks: Richard Paul and Linda Elder on critical thinking, Bloom's taxonomy of educational objectives, and the Reading Apprenticeship Framework for critical reading (Armstrong).

The rubric is based on four achievement levels: Beginning (1), Developing (2), Competent (3), and Accomplished (4) and spans seven criteria of Comprehension, Information Literacy: Analysis, Information Literacy: Synthesis, Evaluation, Coherence, Rhetorical Awareness/Style, and Surface Features (for complete descriptions, see appendix 8.A). Both of the two co-researchers for this project read all 150 randomized essays and applied scores using this assessment rubric, resulting in a total of 2,100 individual data points.

RESULTS

In brief, our results show a statistically significant difference between DE and SE student projects as assessed through this rubric. The averages between the two researcher-readers in the seven assessed goals are shown in table 8.1. These data show that, in the aggregate, DE students were unable to meet the course objectives (defined as a score of 2) in all but the two most basic criteria: Comprehension and Surface Features. SE students *were* able to meet the course objectives in all but the most advanced of the criteria: Evaluation. A statistically significant difference exists between Surface Features (defined in our scoring rubric

Table 8.1. Average rubric scores of DE and SE papers

	Dual Enrollment	*Standard Enrollment*
Comprehension	2.184210526	2.459459459
Information Literacy: Analysis	1.743421053	2.108108108
Information Literacy: Synthesis	1.684210526	2.182432432
Evaluation	1.539473684	1.925675676
Coherence	1.875	2.290540541
Rhetorical Awareness and Style	1.986842105	2.216216216
Surface Features	2.684210526	2.567567568
Average Total	1.956766917	2.25

as concerns of punctuation, grammar, capitalization, and relevant citation formatting with an eye toward a relationship with clarity) and the other six criteria for DE students in a test of Between-Subjects Effects.[2] Moreover, the average score for Surface Features is *higher* for DE students than for SE students.

If we look at the data (presented in table 8.2) through the lens of whether individual students meet the watermark score of 2, we see a slightly different perspective. Despite the anomaly that DE and SE students scored 2 an equal number of times (558), these data clearly indicate that SE scores skew higher, with fewer 1s and significantly more 3s and 4s.

An assessment of these scores from the perspective of whether individual students scored *below* the benchmark of a 2 (in other words, scored a 1) or *above* the benchmark of a 2 (a score of 2, 3, or 4) shows a similar result, as demonstrated in table 8.3. SE students met the benchmark with 88.2 percent of their scores, while DE students only met that benchmark 73.19 percent of the time. In the SE data set, there are only 122 total occurrences of a score of 1 (11.80%) and 282 occurrences of 1 DE data—a whopping 26.81 percent of the total DE scores.

We also discovered major differences in content and approach, indicating dramatically different assignments that vary from course expectations and learning outcomes of the FYC program. In particular, we found thirty-eight essays that took the form of job or major reports, in which students had apparently been asked to "research" their future majors or careers. A majority of these projects involved simple copy-and-pasting of degree information or interview transcriptions, with little attention to integration of source material, transitions, audience needs, or use of academic writing conventions. After completing our

Table 8.2. Score distribution

Scores	*Dual Enrollment*	*Standard Enrollment*
1	282	122
2	558	558
3	212	331
4	0	23

Table 8.3. Number of scores meeting (or not meeting) benchmark of 2 or above

Students	*Score of 1*	*Score of 2, 3, or 4*
Dual Enrollment	282 26.81%	770 73.19%
Standard Enrollment	122 11.80%	912 88.20%

assessment and revealing which essays were DE and which were SE, we found that all thirty-eight of these essays were from DE courses.

A smaller number of essays deviated from the FYC curriculum in other substantial ways, including seven literary analysis essays (all written by DE students) and five history reports (three written by DE and two by SE students). The presence of these essays, rather than the inquiry-focused projects called for by our FYC program, suggests that while the DE courses are required by the Kentucky CPE to use a syllabus that matches the university FYC syllabus, some instructors may be following traditional high school curricula instead.

DISCUSSION

This research shows a strong negative correlation between required college-level student learning outcomes and DE courses. Two related points stand out for discussion: first, DE students scored significantly higher on Surface Features than SE students, and second, evidence shows a need for greater alignment of curriculum expectations between DE and SE sections. Seen holistically, these discrepancies perhaps indicate varied understandings of college preparedness—understandings shaped by institutional and regional contexts.

DE students performed highest on Surface Features; this is also the only area in our assessment where DE students on average scored higher than SE students. While Surface Features contribute to clarity and style, the fact that DE students performed highest in this area raises concerns about the emphasis of DE curricula; most important, this focus may distract students from spending time on other critical, higher-order concerns, such as source analysis and synthesis. In separate studies, both Christine R. Farris and Christine Denecker identify superficial engagement with texts in high school student writing as a result of a focus on preparation for on-demand writing and a teaching style that emphasizes format and surface-level features. Taking into account the tendency for high school English to emphasize Surface Features as part of a strategy to prepare students for federal and state competency and college entrance exams, it is unsurprising that the DE students' writing exceeded SE student performance in this area. Indeed, the exigence of needing to help students prepare for testing is likely one of the contextually necessary differences between a high school DE and a traditional FYC course. Denecker identifies "factors of content coverage, [state and federal] testing mandates, and the grading load" as three major drivers of difference between high school and college English instruction (32). This harkens back to the socioeconomic and cultural variables at play in our region as well: the rural, working-class "sociocultural perspective means that some students are not born into conditions that easily allow them to acquire linguistic practices that are understood as norms leading to common academic assessment standards" (Poe et al. 7). Through a social justice lens, we can both interpret and contest these scores as a move by teachers to prepare students for what they perceive as the standards of the academy necessary for future student success.

Other divergences from programmatic FYC goals reinforce an interpretation that score discrepancies come from—at least in part—a lack of alignment with college-level curriculum objectives. While we applaud the likely impulse behind the writing prompts that ask students to research a topic of personal importance and encourage them to take their own primary research seriously, we are deeply concerned by the apparent lack of engagement with library research methods as well as by the above-mentioned problems found in most of the projects. The reality that these final, revised projects included significant problems with ethical source use, integration, organization, and attention to audience indicates that instructors using these prompts have different learning objectives in mind than those endorsed by the FYC program. While genres such as historical or literary reports allow students opportunities to succeed in certain areas of writing, they do not provide opportunities to demonstrate excellence in the other important evaluation areas valued by college-level programs, notably Analysis and Synthesis.

Our standard of evaluation is not 100 percent identicality between DE and SE courses and assignments. Variation between courses is expected and likely necessary to promote student success. As Anson notes, "Although the high school course may not exactly replicate the college course in every respect, it must maintain the same educational standards, teach to the same general outcomes, and provide the same sorts of intellectual experiences as the college course" (254). At the same time, "Simply replicating a college course, reading for reading and assignment for assignment, may not be enough to realize its underlying goals in a different context" (254). Similarly, NACEP uses phrases such as "same quality and rigor" and "same standards" as opposed to phrases that might indicate identicality. However, our reading of essays found that at least some of our partner DE courses leave behind equivalency as well as identicality.

As we note in this chapter's introduction, dual enrollment is marketed as a way to increase student access to and preparedness for college, but pushing students too quickly from under-funded public schools such as those in our rural Appalachian region into college courses for which they are ill prepared may put them *in* classes but also decreases the likelihood of success for higher-order intellectual work such as Analysis, Synthesis, and Evaluation. Indeed, "While dual-enrollment programs have been shown to have a positive effect on the persistence of some students and on their decision to continue into college, such programs have not been proven to enhance student learning" (Tinberg and Nadeau 706). Schwalm's fear that DE courses will "eliminat[e] the demand for college composition without eliminating the need" resonates (52).

One possible response to the differences in assessment scores between DE and SE students is that more students should take composition at the university rather than on high school campuses. Columbia University's Community College Research Center's 2012 report concludes with seven suggestions to improve DE programs, including "whenever possible, [to] offer dual enrollment courses on college campuses" (6). In addition to increased access to instructors who are explicitly trained in college-level writing pedagogy, DE students who take courses on campus have access to resources such as libraries, writing centers, and student success support. However, their schedules and limited time on campus mean they have less consistent access than SE students, and access is even more limited for DE students taking courses in the high schools—an issue that plagues many DE programs in our region and beyond.[3] This lack of access is a likely contributor to the lower assessment scores of DE student work in Information Literacy (both Analysis and Synthesis) and Evaluation. We join others in the call for additional services for DE programs—particularly the need for library resources, training for librarians, writing center support (Anson 260), and "tutoring opportunities" coordinated between the secondary and postsecondary partner institutions (Stephenson 847). To achieve equivalency of learning between DE and SE courses, partner institutions must find ways to provide equivalent resources or enable consistent remote access (Anson 260). While we believe that moving DE students onto a university campus as much as possible is optimal in many ways, such a solution raises concerns about equity: offering DE courses only on college campuses limits access to students in schools geographically close to a college or university.

Rather than conclude that all DE students must come to campus, our data point to a need for greater communication, collaboration, and clarity of expectations between the university and the partnering high schools. Moves such as syllabus review and general adherence to university or college policies in the high school DE course by itself are insufficient (Piontek et al.). Implementation of quality checks such as syllabus review and teaching observations of DE instruction is problematic at institutions such as ours, where hiring DE instructors and approval of DE courses are handled largely by the university's DE coordinator (who oversees *all* DE programs) rather than by the writing program administrator or another program-specific coordinator.[4] To improve programs, Anson recommends a dedicated, program-specific coordinator: not just a DE coordinator but very specifically a coordinator for the DE composition program (259). A dedicated coordinator (what NACEP calls a "faculty liaison") can provide professional development that sets clear pedagogical standards for *all* instructors in the discipline and that includes conversations about student needs and learning outcomes.

One way to do that is to include all DE instructors in programmatic professional development, as greater collaboration involving college faculty and high school DE instructors builds greater equivalency between sections. We admire the DE mentorship program in place at the University of Findlay, which involves supported opportunities for conversations about the shared and different needs and expectations of the two settings, including "a week-long intensive course in composition theory" followed by twice-yearly meetings "to calibrate grading, share pedagogical techniques," design assignments, and "discuss the challenges of teaching writers from high school to college-level expectations" (Denecker 43–44).

To maintain programmatic integrity, our writing program holds a two-day professional development workshop before the start of each academic year as well as shorter opportunities throughout the year, open to all composition instructors and to which DE instructors are invited; however, only a handful of the DE instructors attend, as many are limited by travel expenses we are unable to reimburse. Indeed, herein lies a major problem: schools in our state (as in others) are mandated to participate in DE programs yet are not provided with the necessary funding to do so at the level of quality promised. While we will continue to reach out to our DE partners and provide support to those who respond, it is untenable to expect these already overtaxed public school teachers to take on additional uncompensated work. To support the state's enthusiasm for DE programs, more appropriations should be directed to ongoing professional development for the high school–based instructors—program development planned and conducted in coordination with the university partners.

CONCLUSIONS

Our study draws attention to several needs particular to Eastern Kentucky University's DE program—needs the existing literature suggests are shared by many institutions and programs and that will doubtless be exacerbated as the popularity of DE increases among state policymakers, administrators, parents, and students for the varied and complex reasons we have discussed. The question of how we respond now, in the midst of growth in DE enrollment and a downturn in funding for education, remains.

The DE essays we evaluated demonstrate students' willingness to strive to meet the expectations set by their instructors: polished Surface Features and detailed summaries that evince reading comprehension suggest that these students are earnestly engaging with courses that promise them not only college credit but equivalency of a college-learning experience. From the quality of work evaluated, particularly the attention to citation styles (a skill strongly associated with successful college-level writing), we are encouraged that DE instructors are invested in preparing their students for college success. However, our assessment shows the *opportunity* for equivalencies that correlate with college preparedness, not the attainment of it. Stakeholders should heed these results in calculating the success of DE programs and in planning for how to live up to the promises these programs make to students, parents, teachers, and the taxpayers who ultimately support public high schools and state colleges and universities.

Our data also illuminate our own institutional paradigm while providing insight for administrators, instructors, and students about the gap between the goals we have for these courses and their success. Student writing in DE courses can and should be meaningfully assessed using college-level assessment rubrics as we continue to discuss equivalency in an effort to identify and manage discrepancies. When college and *access to* college are touted as potential avenues out of poverty, as they are in our region, we must consider whether the institutions with which we collaborate value *degrees* or value *education*, and we must reiterate that these goals are not the same.

APPENDIX 8.A

REVISED: GENERAL EDUCATION SCORING GUIDE FOR WRITTEN COMMUNICATION

COURSE ASSESSMENT RUBRIC

Criteria	*4—Accomplished Exceeds Course Expectations*	*3—Competent Meets Course Expectations*	*2—Developing Incomplete in Meeting Course Expectations*	*1—Beginning Does Not Meet Expectations*
Comprehension (GE Goal 2, 8) (QEP Comprehension)	Demonstrates accurate, clear, and precise comprehension of significant concepts in the text(s).	Demonstrates accurate comprehension of significant concepts in the text(s).	Demonstrates limited or inexact comprehension of significant concepts in the text(s). (Not always *accurate*.)	Fails to demonstrate comprehension of significant concepts in the text(s). (Not *accurate*.)
Information Literacy: Analysis (GE Goal 1) (QEP Analysis)	Provides *accurate, relevant*, and *precise* analysis by recognizing the parts or aspects of the text that contribute to understanding the purpose of the text(s).	Provides *accurate* and *relevant* analysis by recognizing the parts or aspects of the text that contribute to understanding the purpose of the text(s).	Provides limited *relevant* analysis by recognizing the parts or aspects of the text that contribute to understanding the purpose of the text(s). (Not always *accurate*.)	Fails to provide relevant analysis by recognizing the parts or aspects of the text that contribute to understanding the purpose of the text.
Information Literacy: Synthesis (GE Goal 1, 2, 8) (QEP Synthesis)	*Accurately, deeply*, and *broadly* connects and integrates relevant and significant concepts from text(s) to construct and support explanations, conclusions, or arguments.	*Accurately* connects and integrates relevant and significant concepts from text(s) to construct and support explanations, conclusions, or arguments.	Accurately connects and integrates some relevant and significant concepts from text(s) to construct and support explanations, conclusions, or arguments. May attempt to develop argument through vague generalizations.	Fails to or inaccurately connects and integrates relevant and significant concepts from text(s) to construct and support explanations, conclusions, or arguments.

continued on next page

Appendix 8.A—continued

Criteria	*4—Accomplished Exceeds Course Expectations*	*3—Competent Meets Course Expectations*	*2—Developing Incomplete in Meeting Course Expectations*	*1—Beginning Does Not Meet Expectations*
Evaluation (GE Goal 1, 2) (QEP Evaluation)	Demonstrates the use of methods, models, or perspectives to evaluate the *accuracy*, *relevance*, *logic*, or *significance* of the text(s).	Demonstrates the use of methods, models, or perspectives to evaluate the *accuracy* and *relevance* of the text(s).	Demonstrates limited success in the use of methods, models, or perspectives to evaluate the *relevance* of the text(s). (Not always *accurate*.)	Fails to demonstrate the use of methods, models, and/or perspectives to evaluate the *relevance* of the text(s). (Not *accurate*.)
Coherence (GE Goal 1)	Organization is *clearly* and *logically* developed around a significant topic, claims, and supporting evidence. Presents seamless transitions between paragraphs.	Organization is developed around a thesis, claims, and supporting evidence. Presents effective transitions between paragraphs.	Defines a topic leading to a thesis, although it may not be stated or maintain consistent focus. Transitions between paragraphs are inconsistent or awkward.	Organization is ineffective. No attention paid to transitions.
Rhetorical Awareness/Style (GE Goal 1, 2)	Presents writing that is sophisticated and engages reader with a distinctive voice. Demonstrates sophisticated recognition of rhetorical situation and audience.	Presents writing that is *clear*, *accurate*, and *precise* most of the time. Develops voice through paragraphing, sentence structure, variation, rhythm, phrasing, and word choice. Demonstrates recognition of rhetorical situation and audience.	Presents writing that is *clear* and *accurate* some of the time. May have some awkward sentences. Attempts to develop voice. Treats rhetorical situation and/or audience inconsistently.	Fails to reach developing level.
Surface Features (GE Goal 1)	Uses nearly error-free and *accurate* punctuation, grammar, capitalization, *relevant* citation format, etc.	Uses *accurate* punctuation, grammar, capitalization, *relevant* citation format, etc., with minor or minimal errors that do not interfere with *clarity*.	Presents major and/or frequent errors in use of punctuation, grammar, capitalization, *relevant* citation format, etc. Errors sometimes interfere with *clarity*.	Fails to reach developing level.

NOTES

1. Credit to Caroline Wilkinson's presentation "Shifting Spaces of Composition: Co-Teaching in the Dual Enrollment Classroom" at the Twelfth Biennial Thomas R. Watson Conference at the University of Louisville on October 26, 2018, for helping us better understand the relationship between equivalency and identicality.
2. Surface Feature total = 0.124 compared to Comprehension at 0.002, Rhetorical Awareness and Style at 0.007, and all others at 0.000.
3. Piontek et al. found that support in the Kentucky school districts they studied was limited and should be enhanced (9).
4. Piontek et al. report that "postsecondary institutions serving four districts [out of six studied] reported that program administrators are supposed to observe dual credit courses annually but that implementation of this requirement is inconsistent in two districts" (9).

WORKS CITED

Allen, Drew, and Mina Dadgar. "Does Dual Enrollment Increase Students' Success in College? Evidence from a Quasi-Experimental Analysis of Dual Enrollment in New York City." *New Directions for Higher Education*, no. 158, Summer 2012, pp. 11–19.

Anson, Chris M. "Absentee Landlords or Owner-Tenants? Formulating Standards for Dual-Credit Composition Programs." In *College Credit for Writing in High School: The "Taking Care of" Business*, edited by Kristine Hansen and Christine R. Farris. NCTE, 2010, pp. 245–271.

Armstrong, Patricia. "Bloom's Taxonomy." Center for Teaching, Vanderbilt University, 2022. https://cft.vanderbilt.edu/guides-sub-pages/blooms-taxonomy/. Accessed May 13, 2022.

Columbia University, Community College Research Center. "What We Know about Dual Enrollment: Research Overview." Community College Research Center, Columbia University, Feb. 2012.

Crouse, Jill D., and Jeff Allen. "College Course Grades for Dual Enrollment Students." *College Journal of Research and Practice*, vol. 38, 2014, pp. 494–511.

Denecker, Christine. "Transitioning Writers across the Composition Threshold: What We Can Learn from Dual Enrollment Partnerships." *Composition Studies*, vol. 41, no. 1, 2013, pp. 27–50.

Elam, Constance. "Culture, Poverty and Education in Appalachian Kentucky." *Education and Culture*, vol. 18, no. 1, 2002, pp. 10–13. *JSTOR*. www.jstor.org/stable/42922461. Accessed May 13, 2022.

Estip, Bill. " 'Not Enough Jobs:' Nine of the Poorest Counties in U.S. Are in Eastern Kentucky." *Lexington (KY) Herald-Leader*, Dec. 4, 2017.

Evenbeck, Scott, and Kathy E. Johnson. "Students Must Not Become Victims of the Completion Agenda." *Liberal Education*, vol. 98, no. 1, Winter 2012, p. 26.

Farris, Christine R. "Minding the Gap and Learning the Game: Differences That Matter between High School and College Writing." In *College Credit for Writing in High School: The "Taking Care of" Business*, edited by Kristine Hansen and Christine R. Farris. NCTE, 2010, pp. 272–282.

Fink, John, Davis Jenkins, and Takeshi Yanagiura. "What Happens to Students Who Take Community College 'Dual Enrollment' Courses in High School?" Community College Research Center, Teachers College, Columbia University, Sept. 1, 2017.

"Graduation Rate More than Doubles in 8 Years." *EKU Stories*, Oct. 26, 2018. https://stories.eku.edu/people/graduation-rate-more-doubles-8-years. Accessed May 13, 2022.

Kelley, Rosemary. "Lack of Representation: EKU Struggles to Diversify Students, Employees." *Eastern Progress*, April 15, 2022. https://www.easternprogress.com/news/lack-of

-representation-eku-struggles-to-diversify-students-employees/article_7fe2767e-38e6-11ec-a3ef-9f32a4ab50c2.html. Accessed May 20, 2022.

Kentucky Center for Education and Workforce Statistics. *2018 Postsecondary Feedback Report.* Jan. 27, 2020. www.kystats.ky.gov. Accessed May 16, 2022.

Kentucky Council on Postsecondary Education, Department of Academic Affairs. *Dual Credit Policy for Kentucky Public and Participating Postsecondary Institutions and Secondary Schools.* Fall 2016. http://cpe.ky.gov/policies/academicaffairs/dualcreditpolicy.pdf. Accessed May 16, 2022.

Lochmiller, Chad R., Thomas J. Sugimoto, Patricia A. Muller, Gina G. Mosier, and Steven E. Williamson. "Dual Enrollment Courses in Kentucky: High School Students' Participation and Completion Rates, REL 2016–137." Regional Educational Laboratory Appalachia, June 1, 2016.

McCrimmon, Miles. "Contesting the Territoriality of 'Freshman English': The Political Ecology of Dual Enrollment." In *College Credit for Writing in High School: The "Taking Care of" Business,* edited by Kristine Hansen and Christine R. Farris. NCTE, 2010, pp. 208–226.

National Alliance of Concurrent Enrollment Partnerships. "2017 National Concurrent Enrollment Partnership Standards." *NACEP,* May 2017. www.nacep.org/docs/accreditation/NACEP_Standards_2017.pdf. Accessed May 13, 2022.

National Alliance of Concurrent Enrollment Partnerships. "NACEP Accredited Programs 2019." *NACEP,* May 1, 2019. www.nacep.org/docs/accreditation/NACEPAccredited Programs2019.pdf. Accessed May 13, 2022.

Paul, Richard, and Linda Elder. *The Miniature Guide to Critical Thinking: Concepts and Tools.* Foundation for Critical Thinking, April 19, 2019. https://www.criticalthinking.org/files/ConceptsTools.pdf. Accessed May 13, 2022.

Piontek, Mary E., Patricia J. Kannapel, Michael Flory, and Molly S. Stewart. "The Implementation of Dual Credit Programs in Six Nonurban Kentucky School Districts, REL 2016–136." Regional Educational Laboratory Appalachia, June 1, 2016.

Poe, Mya, Asao B. Inoue, and Norbert Elliot, eds. *Writing Assessment, Social Justice, and the Advancement of Opportunity.* Perspectives on Writing Series. UP of Colorado, 2018.

"The Reading Apprenticeship Framework." *Reading Apprenticeship.* West Ed, April 19, 2019. https://readingapprenticeship.org/our-approach/our-framework/. Accessed May 13, 2022.

Schwalm, David E. "High School–College Dual Enrollment." *WPA: Writing Program Administration,* vol. 15, no. 1–2, 1991, pp. 51–53.

Stephenson, Lisa G. "Dual Credit in Kentucky." *Community College Journal of Research and Practice,* vol. 37, no. 11, 2013, pp. 844–850.

Thomson, Alec. "Dual Enrollment's Expansion: Cause for Concern." *Thought and Action,* vol. 33, no. 2, Jan. 2017, pp. 51–62.

Tinberg, Howard, and Jean-Paul Nadeau. "Contesting the Space between High School and College in the Era of Dual-Enrollment." *College Composition and Communication,* vol. 62, no. 4, June 2011, pp. 704–725.

Watkins, Morgan. "Kentucky's 1 of Only 5 States to Cut Money for Higher Education This Year." *Courier Journal* (Louisville, KY), Feb. 11, 2019. https://www.courier-journal.com/story/news/politics/2019/02/11/kentucky-colleges-university-louisville-uk-face-budget-cuts/2704766002/. Accessed May 13, 2022.

Wyllie, Julian. "Kentucky's New Budget Carries Big Consequences for Public Colleges." *Chronicle of Higher Education,* Apr. 3, 2018. https://www.chronicle.com/article/Kentucky-s-New-Budget/243025. Accessed May 13, 2022.

9

DISLOCATING FIRST-YEAR COMPOSITION

Beyond the Deficit Model

Miles McCrimmon

Given the increasing popularity of dual enrollment (DE) and other means of satisfying first-year composition (FYC) writing requirements while in high school, those who have spent their careers helping to professionalize the discipline of composition can perhaps be forgiven for drawing an imaginary starting line for college-level literacy acquisition at the outset of college. In 2009, Kara Taczak and William H. Thelin argued that we should "slow down this seeming race to adulthood and allow children to be children" (22). The writers of each bookend of Kristine Hansen and Christine R. Farris's 2010 National Council of Teachers of English (NCTE) collection (*College Credit for Writing in High School*), David A. Jolliffe (in his foreword) and Douglas Hesse (in his afterword), asked students eager to "take care of" first-year college writing requirements in high school the same question: "Good God, what's the hurry" (Jolliffe ix) and "why the hurry" (Hesse 291). A 2013 NCTE Policy Research Brief, "First-Year Writing: What Good Does It Do," flatly claimed that "allowing college credit for writing courses completed while in high school will not help students to fully develop capacities for engagement, persistence, collaboration, reflection, metacognition, flexibility, and ownership that will help them to grow as writers and learners" (3). For all their objections, gatekeepers of FYC may have failed to check their privilege in assuming that motivated students and their families are willing to push the pause button so an increasingly expensive and antiquated master narrative (where life begins at college) can be played out according to a timetable of the university's choosing.

Using a deficit model that characterizes what happens in high school as "less than" forestalls a meaningful conversation about what might be best for the increasing number of first-year students who arrive at a university with legitimately earned college writing credits. This ideology

https://doi.org/10.7330/9781646422531.c009

also silences a discussion about what might actually be in the best interest of the universities that eagerly accept these high-achieving students. Could the loss of an FYC enrollment be offset with the gains a more advanced writer might bring to the university community upon entry? In the decade-plus since Hansen and Farris's collection explored the array of accelerated means of "taking care of" the traditional FYC requirement, it's safe to say that FYC has become even less site- or time-specific. As FYC continues to pick up stakes and move itself into high school in increasing numbers, can we find a different way to characterize—and perhaps even welcome—students who happen to have been industrious enough to take FYC prior to their university experience? Can we leverage the presence of FYC pedagogy in the daily arsenal of an increasingly large corps of high school teachers to lift the veil between secondary and postsecondary classrooms once and for all?

This chapter explores the ambitious enterprise of putting college-level writing at the center of DE through research conducted with ninety alumni from the first four graduating classes of the Reynolds Advance College Academies (ACA), in which cohorts of students earn an entire associate degree concurrent with high school graduation. Because alums from this program were not typically required to take FYC at a university, they bring valuable insights about whether their acculturation to higher education would have benefited from an FYC requirement after high school. Are they as impoverished in demonstrating the "habits of mind" as the NCTE's own College Section Research Policy Brief claims they are, by having missed out on taking FYC in a university setting? Their high school–based academy instructors who have taken on the credentials and training to teach first-year composition bring equally compelling testimony about how teaching college-level writing has changed their professional lives and transformed their schools. Together, these two populations, the students and instructors themselves, engaged on a daily basis with DE, may help us recognize that "dislocating" first-year writing may in fact serve to expand its reach and influence well beyond, before, and after the first term of college.

THE ACADEMY MODEL: GOING FROM SIX TO SIXTY CREDITS

In the past decade, the Reynolds ACA has transformed its DE offerings from a collection of "one-offs" (usually two terms of decontextualized FYC) to an "academy model" in which FYC is nested in the context of an associate degree designed for university transfer. Each academy is designed around the Three Cs: **cohorts** of twenty-five–fifty students

Table 9.1. The Associate of Science (AS) in social science degree plan: J. R. Tucker High School

Grade 9	*Grade 10*	*Summer Session*	*Grade 11*	*Grade 12*
Honors English	Honors English	**Student Development 100**	**English 111 and English 112**	**English 224 and English 242**
Honors Biology	Honors Chemistry	**Health 115**	AP physics or AP chemistry	**Biology 101 and Biology 102**
Pathway 1: Honors Geometry Pathway 2: Honors Algebra II	Honors Algebra II Honors Math Analysis	**Approved Reynolds elective**	**MTH 167 and MTH 245** **MTH 167 and MTH 245**	AP stats AP calculus A/B or B/C
Honors World History II	AP European history	**Approved Reynolds elective**	**History 121 and History 122**	**Political Science 211 and Political Science 212**
World language	World language	**Approved Reynolds elective**	**Spanish 101 and 102 or 102 and 201**	**Psychology 200 and Psychology 230**
Health and physical education	Health and physical education	**Approved Reynolds elective**	High school elective	**Biology lab**
High school elective	High school elective	**Approved Reynolds elective**	High school elective	High school elective

per grade enrolled in sections of no more than twenty-five students per course as full-time Reynolds students in a **curriculum**, supported by intrusive and intentional **coaching** that begins more than two years before any of the college coursework and continues through graduation and beyond. Instead of accepting students out of tenth grade and delivering only a two-year slate of college courses, the academy model builds in two years of college-prep coursework and coaching interventions in ninth and tenth grades before the Reynolds curriculum begins in the summer before eleventh grade. These academies offer complete AS degrees in social sciences and business administration, each anchored by twelve credits of English (six of FYC during the junior year and six of 200-level literature survey courses during the senior year). All but one of these seven academies are high school–based, and they are taught by Southern Association of Colleges and Schools Commission on Colleges–credentialed high school faculty, who themselves form a powerful interdisciplinary teaching cohort that transforms the culture of their school.[1] A typical four-year curriculum appears in table 9.1. Please note that the Reynolds courses are in bold.

From the outset, the "habits of mind" described in the WPA's Framework for Success in Postsecondary Writing are made manifest

(Council of Writing Program Administrators et al.). The application essay, administered to hundreds of eighth graders, quotes and defines the eight habits directly: "Success in college-level work requires certain **habits of mind**: **curiosity**; **openness**; **engagement**; **creativity**; **persistence**; **responsibility**; **flexibility**; and **metacognition**. Reflecting on your school years, in an essay, describe how you have already developed up to three of these habits, and identify at least one habit you will need to develop further as a student in the Advance College Academy."[2] These same habits—characterized by the 2013 NCTE Research Policy Brief as invisible, occult, secret, and elusive to all but those to whom they are revealed in FYC at a university—are introduced as part of the application process and revisited throughout. High school seniors return to their eighth grade admissions essays to reflect on what habits they have developed over the past four years and which ones they may still need to develop before leaving for the university—a longitudinal exercise providing insights folded back into the design of the program.[3]

SURVEYING ALUMNI: ASKING "WHAT ELSE TRANSFERS?"

Once we had a pool of 261 academy alumni from the first four years of graduating classes (2015–2018), we were ready to ask what else transfers besides the credits and, by extension, to ponder whether taking FYC before the "first year" affected students' acculturation to the university. Quantitative data collected from 90 alumni surveys indicated that 90 percent of our alums strongly agreed (46%) or agreed (44%) with the statement that "by taking ACA courses, I was better prepared academically for college," while only 3 percent disagreed. But such satisfaction data, while impressive, told us only so much. We decided to dig a little deeper to find out whether and how ACA alums were navigating their dual role of acculturating to adult residential life at a university as social first years while taking upper-division coursework as academic third years. Ultimately, as in any assessment, the results of this study will be used to refine career coaching, counseling, and teaching methods for current and future students in the academies.[4]

For this more focused study, we surveyed the 200 or so alumni among the first four graduating classes from whom we had reliable contact information (see appendix 9.A for the survey instrument). Because our initial questions were intentionally open-ended, quantitative coding of data proved elusive. Even so, after collecting and evaluating twenty-seven detailed responses from these alumni (roughly a 13.5% response rate), we were pleased to see a pattern confirming previous quantitative data.[5]

Several responses demonstrated a capacity for meta-cognition, nuanced self-awareness, and an entrepreneurial stance toward higher education:

> I realized that I had a lot more to learn about time management, focus, and being resilient to failure. I realized that most of these concepts are based on experiential learning for the student compared to courses. For example, a student has to learn how to optimize their time management through deliberate practice instead of having a course that forces it to them.

> I've learned that my environment has a significant effect on my productivity and my mindset; both my physical environment as well as the type of place I'm in geographically . . . I've also learned that it's unreasonable to expect myself to be perfect at everything all the time, and that as long as I'm giving my all to the things that I'm passionate about, that is a success in itself.

> I have learned that I am more forward-thinking and self-motivated than many of my peers. Because ACA afforded me the opportunity to graduate two years early with my undergraduate degree, I had to make plans for post-graduate life well before my peers and figure out for myself how to accomplish those goals. For example, in my first semester at university, I made the decision to apply to law school, so I signed up for and started studying for the LSAT, started working to make connections with professors who could write me letters of recommendation, and researched what elective courses would best prepare me for law school.

Sometimes, the shortest responses were the most profound:

> After going to high school for 9 hours straight, taking college courses, and still having time for athletics and a social life, I was definitely able to do better as a student at university.

> I'm a lot stronger than I thought I was.

> I can do a lot more with my life than I thought I could.

Answers to one question ("What would you change about the ACA design or philosophy based on what you now know about university life?") did elicit some concern about rigor:

> I never would have wanted to hear this in high school, but I think that ACA isn't necessarily as tough on students as college professors are. If we want to mimic college life, I think this is the biggest difference.

> Don't coddle the kids too much.

Another respondent argued that scaffolding college-level rigor in a high school setting can sometimes take the form of too much busy work:

> The workload that ACA teachers give is unrealistic. They gave us college-level work but gave us a high school workload. They also encouraged us to participate in sports, extracurricular activities, and part-time jobs. We

were in class for 7 hours a day, but in college we only have 2–3 classes a day. We got too much work considering the amount of time outside of class we had to work on it. I know a lot of us were sleep-deprived the majority of senior year. *There needs to be a better balance between work volume and difficulty.* (emphasis added)

Curious to probe further, we scheduled focus groups with the twenty-one respondents who had chosen to identify themselves and were geographically accessible. We returned to the question of rigor in detail in a particularly interesting focus group exchange, an excerpt of which appears here, using pseudonyms in accordance with the participants' signed consent forms:

Q: What about the relationship between [*sic*] homework, assignments, grading, and rigor in university v. high school? How did you make the transition, and how might the design of the ACA be tweaked to encourage a greater sense of personal responsibility, understanding that we're still operating within the high school environment?

PATRICK: In college, some teachers they don't give out much graded homework, but they give out practice examples. But some students don't use that to their benefit because it's not graded. They're only worried about the test or quiz. So, it is beneficial in high school to make it graded. That way they do it and then when they come to college if it's not necessarily graded they can still do it to get practice from it in order to make themselves better.

JENNIFER: I guess it just depends on how much you can simulate the college experience. On the other hand it might be nice to learn that lesson in high school. Because I had friends in college who were like, "Well I did the econ reading or whatever but I didn't do the problems" and then they got bad grades. Or one person would say, "Well I went to class every day." I was like, "Well did you read the textbook?" And she said "Well, no." I was like, "Well you have to do it." It wasn't graded so she didn't do it. So if you maybe fall one time in high school and realize that you actually have to do the extra work, college might be less.

JESSIE: They say that active learning is where you learn the most, instead of passive learning where you just sit in class. You just hear it, you think you know it, but you don't. You have to put yourself to work.

DENNIS: Yeah, I would agree with that. Depends on how you want to simulate, like if you want to give them those training wheels in high school and that foundation to give them that drive to do that work that's not graded because I feel that high schoolers do need to learn how to do homework that's not graded. If a teacher gave me homework in high school and said that it's not for a grade I promise you I wouldn't have done it.

JENNIFER: I probably wouldn't have done it the first time and then I probably would have picked it up.

JESSIE: I think that's what you should do, maybe make some of the teachers say "okay this will not be graded, worry about the test" and those people who didn't study, they'll realize soon on that it's on the test. I had to learn that in college also where like orgo (organic chemistry) you have to do the practice problems even though it's not graded but you have to do them. And so, even if they don't catch on they will eventually. Expose it to them early on. The second they see the test they'll see it's exactly like the practice problems that weren't graded and you trick them. Trick them first and then they'll figure it out.

There's a lot to unpack in this fascinating exchange. These students, on the other side of a waived FYC requirement that might have helped orient them to the university, seem nonetheless to have learned sophisticated acculturative lessons about the multifaceted assessments and assignments that characterize university-level study. How so? Perhaps because the FYC requirement was not "waived" or "taken care of" (to borrow the phrase from the title of the Hansen and Farris collection) but in fact *satisfied*—in a systematic, embedded, and cross-curricular manner. The twelve credits of English (two courses in composition and rhetoric, two courses in American and British literature) taken across all four semesters of the final two years of high school function as the critical thinking, reading, and writing glue for the associate degree program. More than any other discipline in the program, English is the curricular constant responsible for the fact that from 2015 through 2019, 434 of the 515 students who began this program completed the entire AS degree in two years, an 84.3 percent graduation rate.

Such centrality for English studies is increasingly elusive in university core curricula. A four-course English sequence butts heads with counterclaims that even two courses of English are a burden to the completion agendas of majors across the university. The ACA's twelve-credit core, even though it takes place prior to and outside the university setting, as least ensures that English studies hold a position of primacy. With each English course in conversation with other disciplines of the curriculum, the process pedagogy of meta-cognition and scaffolding that is the proud tradition of FYC ingrains itself in the way these students view themselves and their classmates long after they leave the program. ACA alums like "Jennifer" appear to have positioned themselves as the most academically acculturated members of their entering class at the university. Their insight about the importance of doing ungraded work extends well beyond the composition pedagogy where that value first takes root. It extends to disciplines as far flung as "econ" and "orgo," as a foundational practice other university students might be encouraged to emulate. That's why even without formal peer-mentoring programs in place to leverage their experience, ACA alums are already coveted by university admissions officers for the example they set.

Those who were not available in person for focus groups were given a follow-up survey by email or an opportunity for a phone interview (see appendix 9.B for this instrument). These emails and phone conversations also produced some deeper insights. Alums reported that the dual role they had occupied as high school students taking college courses transformed into a similarly divided identity of being a social first-year student and an academic third-year student at the university:

> The other first year students in my residential hall did not seem to be as concerned about their academics. They had more time to make decisions about their future. While I was finding ways to become involved on campus, they were living out the new-found college freedom.

> I have viewed the pursuit of my bachelor's degree as a stepping stone. My end goal is to earn my Master's in Healthcare Administration. Because I will be graduating college two years early, time is a factor that has actually influenced me to do more.

> I kind of had at the beginning, more of a freshman experience: I call it my freshman semester. Then I moved on. I think the kids that come out of this program are mature enough to understand how to get involved on campus and how to balance what they're doing.

There's a quality of no-nonsense pragmatism in these responses that may not appeal to those whose cultural sensibilities have led them to presume that a bacchanalian first year "living out the newfound college freedom" should follow on the heels of a year's worth of senioritis. ACA students are savvy enough to squeeze two years out of this inflated and expensive accordion from eleventh to fourteenth grade by instead earning up to sixty real college credits in eleventh and twelfth grades and taking 300-level coursework in their major as first-year students at a university. If they happen to save $50,000 on those two years of undergraduate tuition, room, and board at a public university in the process or they choose to use their four years at a university to earn multiple baccalaureate degrees or even a master's degree, all the better. Our alumni surveys also reveal that 72 percent of our graduates intend for their highest earned degree to be not the baccalaureate (the goal of the other 28%) but in fact a post-baccalaureate credential. When nearly three-quarters of our student population have moved the postsecondary finish line to graduate school, is it any wonder they aren't keen on keeping the starting line for college where it's traditionally been?

In the initial Google survey, we encountered a number of observations about mental health, so we followed a hunch that we might be able to glean some insights on self-care challenges faced not only by our own alums but by their roommates, suitemates, and classmates at the university. One respondent went into great detail in a phone interview about the challenges of "taking care of myself mentally":

> I never had to actively think about my mental state until I got to college. I now have a different understanding of the same concept I talked about after my first year at college. When students come out here—especially minority students—they feel like they have to uphold their whole community. The belief that you are a reflection of your family and community is what creates the burden in the first place. "Don't mess it up for us." That community weight can work for you or against you. Minority students have to do certain things non-minorities don't have to do—things like code-switching. No matter how rough their backgrounds were, they're still leaving support systems in their communities behind.

How much of this insight would have been gleaned by a typical student after just fifteen months of university experience—and what role a traditional FYC requirement in the first semester at a university might have played—is difficult to determine. But for this student who arrived with sixty credits and academic junior status, solutions based on strategies for self-reflection and meta-cognition were readily at hand:

> Since I've been back for my sophomore year, living a mile and a half off campus, I've been compartmentalizing my energies. I leave the apartment to take the shuttle into campus at 9am and I take the last shuttle home just before midnight. I spend 15 hours a day on campus, so that all I do at the apartment is watch TV, watch youtube [*sic*], and sleep. That way, I don't associate home with school or vice versa . . . While I'm on campus all day [and] into the evening, it's classes and the organizations that are important to me: the Black Culture Center, where I'm doing program management, and Student Government, where I'm working on a strategic planning committee to write legislation for student mental health and retention. I've also gotten some good mentoring from an alum who works for Microsoft. He's taken me under his wing and shared some of his story.

Was this ACA alum in as good or better a position academically and socially as a typical second-year university student to work through this existential crisis and reemerge as a leader on campus? We'd like to think so.

Follow-up questions also explored the impact of leaving the visibility of "the bubble" of an intensely coached high school cohort, leapfrogging the temporary safe space and acculturation of a traditional FYC course, and landing as an eighteen-year-old in a presumably more anonymous environment:

> You go to college and you realize that it's now all on you, and you have to seek out opportunities. Not all opportunities will come to you. In high school a lot of opportunities came to you like "Oh, here's some scholarships and here's an organization you should join" as opposed to college where you have to seek that out yourself. When I wanted to shadow a doctor or be involved in research I had to look it up myself and do a lot of emailing to eventually build a new connection with people.

> I took advantage of the invisibility and didn't join as many things as other people did but I think I just needed a break after high school. Then I think I sought visibility out for myself. I probably went to too many appointments with my adviser. He really knew who I was by the time I graduated, which was good for recommendation letters.

Even though these ACA alums are social first-year students, their upper-division academic undergraduate standing coupled with their capacity for self-advocacy prove to be a hedge against the invisibility and anonymity our cultural narrative tells us comes with the territory of the transition from high school to college.

SURVEYING FACULTY: PROFESSIONALIZING SECONDARY EDUCATION

As with the alumni surveys, we have drawn insights from ACA faculty from a variety of academic disciplines on how an academy is transformational in their school. Teaching a two-year college degree program to a shared cohort of twenty-five–fifty students in a high school setting creates horizontal relationships across the disciplines. Building an expectation that ninth and tenth grade high school courses will prepare academy students for their college coursework in eleventh and twelfth grades creates vertical relationships across grade levels. One faculty member attested, "We do a good job of integrating cross-curricular assignments and interacting as a teacher cohort to stress the ideas of different types of writings based on the writing situation. We read a common novel in ninth grade with science and do group projects connected to both subjects. We also read a common novel in eleventh grade and connect with all subject areas. Both culminate with group presentations and critiques involving text, visual media, and oral presentations as well as peer evaluations." Another responded in a similar vein: "The most obvious cross-disciplinary interaction is the junior year *Something Must be Done about Prince Edward County* project, in which students use English history, math, and Spanish language skills in a culminating inquiry about school segregation in the 1950s versus school segregation in 2019. Students use visual rhetorical analysis to create a rally or protest sign, and they also use their composition skills to create and deliver the final presentation."

Interdisciplinary faculty cohorts have also been able to use a common reading, Kevin Bales's *Blood and Earth*, to engage students and faculty across the disciplines of political science, psychology, biology, and English. The first phase of this months-long project that carries credit across all four classes asks students to choose one of the three non-English disciplines as a lens through which to read and annotate the book. The second phase groups all the students by their chosen discipline to collaborate and prepare a public lecture and discussion held at our college. To prepare for the final phase, a ninety-minute performance, each student in each group holds responsibility for certain tasks—from oral presentation to copyediting and scriptwriting to visual design (including proper attribution of images) to fielding questions from the audience. Because ACA students are still a captive population enrolled in the same associate degree program through the end of twelfth grade, it's a capstone project far more ambitious than what a commuter community college with a 16 percent full-time student population could even dream of pulling off.

Even though (or perhaps because) the ACA is a "school within a school," its presence has a much more profound and lasting impact on the larger school environment than, say, increasing the percentage of students who take at least one Advanced Placement (AP) class. This distinction was borne out even more clearly at a granular level once we asked ACA English instructors, "How do DE composition courses differ from your other teaching? What are you able to do with DE students that you can't do with your other students? What, if anything, are you not able to do?"

> I feel like I have the freedom in a composition course to prepare them for college writing. I don't have to focus on literature analysis. Instead I can give them a variety of writing assessments that incorporate analysis without the novel approach.
>
> In general, DE courses are much more rigorous, demand more student engagement, and are more sophisticated.
>
> In secondary education, high school teachers are teaching students to help them pass a "minimum competency test." Because of this, classroom instruction includes a high volume of classwork, discipline management, and a high volume of grades designed to help students pass high school rather than assess their skills. In the DE context, we do not have these pedestrian constraints. We can run a syllabus that includes 5 or 6 major tests or papers much like one would do in the university setting.

> I can't say that I had any limitations. If I wanted to conduct a Skype chat with a person from Nigeria to discuss *Things Fall Apart*, I did. If I wanted to take a field trip to the Richmond Art Museum, I could. If I wanted to organize an international communication between my students in Richmond and students in Alberta, Canada, I could and did do that. If I wanted students to go out into the world and meet people in the fields that interested them, I supported that.
>
> I focus the comp courses on writing, specifically responding to non-fiction—all types. We spend a lot of time breaking down writing from specific sentence structures to specific word choices, and why the writer may or may not have chosen these—for what purpose? This is different from my ninth grade courses[,] which are locked in to specific reading and curriculum requirements. The DE courses give me much more freedom in choosing works to analyze, and since the students are generally high achievers, I don't have to worry about "skill and drill" activities.
>
> There's not much I can't do with DE. They are receptive and motivated enough to complete nearly every assignment with rigor and intelligence. I do have a certain responsibility to teach different types of writing to my DE class. Knowing DE students will be attending college, and many will be majoring in careers that use APA writing, I teach APA and Chicago style as well as MLA. I also teach them how to use the Reynolds databases and library because these are skills they'll need in nearly every class in college.

There's something compelling to teachers about the subtle but significant shift to the presence of college-level rather than merely college-prep courses in the high school setting. One of the many ACA English instructors who came from an AP background put it this way:

> Knowing that their courses transfer tends to calm their nerves. They don't have the stress of the AP test on them. They can work and revise without the pressure about credit depending on one test. My numbers in DE are growing each year because of that. Students want the guaranteed credit for all the hard work. They know that six English credits will follow them after a year of intense writing. In AP their final assessment score determines if credit will happen.

This very distinction between AP and DE—the lack of a final timed assessment from on high, graded by a panel of strangers thousands of miles away—is what has convinced education influencers like Jay Mathews to discount DE as somehow less reliable: "AP exams are at least three hours long. They are written and graded by outside experts. Dual-enrollment exams are usually shorter and the teachers who grade them often taught the students. That makes them more likely to go easy." But our experience is that fostering the semester-long (and often year-long) relationship between student and teacher that is fundamental to FYC—and encouraging high school faculty members to own their courses as the professionals they are rather than teach a standardized curriculum—is precisely what makes DE more authentic than AP.

IMPLICATIONS FOR "COLLEGE ENGLISH"

To his credit, elsewhere in his foreword to the Hansen and Farris collection, David Jolliffe offers an olive branch in place of insisting on FYC as a duplicative curricular requirement for those students who arrive with the credits in hand: "If not a complete course, why not require students entering with credits or waivers to participate in an intensive workshop . . . so they can learn about the culture of reading and writing that successful students inhabit at the college or university" (xii)? In his contribution to another 2010 NCTE collection, the *What Is "College-Level" Writing, Volume* 2, Jolliffe expands on his idea, specifically in reference to students arriving with qualifying AP scores: "Rather than simply complaining about the AP students placing *out* of composition, why not work to get a more advanced writing course in place for the students to place *into*? . . . Why not try to recruit these students into peer tutoring programs in writing centers? . . . In short, why not take advantage of better-than-average students showing up at the door" (73–74, original emphasis)? The ACAs—specifically, composition's central place in them—are efforts to produce graduates ready to populate and animate the kind of advanced college literacy role Jolliffe proposes. In the process, the professional identities of the cohort of high school educators delivering this program have been transformed as well. These teachers are illustrating every day how it's possible to create a high school–based DE program that still claims FYC as one of its chief academic disciplines.

More broadly, we might ask how this "dislocation" of FYC might actually have a profound and productive impact on the discipline of composition. Its self-assigned moniker, FYC, was meant to ensure its existence as part of the fulcrum of general education, but that name may also be what is preventing it from conceiving of itself in more institutionally agile ways. Are there other disciplines in higher education that have been as contingent on place and time as FYC? Would our colleagues in STEM fields insist that every entering university student take first-year math, regardless of their K–12 preparation and experience? Higher education already has an infantilization problem, and insisting on a specific time and place for FYC risks making FYC its central enabler. Today's entering college students have neither the patience nor the funds to allow college to work its four-year time-release magic on them. They may still be coming for the four-year experience, but they expect more out of those four years than ever before, and they don't expect to be treated as if they are starting their adult lives at orientation. Exploring what DE has done by necessity to legitimize itself outside the temporal and spatial kingdom of FYC may ironically lead us to insights about how to save FYC from itself.

NOTES

1. For more on the Reynolds Advance College Academies, visit the website at www.reynolds.edu/aca. Specific curricula for each location are available at the Curriculum and Courses tab.
2. While all of the academies use a variation on this application essay prompt, admissions criteria vary widely across Reynolds's service area depending on the culture and aims of the school district partners. As an open admissions institution, Reynolds does not make admissions decisions directly; successful placement into college-level writing is required, however. Of the eight associate degree-granting academies, three use a lottery system, three are very nearly open admissions themselves, and two are highly selective. Demographics of gender, race, ethnicity, and economics across the eight academies closely resemble those of the highly diverse adult population of Metro Richmond, save the one factor of age, of course. Thresholds for continuation in the program after admission also vary by school division, but in general, a non-weighted GPA of 2.5 is required after junior year.
3. For example, our longitudinal research has told us that of the eight WPA "habits of mind," flexibility is the only habit that increases from eighth to twelfth grade as both a strength and a habit in need of development. Reflection plummets as a habit in need of development, while engagement spikes over the same four-year period, suggesting perhaps that students develop meta-cognitive strategies in the program but also finish high school knowing they will need to find ways to engage with the outside world as they move on to a university. My thanks to Rob Meister, ACA English teacher at the time, for his collaboration on this 2016 research study.
4. I want to acknowledge the collaborative assistance in developing and administering this survey and the resulting focus group I received from two of the site directors in the Reynolds ACA: Sheralyne Tierseron, biology instructor at J. R. Tucker HS, and Allen Riddle, ITE instructor at Highland Springs HS. Students in all phases of this study signed consent forms ensuring their anonymity.
5. Alumni were given the option of responding to the initial Google survey anonymously; six of the twenty-seven chose to do so.

APPENDIX 9.A

INITIAL GOOGLE SURVEY ADMINISTERED TO ALUMNI

1. How did you adjust **socially** as a university student with a significant number of transfer credits?
2. How did you adjust **academically** as a university student with a significant number of transfer credits?
3. What was the most difficult challenge you faced in your first year at university?
4. What surprised you the most about being a university student?
5. Thinking back, what would you have done differently in the summer between graduating from high school and starting at university?
6. What have you learned about yourself since finishing the ACA?
7. What would you change about the ACA design or philosophy based on what you now know about university life?
8. Is there anything else you'd like to share that is not covered by the questions above?

APPENDIX 9.B

FOLLOW-UP ALUMNI SURVEY FOR FOCUS GROUPS, PHONE INTERVIEWS, AND EMAILS

1. Belonging to a learning cohort is integral to the ACA design. How (well) did you create or identify a cohort at university?
2. How (well) did you navigate being advanced (third-year) academically and on pace (first-year) socially and residentially?
3. In the ACA, you were coached to be in future mode, always thinking a few moves ahead on the chessboard of your academic life, even though the design of the program allowed you to be a typical high school student. When you got to university, (how) did that future orientation continue? (When/how) did you live in the present and (when/how) were you a "typical" college student?
4. How have you viewed the pursuit of your baccalaureate degree? As an end goal or as a stepping stone? Why/what influenced that view?
5. How attuned were you to your own and others' mental health during your first year at university?
6. How is student mental health addressed differently in a university vs. [a] high school setting, not only by the administration but by the students themselves?
7. How did you adjust from the intense level of scrutiny and visibility of a high school setting to the relative anonymity and invisibility of a university environment?

8. What in the ACA design specifically gave you an advantage relative to your fellow first-years? What in the design could be changed to make you better prepared?
9. Absent the requirement to complete certain gen ed coursework that traditionally purports to assist with acculturation to university life (e.g., curricular rites of passage like "first-year composition"), what did your university do, if anything, whether curricular or otherwise, to ensure that you were acculturated?
10. What would you recommend universities do to accommodate the special needs of students such as yourself (e.g., first-year, first-time-in-college students who arrive with 30–60 college credits completed)?

WORKS CITED

Bales, Kevin. *Blood and Earth: Modern Slavery, Ecocide, and the Secret to Saving the World.* Spiegel and Grau, 2016.

Council of Writing Program Administrators, National Council of Teachers of English, and National Writing Project. *Framework for Success in Postsecondary Writing.* Jan. 2011. http://wpacouncil.org/files/framework-for-success-postsecondary-writing.pdf. Accessed May 13, 2022.

Hansen, Kristine, and Christine R. Farris, eds. *College Credit for Writing in High School: The "Taking Care of" Business.* NCTE, 2010.

Hesse, Douglas. "Afterword: Of Cellists and Writers, Getting Better and Getting On." In *College Credit for Writing in High School: The "Taking Care of" Business*, edited by Kristine Hansen and Christine R. Farris. NCTE, 2010, pp. 283–292.

Jolliffe, David A. "Advanced Placement English and College Composition: 'Can't We All Get Along?'" In *What Is "College-Level" Writing? Volume 2: Arguments, Readings, and College Writing Samples*, edited by Patrick Sullivan, Howard Tinberg, and Sheridan Blau. NCTE, 2010, pp. 57–76.

Jolliffe, David A. "Foreword: Tough Questions for Thoughtful Educators." In *College Credit for Writing in High School: The "Taking Care of" Business*, edited by Kristine Hansen and Christine R. Farris. NCTE, 2010, pp. vii–xiii.

Mathews, Jay. "Dual Enrollment High School Programs Are Oversold, but They Do Have Value." *Washington Post*, Sept. 18, 2016. https://www.washingtonpost.com/local/education/dual-enrollment-high-school-programs-are-oversold-but-they-do-have-value/2016/09/18/c2faeb5c-7ba5-11e6-ac8e-cf8e0dd91dc7_story.html. Accessed May 13, 2022.

NCTE Policy Research Brief. "First-Year Writing: What Good Does It Do?" National Council of Teachers of English, 2013. http://mjreiff.com/uploads/3/4/2/1/34215272/ncte policybrief.pdf. Accessed May 16, 2022.

Sullivan, Patrick, Howard Tinberg, and Sheridan Blau, eds. *What Is "College-Level" Writing? Volume* 2. NCTE, 2010.

Taczak, Kara, and William H. Thelin. "(Re)Envisioning the Divide: The Impact of College Courses on High School Students." *Teaching English in the Two-Year College*, vol. 37, no. 1, 2009, pp. 7–23.

10

COLLEGE COMPOSITION AT MIDWEST HIGH

Field Notes from a Concurrent Enrollment Classroom

Tyler Branson

Dual enrollment (DE), as many in this collection have pointed out, is poised to fundamentally change the way we research, teach, and administer college writing. According to the National Alliance of Concurrent Enrollment Partnerships (NACEP), 1.4 million high schoolers took more than 2 million college courses in 2010–2011, which represents about 10 percent of all high school students ("Fast Facts"). These numbers have been rising steadily over the nearly four decades since 1983's *Nation at Risk* report, which characterized the nation's schools as failing and precipitated a rise in policy reform initiatives linked to holding schools accountable (National Commission on Excellence in Education). President Barack Obama's Every Student Succeeds Act (ESSA) of 2015 was the first federal legislation that asked schools to factor high school student participation into college coursework as part of calculating state report cards. After ESSA, legislators in states like Ohio, where I currently teach, began revamping their DE policies. In 2015 Ohio created "College Credit Plus" (CCP), which was designed to "enhance students' career readiness and postsecondary success" and effectively opened the floodgates for DE partnerships across the state ("About"). Since then, the number of Ohio students participating in DE rose from about 14,000 in 2014 (Blanco) to over 70,000 in 2017. In the ESSA era, Ohio's annual report claims that over 21.3 percent of Ohio seventh- to twelfth-graders participated (*Annual Report 2020–2021*).

This chapter shares the results of a semester-long observation of a concurrent enrollment (CE) CCP composition classroom at "Midwest High," located in a suburb of a large city in northwest Ohio; Midwest High partners with the institution of higher education at which I work. Through site visits, my goal as a researcher was to understand, qualitatively, stakeholder experiences with DE in the day-to-day operations

https://doi.org/10.7330/9781646422531.c010

of schools and classrooms. For instance, while K–12 education policies like DE are negotiated and enacted by institutions and politicians long before students and teachers even enter the classroom, those students and teachers are nevertheless levers of policy. And while students and teachers are imbued in the complex governing arrangements that shape the durability and legitimacy of education policies, they also interact with, interpret, individualize, and sometimes push back against those policies.

While this chapter primarily analyzes the way one CCP-credentialed instructor at Midwest High and her students experienced DE policies, those experiences only matter insofar as they can be situated within a broader ecosystem. Therefore, this chapter unfolds through three distinct views of Midwest High and its CE composition course. First is the macro-level, or rather, the perspective of my university, in which a team of administrators forge partnerships with local school districts in the region, drawing on the broader mandated DE legislation in Ohio. Second is the *meso*-level at which the DE partnership is executed. Here we see some of the more pernicious issues that lie beneath the surface of DE in Ohio, particularly that of equity. And finally there's the *micro*-level, or the experiences of teachers and students on the ground floor. Through ten site visits throughout one semester at Midwest High, I found that the CE students (referred to using pseudonyms) and their instructor, whom I am calling Ms. Elliot, all demonstrated kairotic rhetorical savvy in the ways they worked with, around, and sometimes against DE policies.

THE MACRO-LEVEL: DE IMPLEMENTATION BY INSTITUTIONS OF HIGHER LEARNING

In Ohio, CCP mandates and the massive influx of students have resulted in a new infrastructure for implementation at the university level. These institutional efforts work broadly to bureaucratize DE so that students and parents see the policy as a natural and inevitable solution to the high costs of education. For example, at my university, offices of enrollment management are required to pursue and broker partnerships with secondary schools, securing contracts that set the terms, tuition rates, and methods of DE instruction. Once they agree to a partnership, money for tuition is then transferred from the participating school district's budget into the university's budget. While CCP annual reports indicate this as "tuition savings" for families (Annual Report 2019–20 29), it comes by way of significant revenue *loss* for secondary districts. Ohio colleges and universities, which often offer reduced tuition for CCP courses, also experience this as a revenue loss. In other words, while students and parents experience CCP as "free," their secondary school districts foot the bill for tuition while the participating universities receive fewer tuition dollars than they would for otherwise traditionally enrolled students.

Higher education administrators in Ohio, however, often invoke a rhetoric of market-based education reform to defend these policies, noting that while secondary schools experience CCP as a revenue loss, the *state* is still saving money. For example, since public universities still rely on state funding for a share of their operational revenues, the state calculates how much to fund universities based on Full-Time Equivalent (FTE) students. With a program like CCP, in which over 70,000 high school students across the state are participating, this significantly lowers the amount of funding the state provides per FTE student in public universities across Ohio, since secondary school districts are now taking on that burden. University administrators are also inclined to see this arrangement as "profitable," since the seats CCP students fill would have otherwise remained empty. Our university also sees more revenue-positive CCP partnerships if a significant chunk of those courses is taught at the high school by high school instructors (like Ms. Elliot), since they receive no extra compensation for their labor. In other words, enrollment management plays a fundamental role in maintaining the durability of DE, not just in the ways its offices implement the mandated policy but in the ways those implementation procedures serve to legitimize a paradigm of choice, efficiency, and market-based logics that define "successful" or "effective" policies as those that save money.

Another way dual enrollment policy is implemented in Ohio is through the administration of the courses themselves. At my home institution, internal data from fall 2019 show 1,023 high school students enrolled in CCP courses throughout the entire university. With an overall student population of 19,759, that represents about 5 percent of the student body. Department heads are tasked with overseeing, staffing, and taking care of other minutia of DE policy implementation. Our department chair, for example, manages staffing for 444 dually enrolled students in our freshman- and/or sophomore-level composition courses. Of those students, 135, or about 30 percent, took composition through courses taught at a high school by a credentialed high school teacher. As part of the state-legislated CCP mandate, the composition program administrators (which, in my context, includes myself and one other person) provided mentorship to nine high school teachers credentialed to teach our courses on their campuses. This mentorship included providing workshops, traveling to the high schools to conduct teaching observations, and offering other professional development opportunities throughout the year. At my university, all of this represents a fundamental shift in both the student makeup of our composition courses and the job duties of department chairs, writing program administrators, and individual composition instructors.

THE MESO-LEVEL: DUAL ENROLLMENT POLICY IMPLEMENTATION AT MIDWEST HIGH

DE policies at the level of the schools tend to complicate the policy paradigm that frames DE as cost-effective and equitable. Even though past Chancellor John Carey (2014) recommended equity as one of the key concerns of the then new DE program, stating that CCP would provide "seamless and equitable pathways . . . across all demographic populations" (3), CCP has consistently benefited mostly white high school students in Ohio. For example, a recent annual report stated that 68.1 percent of all CCP students were white, which shows that in Ohio, high school students of color are underrepresented in this statewide policy (*Annual Report 2019–2020* 9).

Moreover, Midwest High, the site of the participant observation research shared below, is located in a suburb just outside the city where my university is located. A vast majority of Midwest High's student population is white, as is its broader school district. Of the ten schools my university partnered with in fall 2019, only one was in the actual district in which the university is situated. The others were in towns where more students are white and in districts that score higher on state annual report cards. Half of the top ten high schools my university partnered with in fall 2019 had white student populations of 90 percent or higher. Several of the partnered high schools had no Black students, and only one had a Black student population above 10 percent. In other words, despite the so-called equitable pathways on which CCP is predicated, my university tends to partner with schools that are predominately white—schools that also tend to have better annual report cards and more so-called college-ready students.

Unsurprisingly, these statistics on educational inequality are reflected in most studies of DE policies nationwide. For example, the US Department of Education's February 2019 report on DE participation showed that Black and Brown students were around 30 percent less likely than white students to take DE courses ("Dual Enrollment Participation and Characteristics"). Other studies show that affluent students are overrepresented in DE numbers as well (Zinth and Barnett). While this chapter analyzes just one classroom, these broader systemic issues impact all students' experiences before they even enter the classroom.

THE MICRO-LEVEL: MS. ELLIOT'S CONCURRENT ENROLLMENT CLASSROOM

Site Selection and Methodology

First, it is important to describe why I chose *participant observation* as a way to study the lived experience of teachers and students in this CE classroom. Taking my cues from ethnographers like Howard S. Becker and Blanche Geer, I utilized observation as a way to participate "in the daily life of the people under study . . . observing things that happen, listening to what is said, and questioning people, over some length of time" (28). Other scholars, such as Frank W. Lutz and Laurence Iannaccone, define participant observers in three ways: (1) the participant *as* an observer, (2) the observer as a limited participant, and (3) the observer as a non-participant. At Midwest High, I mostly utilized the second of these, wherein I worked as an observer with *limited* participation in the activities of the classroom. This limited participation meant I was a "quasi-member" of the classroom. Therefore, in my site visits, I ensured that interactions with Ms. Elliot and her students included only conversations initiated by students or the teacher or interactions that, according to Janice Ahola and Barry G. Lucas, "focus[ed] on the research project, either demonstrating curiosity about the purpose of the study or asking about the progress of the research" (81). Moreover, I also ensured that any responses to student inquiries and the teacher in this capacity were made so as to only "establish and maintain rapport" (78).

While I maintained these ethical commitments as a limited participant, it is important to mention that the boundaries of these techniques are always blurry, especially considering students' natural curiosity about the consistent presence of a researcher in their classroom. From students gazing at my observation journals and playfully exclaiming "one day I'm going to find out what you're writing in there" to students turning to me during class to ask for help on their papers, I found that that the more wary I was in response to their inquisitiveness, the more awkward my presence could be, which might have had more of an impact on the way students engaged with their instructor and the course material than if I were directly involved. Thus, as the semester progressed, I found myself saying hello to the students each morning, chatting with them and Ms. Elliot before class began, and occasionally taking part in class discussions.

As a participant observer, though, my main responsibility was to gauge the ways DE was felt and experienced at Midwest High. To document this, my data consisted of recording the day-to-day classroom activities in the form of extensive descriptive notes, including verbatim remarks when possible, which I subsequently turned into observation journals after each visit that summarized my own thoughts, comments, feelings, and interpretations of the events of the day. I also conducted follow-up interviews with four assenting students at the end of the semester. In this way, I was able to become familiar with classroom routines, materials, policies, activities, dynamics, and student/teacher interactions. I also described in my notes the learning process of college-level writing in a high school classroom (though a formal critique of Ms. Eliot's pedagogy was not the intention). Ultimately, these efforts worked toward a broader goal of describing day-to-day policy implementation.

Not surprisingly, the day-to-day activities of Ms. Elliot's DE classroom constituted an overall positive experience that semester. All of the students I interviewed after the semester was over spoke highly of Ms. Elliot, their high school, and CCP as an educational policy. The temptation here is to surmise that based on these results, DE at Midwest High is a *good* policy. While it is probably true that DE was indeed a positive experience for this group, what sticks out the most from my observations is that both the students and their teacher navigated DE in unique ways, regardless of whether they felt they benefited from the policy. More important, as I describe at the end of this section, when we consider whether DE is *good* policy from the perspective of a paradigm of equity as opposed to one of accountability, the question then becomes, good for *whom*? The rhetorical practices identified below, while illuminating, should nevertheless give us pause when we consider how we carry out, navigate, and resist policies like DE at our home institutions. For example, if DE and accountability are going to be the prevailing policy arrangements for the foreseeable future, then the individualized and interpretive rhetorical practices below might help administrators consider the ethical questions we should be asking when we pursue DE partnerships with schools in more or less academically successful districts—distinctions that are often conflated with race.

College Composition Is a Different Experience in the High School

Although policy in Ohio mandates that DE courses should be the same as those taught on campus, my research showed that the embodied classroom experience is one of being in high school, and this social world fundamentally changed the way the course was taught. In the most obvious way, the course is in a different physical location than the university. In other ways, though, the spatial arrangements of the high school, the physical artifacts in the room, and the strict focus on routine, structure, and safety all resemble a different social world than my university's campus.

Midwest High, for example, operates at the regimented pace one would expect of a mid-size high school: a bell rings to start first period promptly at 7:30 a.m. The weekly schedule alternates between *blue* and *red* days, with different schedules each day. Young people wearing school IDs on lanyards exchange books and papers from their lockers before hurrying to class. Teachers and administrators diligently patrol the halls, ensuring student safety and making sure nobody is left wandering around after the bell rings. Security at Midwest High is a high priority. After being questioned and waved on by a security guard in the parking lot, all guests sign in at the front office and obtain temporary passes to enter the building. On my first day observing, the principal escorted me to Ms. Elliot's room and knocked on the door, which was locked from the outside. When I was let into the room, Ms. Elliot pointed me to a seat in the back, where she had made a name tent that said "Dr. Branson." Around the room were other artifacts that designated the space as a high school. On the days that I observed, for example, Ms. Elliot's classroom was a university-level composition course. On other days, it was an AP literature or drama classroom. After school, the space became a meeting place for the Midwest High Chess Club. The walls of Ms. Elliot's room reflected these differing purposes: MLA style posters, examples of student work, chess trophies, bookshelves adorned with Norton Anthologies, a laminated handmade sign above Ms. Elliot's desk that read "No whining." The spatial arrangements, an overt focus on student safety, the distribution of power and authority, and the physical artifacts all felt different from my university's students' experience. For all intents and purposes, it *felt* like high school. These characteristics that designate the space as a high school did not necessarily preclude the content from being delivered at a college level, though. In fact, Ms. Elliot demonstrated that she was a more than competent writing instructor. And the students, for the most part, seemed intellectually capable of handling the material. However, the sights, sounds, and embodied experience of DE at Midwest High quickly revealed a discrepancy between the policy of DE in Ohio and the reality, which is that in this CE classroom, the experience is fundamentally different from that of a college campus.

Pedagogy Was Often Aimed at Transitioning Students from High School to College
The above characteristics that marked the CE classroom at Midwest High as a *different kind of space* than college necessarily changed the learning experience as well. In general, this was not a college classroom per se but a dedicated space in which a group of college-bound high school students worked closely with a college-writing mentor who helped them transition from high school to college. On the first day, for example, Ms. Elliot assigned the essay "Bam" by Amanda Winalski from the book *What Is "College-Level Writing,"* edited by Patrick Sullivan and Howard Tinberg. The essay was a firsthand perspective on transitioning from high school– to college-level writing. Ms. Elliot pointed to a quote from the essay, where the author realized that in college, "What I wrote was more important than *how* I wrote" (303, emphasis added). Ms. Elliot asked the students to unpack what Winalski meant. One student, Nick, said the piece argued that in college, it's a matter of "function over form." Nick went on to say that in high school, writing is mostly about "making six words out of two" to meet a word count, gussying up a text to make it "seem smart." Another student chimed in and said that in high school, writing a paper is a matter of making sure the beginning thesis and concluding paragraph aligned, and it didn't really matter what was in the middle. Then, Ms. Elliot moved the conversation toward the main idea of Winalski's essay, which was that transitioning to college-level writing means considering argument as opposed to the veneer of correctness that is characteristic of high school writing. These activities and discussions started a conversation about their fears and expectations for transitioning to college-level writing. One student, Ricky, pointed out that the essay made her feel better because it gave her a map of things "to look out for" once she got to college.

This notion that DE composition involves ensuring a successful transition from high school to college arose again later in the semester, when Ms. Elliot was working with handouts from the textbook *They Say I Say* by Gerald Graff, Cathy Birkenstein, and Russel Durst. Ms. Elliot provided the authors' appendices for students to use as a reference as they polished their writing on a rhetorical analysis assignment. Ms. Elliot described how templates like these can help their writing achieve a more college-level quality. She provided other worksheets, too, including an example of a college-level paper and a handout of rhetorical strategies. One student began reading the sample paper and exclaimed, "Woah, this is what they write like in college?" Even though everyone in the room was technically *already* in college, this student apparently saw the course as merely a prelude to the "real thing." And while students struggling with college-level writing expectations is not necessarily unique to high school, it does show that in the CE classroom, Ms. Elliot's students had the benefit of a small, intimate space to work one on one with a dedicated mentor who could guide them through not just the process of critique but also the social and cultural transition from the high school to the college writing process.

Dual Enrollment Functions as a Liminal Space

Another finding from this case study is that the CE classroom at Midwest High resembled neither high school nor college but a "liminal" space where students worked on problems in college writing. Victor W. Turner famously called liminality a "realm of pure possibility whence novel configurations of ideas and relations may arise" (236). In this transitional stage, which Turner also calls "betwixt and between" or a period of "fruitful darkness" (243), traditional boundaries and rules can be dissolved, creating a kind of uncertainty where new possibilities are imagined. Accountability-based policies like DE can also create pockets of liminal spaces as Turner described: for example, Ms. Elliot's class is *supposed to be* college but is *essentially* high school, to the extent that the *actual* experience is something not quite one or the other. This liminal space creates unique opportunities for teachers and students to critically analyze, interpret, and even potentially remake policy arrangements.

Ms. Elliot's DE classroom resembled Turner's liminal world of "fruitful darkness" because it gave her wiggle room to think more broadly about the needs of individual students and to question the boundaries between college and high school. Some of the best examples of this liminality are from the students' one-on-one conferencing with Ms. Elliot, juxtaposed with students' free discussion in the back of the room. In their first conferencing session early in the semester, for example, Ms. Elliot conferred with students about a literacy narrative assignment. These sessions were done in class, and Ms. Elliot would simply call on each student to conference with her in the front of the room while the other students worked on their papers in the back. The first student she met with was named Joel. Ms. Elliot asked, "What are three questions and what are three concerns?" Instead of responding, Joel wanted to know what he needed to do to pass, and he didn't seem invested in taking ownership of his essay. Ms. Elliot asked him to read his paper out loud so she could "interrupt" when needed. As she interrupted, she asked him to "show, not tell" in his narrative. She also guided Joel line by line through structure and coherence, providing feedback such as "you mention this here, but further down the page I don't see this again" or "I thought you were talking about Harry Potter in the beginning, but now it seems you've switched to a different book." Other times she helped him with his ideas. "What idea are you trying to convey here?" she asked him once, as well as "what's the goal of this paragraph?" Next up was Dan. Ms. Elliot worked with Dan just as she did with Joel, interrupting as he read to make comments such as "what do you want people to take from this part" or "how do you incorporate this idea into the body paragraphs later on?" With Brian, a struggling student, Ms. Elliot said, "Some people don't know what this term is, so you need to spell it out." Meanwhile, at the other side of the room, students Corey and Karlie were reviewing one another's papers, as were Ricky and Sara. I overheard Karlie say, "I need to redo my whole paper now!" Later, I overheard Ricky say, "I need to put this on my blog—not [in] my paper." And then Corey: "What can I do to make my paper better, Ricky?" After a while I heard a frustrated Karlie say, "I think I just don't have good ideas." At the front of the room, Nick, conferencing with Ms. Elliot, said, "I think mine is a mess, Ms. Elliot."

Ms. Elliot's one-on-one conferencing with students showcases how DE composition at Midwest High functions as a liminal space. On the surface, these conferences resembled other first-year composition writing conferences. But her format of doing them in class for every assignment was a pedagogical tool she could use thanks in large part to the *structure of the DE classroom*. For high-achieving students like Nick, who needed help with development, to frustrated students like Karlie, who needed confidence, or struggling students like Brian, who were capable but lacked motivation, Ms. Elliot dedicated enormous amounts of time to meet their individual needs while also granting downtime for others—time that led to meaningful investment in writing. Karlie, for example, who at one point had told her classmate that her paper "sucked," used the time to eventually discover a new topic.

Ms. Elliot wasn't the only one who recognized the liminality of DE composition at Midwest High. Karlie said she worked with Ms. Elliot one on one in class, at lunch, in study hall, and at any other opportunity she had. "For one of the assignments," she said, "I did come to [Ms. Elliot] almost every day." Since Karlie was a senior who would be starting college in the fall, I asked if she would feel comfortable next year going to her professors' office hours every day the way she went to see Ms. Elliot. She responded: "Honestly, I [wouldn't]. I think it'll be different because I'm here [in high school] all day. Like, I would've seen [Ms. Elliot] in . . . study hall. But, like, in college I'm sure I'll have my things going on, and [my professors] will have things going on, and I don't know if I'll go [to office hours] that often. But I'm hoping that this class is helping me to figure it out and I won't need to do that."

Here, Karlie is recognizing and acting on the liminal space of DE composition. She knew Ms. Elliott would be around in study hall or in class to work with her one on one on her writing. She also speculated that once she got to the *real thing*, her professors might be too busy, and so she recognized DE as an opportunity to work on her writing so she "wouldn't need" to go to office hours once she gets to college. The DE classroom, in other words, was a different kind of space for students like Karlie to learn in between high school and college. Students recognized this and purposefully leveraged their educational experiences to help them work through different stages of liminality.

Dual Enrollment Students and Teachers Made Micro-Political Decisions

To say that Ms. Elliot took advantage of the liminality of the course is also to imply that she was using DE policies *micro-politically*. In "The Micropolitics of Pathways: Teacher Education, Writing Assessment, and the Common Core," J. W. Hammond and Merideth Garcia document the "micropolitical work" of teachers, or rather, the moves educators make as they engage with various education reform initiatives in the classroom, particularly with regard to the Common Core State Standards (CCSS). Through in-depth interviews with nine high school teachers, Hammond and Garcia found that while their participants used the CCSS in their circular planning, none used them in the same way; nor did they personally see the standards as a determining factor in shaping student pathways. "Instead," they write, "participants reported micropolitically interpreting and repurposing the CCSS—drawing strategically on the standards to supplement and support the local pathways they already had in mind for students." Like those in Hammond and Garcia's interviews, Ms. Elliot strategically interpreted DE policies to benefit her students in ways she saw fit.

To this point, in my last observation, Ms. Elliot introduced a multimodal rhetorical analysis assignment and showed Childish Gambino's music video for the song "This Is America" as an example of visual rhetoric. The video, which calls attention to issues of race and racial violence in America, is graphic but well suited for visual analysis in a college composition course. Later, I asked Ms. Elliot if her principal might object to her use of the video in class, since most of her students were minors and some of the content of the video was violent. She said no because "this is a college classroom, not a high school classroom." Ms. Elliot decided independently that her role as a college instructor in this instance superseded her position as a high school teacher. And since Gambino's video *was* suitable for college-level student writers, she felt no qualms about showing it in class. Katie McWain describes CE high school teachers like Ms. Elliot as occupying a "liminal institutional positionality," in which they are "hailed simultaneously as members of high school and college faculty accountable to both sides of the partnership" (406). Similarly, Ms. Elliot was taking advantage of this complex liminality to make pedagogical decisions on a micro-political level.

Follow-up interviews also showed students making micro-political decisions regarding navigating DE policies. For example, each student had varying levels of motivation for signing up for the course. As Joanna Castner Post and her colleagues have written, powerful education reform interest groups like the National Governors Association, the Bill and Melinda Gates Foundation, the Partnership for 21st Century Skills, Achieve, and others all advocate for DE as a cost-saving mechanism for students and parents (167). But the students in Ms. Elliot's class said they took the course because they were "bored" with the classes offered at Midwest High. Karlie told me she signed up because she was "running out of classes to take here" and a DE course was her only option. "I didn't want to just have a bunch of emptiness in my schedule," she said. "If I didn't want to take all electives or just really show up for only what I need—then CCP [College Credit Plus/DE] was the [only] option." Andy told me he was taking DE courses as a way to challenge himself. For him, it was "basically just an honors class . . . that's why I like it." The fact that college credit comes with it was "just the cherry on top," he said. "I'm not taking it for college credit in high school. I'm taking it because it's a challenge for me." Nick said he took the class because he felt it was "good to get the experience of a college class before being thrown into [it]." In fact, he added, "I didn't even know it was worth college credit until, like, halfway through the semester. I'm just like, wait, this goes to my college degree?"

Two students from my interviews, Karlie and Dan, mentioned that getting college credit *was* something they considered. Karlie told me her parents attended an information seminar on earning college credit and factored that into their decision to enroll her in the course. Dan told me he remembered a presentation on DE in the auditorium one fall. For Dan, getting college credit while in high school was one motivating factor to "get these lower-level classes out of the way and then take something more geared toward what I want to do with the semester hours that I get for free there." Students, in other words, were taking DE courses for all kinds of reasons. Some of the reasons, like Dan's and Karlie's, align with the commonsense policy paradigms touted by DE policymakers in Ohio. Other students, however, expressed ambivalence toward getting college credit. Students' varying attitudes show us that policy paradigms that justify education reform initiatives such as DE are not stable, and students who experience these policies bend and shape them to fit their own needs, which sometimes differ from the education reform rationale.

High-Achieving White Students Make up the Bulk of Midwest High's DE Composition

The policy paradigm of DE in Ohio is that CCP is (1) a good way for everyone to save money for college and (2) open to students across all demographics. However, this is not the reality. In fall 2019, of the top high schools my university partnered with, only one was in the adjacent urban public school district. The other partnerships extended to the suburbs where student demographics skew whiter, per-pupil spending trends higher, and student achievement fares better. Relying solely on policy paradigms that focus on cost-effectiveness and expediency thus comes at the expense of equity, access, and inclusion (Moreland and Miller). As an example, all of the students I interviewed at Midwest High were white, and each student was involved in clubs, sports, and outside volunteer opportunities. Andy played football and was involved in multiple clubs and organizations. Nick was involved in drama, choir, and art lessons outside of school. They were also receiving scholarships, and each self-reported that they earned "good" grades. But there were no students of color in the class. While this is representative of the broader student population at Midwest High, the schools adjacent to my university with more Black and Brown students did not have CE courses with my university set up that semester; thus, there is no way to compare experiences with more marginalized districts.

The students in Ms. Elliot's class are not necessarily cognizant of these broader racial considerations of DE's policy arrangements. They have the privilege (no pun intended) of seeing the policy in terms of an opportunity to *get ahead*. As mentioned earlier, one of the reasons Dan signed up for the class was "to experience [college]." The DE course was an opportunity for him to do something *advanced*. Nick provided similar responses. As a high school writer, Nick said, "I knew how to write well . . . I could always write my papers in one go, no rough draft needed . . . because I knew everything a high school teacher was looking for." However, Nick said, "What [Ms. Elliot's class] is teaching me is what college professors are looking for when you write a paper, and that's going to be really useful and it'll help my writing process later." Nick's answers demonstrate that for many of these high-achieving white students at Midwest High, DE is a unique liminal space where they can work closely with a college mentor to successfully transition from high school to college writing and also challenge themselves by going outside traditional English coursework. For school districts closer to my university with higher proportions of Black and Brown students, though, there was no liminality because there was no opportunity.

As alluded to earlier, these responses track with existing research which shows that high-achieving white students are overrepresented in DE participation. Studies from Oregon and Texas show that high-achieving white women from families with higher socioeconomic status were more likely to enroll in DE courses (Pierson et al.; Miller et al.). Other studies that show positive correlations between DE students and college enrollment, persistence, and GPA (such as the 2012 study commissioned by the Community College Research Center ["What We Know"]) nevertheless note that when measuring these data, it is nearly impossible to control for elements such as motivation and aptitude. As Cecilia Speroni argues, this makes assessing the impact of DE difficult because students "who have already decided to go to college would likely consider dual enrollment as an attractive way to obtain a head start" anyway (1–2). This case study, while limited, illustrates what the literature suggests: that DE policies primarily attract and benefit high-achieving white students, and at least in Ohio, universities are economically incentivized to exclude districts with higher proportions of Black and Brown students. While this chapter shows how one group of students and their teacher used rhetorical savvy to negotiate DE policies in their own classroom, the specter of institutional racism shapes the perceptions of students at Midwest High before they even sign up for the course.

CONCLUSION

"Why Wait for Your Future?" This is a question in some promotional literature for CCP in Ohio and represents how insidiously such commonsense rationalizations hide the ideology of accountability-based education reform. As I show in this chapter, the entire DE enterprise is bound up in a broader policy regime of accountability that consists of a policy paradigm that justifies DE partnerships as "free" ways to provide more "options" for all students, "reduce time and costs of attending college," and better prepare students for their "future" (which means their ability to earn income post-college). These rationalizations begin to institutionally bureaucratize and legitimize the policies as Institutions of Higher Education form partnerships with public school districts and then "trickle down" into the perspectives of teachers and students. These rationalizations also reflect changing attitudes about the purpose of higher education—no longer a public good but an economic good, where things like choice, efficiency, and profit are markers of success.

However, my experiences at Midwest High reveal that teachers and students strategically understand and interpret DE in ways not bound to accountability logics. First, the dynamic of college composition is fundamentally affected by the embodied experience of *being in high school*. Second, in addition to meeting first-year composition learning outcomes, the instructor utilized students' experiences in high school to engineer pedagogical activities that helped them transition from high school to college. Third, these distinct efforts at transition were made possible because of the liminality of DE taught in the high school: the class was neither high school nor college but a space in between, where high-achieving college-bound students could practice college-level writing. Fourth, the liminality was furthered thanks to Ms. Elliot's use of micro-political decisions regarding course content. And fifth, racial and socioeconomic homogeneity, both at Midwest High and in DE nationwide, represents a crucial factor the field needs to consider as we evaluate, implement, partner with, and/or resist DE policies at our home institutions.

Nevertheless, the rhetorical strategies Ms. Eliot and her students relied on at Midwest High need to be put into the context of the glaring inequalities in US public education. The students at Midwest High were strong, both in their grades and their ambition for higher education. They clearly benefited from the one-on-one writing instruction by Ms. Elliot. But even for students not in DE courses at Midwest High, their experiences pale in comparison to the racially segregated city only a few miles away—which exemplifies the ways education policies such as DE cater to and disproportionately benefit white students who are already high achieving. In other words, despite CCP's claims of contributing to equity, that equity is not possible when a system purportedly designed to diminish racial and socioeconomic gaps is embedded in a system that perpetuates those gaps. DE by itself is not so much the problem; the case study of mostly positive experiences at Midwest High is a testament to that. Rather, the problem is the broader *policy regime* in which it operates. Ohio's DE policy incentivizes institutions of higher learning to forge partnerships with secondary school districts that are mostly white and high achieving, leaving many districts with majority Black and Brown students at a disadvantage in terms of educational opportunity. One of the ways our field can be most proactive when considering how and whether to forge dual enrollment partnerships is to consider the impact these policies will have on marginalized communities.

Moving forward with future DE composition research, even more questions remain: how might the ways liminality and micro-political decisions that worked so well for Ms. Elliot's students work for *all our students*? How might administrators form coalitions with teachers like Ms. Elliot and others who utilize different strategies, whether through lending expertise and/or power, observing, promoting, training, or working alongside public school districts to ensure quality instruction consistent with best practices in the field? Finally, from these answers, what new research questions might we ask about the field of writing studies and its relationship to education policies? While I do not have all these answers, I do hope that a consideration of the qualitative experience of teachers and students—those on the ground floor tasked with carrying out education policies like DE—is a good first step toward policy research in rhetoric and composition.

WORKS CITED

"About." College Credit Plus. 2022. https://www.ohiohighered.org/content/college_credit_plus_about. Accessed May 13, 2022.

Ahola, Janice, and Barry G. Lucas. "Participant Observation in Educational Research: Dynamics of Role Adjustment in a High School Setting." *McGill Journal of Education*, vol. 16, no. 1, 1981. http://mje.mcgill.ca/article/view/7382. Accessed May 13, 2022.

Annual Report: 2019–2020. College Credit Plus, Ohio Department of Education, Ohio Department of Higher Education, 2020. https://www.ohiohighered.org/sites/default/files/uploads/CCP/CCP-2020-Annual-Report_FINAL.pdf. Accessed May 20, 2022.

Annual Report: 2020–2021. College Credit Plus, Ohio Department of Education, Ohio Department of Higher Education, 2021. https://www.ohiohighered.org/sites/default/files/uploads/CCP/resources/CCP-2021-Annual-Report_FINAL_011022.pdf. Accessed July 5, 2022.

Becker, Howard S., and Blanche Geer. "Participant Observation and Interviewing: A Comparison." *Human Organization*, vol. 16, no. 3, 1957, pp. 28–32.

Blanco, Cheryl. *The Promise of Dual Enrollment: Assessing Ohio's Early College Access Policy*. Western Interstate Commission for Higher Education, 2007.

Carey, John. "College Credit Plus: Chancellor John Carey's Recommendations for Ohio's Dual Credit System." Ohio Board of Regents, University System of Ohio, 2014.

https://www.ohiohighered.org/sites/ohiohighered.org/files/uploads/board/NewCCPlusReport.pdf. Accessed May 16, 2022.

"Dual Enrollment: Participation and Characteristics." US Department of Education, 2019. https://nces.ed.gov/pubs2019/2019176.pdf. Accessed May 13, 2022.

"Fast Facts on Dual and Concurrent Enrollment." National Alliance of Concurrent Enrollment Partnerships, n.d. http://www.nacep.org/resource-center/fast-fact-on-dual-and-concurrent-enrollment. Accessed May 13, 2022.

Graff, Gerald, Cathy Birkenstein, and Russel Durst. *They Say I Say with Readings: The Moves That Matter in Academic Writing.* W. W. Norton, 2009.

Hammond, J. W., and Merideth Garcia. "The Micropolitics of Pathways: Teacher Education, Writing Assessment, and the Common Core." *Journal of Writing Assessment*, vol. 10, no. 1, 2017. http://journalofwritingassessment.org/article.php?article=114. Accessed May 13, 2022.

Lutz, Frank W., and Laurence Iannaccone. *Understanding Educational Organizations: A Field Study Approach.* C. E. Merrill, 1969.

McWain, Katie. "Finding Freedom at the Composition Threshold: Learning from the Experiences of Dual Enrollment Teachers." *Teaching English in the Two-Year College*, vol. 45, no. 4, 2018, pp. 406–424.

Miller, Trey, Holly Kosiewicz, Elaine Lin Want, Elizabeth VP Marwah, Scott Delhommer, and Lindsay Daugherty. *Dual Credit Education in Texas: Interim Report.* RAND Corporation, 2017. doi: 10.7249/RR2043.

Moreland, Casie, and Keith D. Miller. "The Triumph of Whiteness: Dual Credit Courses and Hierarchical Racism in Texas." In *Rhetorics of Whiteness: Postracial Hauntings in Popular Culture, Social Media, and Education*, edited by Tammie Kennedy, Joyce Middleton, and Krista Ratcliffe. Southern Illinois UP, 2016, pp. 182–194.

National Commission on Excellence in Education. *A Nation at Risk: The Imperative for Educational Reform.* National Commission on Excellence in Education, 1983.

Pierson, Ashley, Michelle Hodara, and Jonathan Luke. *Earning College Credits in High School: Options, Participation, and Outcomes for Oregon Students.* US Department of Education, 2017.

Post, Joanna Castner, Vicki Beard Simmons, and Stephanie Vanderslice. "Round up the Horses—the Cards Are Racing Downhill! Programmatic Catch-up to a Quickly Growing Concurrent Enrollment Program." In *College Credit for Writing in High School: The "Taking-Care-of" Business*, edited by Kristine Hansen and Christine R. Farris. NCTE, 2010, pp. 165–188.

Speroni, Cecilia. "High School Dual Enrollment Programs: Are We Fast-Tracking Students Too Fast?" National Center for Postsecondary Research Working Paper, 2011, pp. 1–72. https://ccrc.tc.columbia.edu/media/k2/attachments/dual-enrollment-fast-tracking-students-too-fast.pdf. Accessed May 13, 2022.

Turner, Victor W. "Betwixt and Between: The Liminal Period in Rites de Passage." In *Reader in Comparative Religion: An Anthropological Approach*, edited by William Armand Lessa and Evon Z. Vogt. 4th ed. Harper and Row, 1979, pp. 234–243.

"What We Know about Dual Enrollment." Community College Research Center, Teachers College, Columbia University, Feb. 2012, p. 8. https://ccrc.tc.columbia.edu/media/k2/attachments/dual-enrollment-research-overview.pdf. Accessed March 13, 2022.

Winalski, Amanda. "Bam." In *What Is "College-Level Writing,"* edited by Patrick Sullivan and Howard Tinberg. NCTE, 2011, pp. 302–308.

Zinth, Jennifer, and Elisabeth Barnett. "Rethinking Dual Enrollment to Reach More Students." Promising Practices, Education Commission of the States, May 2018, p. 13. https://files.eric.ed.gov/fulltext/ED582909.pdf. Accessed May 13, 2022.

11

CREDIT WHERE CREDIT IS DUE

Willamette Promise as an Inclusive Alternative to Dual Enrollment

Cornelia Paraskevas and Leigh Graziano

Willamette Promise (WP), a form of accelerated learning in the state of Oregon, was designed specifically as an alternative to dual enrollment (DE) models, with the goal of better serving the students those programs have historically left out. The program offers a range of more than twenty general education courses including college composition, biology, math, psychology, Spanish, and chemistry. WP is fundamentally different from other DE offerings since it is an assessment-based model that most closely resembles and follows the established principles of competency-based education (CBE) programs.[1] Similar to other CBE programs, WP is built around clear, robust, and measurable learning outcomes that align with state and national outcomes; it "reorients the educational process toward demonstrated mastery" of these outcomes, supports formative assessment, and separates mastery from the Carnegie unit (Johnstone and Soares).

The design of WP, therefore, is aimed at addressing some of the growing inequities in Oregon's K–12 education system: access to college credit courses in smaller districts or rural areas and academic achievement gaps between white students and other racial/ethnic groups. In fact, there is a significant gap in the percentage of students earning Advanced Placement/International Baccalaureate (AP/IB) credit among Asian students (72%), white students (40%), and African American students (23%) (Brey et al. 90).

WP differs considerably from other DE programs across the nation but also within Oregon. WP courses are not standalone courses; rather, they are incorporated into existing, traditional high school courses that are taught by high school teachers. Students in these courses have the opportunity to complete appropriately challenging college-level work that allows them to demonstrate competency in college-level learning outcomes; students decide whether they want the course transcripted

https://doi.org/10.7330/9781646422531.c011

after they have received their grade; and the high school courses do not need to be identical to the on-campus course in content and delivery, as DE programs typically do. Instead, the two courses (WP and the college course) must have identical learning outcomes that are met through the high school coursework and classroom activities.

From its inception, WP has focused on equity and access: specifically, WP has sought to remove some of the barriers to obtaining college credit—such as uneven college course offerings and participation by all students, inadequate numbers of qualified instructors able to teach college courses, and financial burden—to provide all high school students with the opportunity to complete college credit courses while in high school. This commitment grows out of the Oregon Equity Lens, which was adopted in 2014 by the Higher Education Coordinating Commission. The HECC asserts that equity "requires the intentional examination of systemic policies and practices that, even if they have the appearance of fairness, may in effect serve to marginalize some and perpetuate disparities" (1). As we consider the full kaleidoscope of DE in the field, a program like Willamette Promise brings us face to face with the students we can reach and the change we can create with innovative models that redress the limitations of DE, particularly those of equity and access.

HITTING THE WALL: BARRIERS TO FIRST-YEAR COMPOSITION

As many DE scholars have noted, DE often touts itself as an opportunity for all students to earn college credit, but large-scale state studies have repeatedly shown the inequities within these programs. For instance, studies have found that affluent white students and students from families in which parents hold a bachelor's degree or higher are overrepresented in these programs (Museus et al.; Friedman et al.; Moreland and Miller). Similarly, a 2011 study on DE in Texas identified two important barriers: first, limited financial resources, which are a "top hindrance" to enrolling in DE course (Friedman et al. 22), and second, the fact that DE courses are usually targeted to talented and gifted students (22%) (20). Casie Moreland and Keith D. Miller argue convincingly that rather than improving equity, the DE courses Lawrence B. Friedman and his colleagues considered actually aggravate "huge socioeconomic and racial disparities" (192).

Despite these problems, DE courses have the potential both to prepare students for higher education by exposing them to college work and to reduce their need for remediation when they get to a college campus (American Association of State Colleges and Universities;

Hughes and Golann; Hoffman et al.; Martinez and Bray). Joanna Castner Post and her colleagues note, "Significant data supports the assertion that participation in concurrent enrollment programs *does* ultimately lead to college success" (169, original emphasis). Furthermore, studies have shown that students who participate in DE programs are more likely to finish high school, are better prepared for college, and are more likely to attain a college degree (Zinth and Barnett). Given our awareness of the opportunities DE offers students, it is imperative that the field continue to address the inequity within traditional DE through innovative programs such as WP.

OPENING THE GATES: REMOVING THE BARRIERS

A consideration of barriers to success in first-year composition (FYC) goes back to Mina P. Shaughnessy's seminal 1976 essay "Diving In: An Introduction to Basic Writing." In this landmark essay, Shaughnessy introduced the field to our practices of "guarding the tower," or gatekeeping, to determine who does and does not belong in college writing classrooms. Although Shaughnessy focused largely on basic writing courses, the principles she introduced are still profoundly relevant to the field and to the DE landscape in particular. Since then, composition studies has continued to explore issues of placement, remediation, readiness, at-risk students, and the effectiveness of basic writing courses in general. In recent years, composition scholarship has grappled with the discomforting notion that an insistence on one Standard English is racist and that our grading practices themselves might reinforce structures of white privilege (Inoue). These are all issues of equity and access within college composition courses.

When it comes to discussing DE credit for college-level writing, much of the conversation returns to the very "guarding the tower" practices that Shaughnessy warned about. Arguments against DE have focused on the immaturity of the students and their readiness for college-level work (Schwalm; Schneider) and on the qualifications of DE teachers and how those qualifications (or lack thereof) may signal the rigor (or lack thereof) of the curriculum (Post et al.). Connected to this, we think, is a territoriality over who owns first-year writing and the space in which that curriculum should be delivered. The authors of this chapter—both tenured faculty in a regional university—urge stakeholders of the DE landscape to stop guarding the tower by purposefully excluding those "perceived not to belong," those, in other words, who are benefiting from programs that expand access—whether in SUNY in the early 1970s

(Moody and Bonesteel) or in DE/dual credit (DC) programs in the 2020s. Opening the gates can include providing multiple entry points for students (not simply GPA), widely distributing information about DE programs to all families, and even translating such information to the students' home languages—ensuring that DE and college courses have the same outcomes and are held to the same standards (Patrick).

The authors of this chapter also urge stakeholders of the DE landscape to embrace Shaughnessy's call of "diving in." Willamette Promise is an accelerated learning[2] opportunity that embodies this "diving in." From the beginning, WP has been grounded in social justice: "Inclusivity and meeting the needs of ethnically and economically diverse student populations" has been at the core of WP (Pierson et al. 1; Ketcham and Davis 19). WP has worked to remove barriers to first-year composition in five particular ways: (1) by broadening access to college credit for more students, (2) by including more teachers, (3) by removing financial barriers and compulsory transcription, (4) by focusing less on terminal degrees and more on experience and partnership, and (5) by rethinking writing instruction and competency.

Including More Students

It has been established that DE has a history of excluding certain populations of students. FYC is just as guilty of excluding students with placement practices that segregate students of color, second-language learners, first-generation students, and economically disadvantaged students into remedial or lower-level writing courses. This is one area in which Willamette Promise is addressing perhaps the most important inequity in our field: who is (and is not) included.

WP provides significant opportunities for historically underserved student populations—in particular, those in rural areas or small districts—to earn college credit. And since WP students represent approximately 50 percent of all Promise students, we argue that WP has contributed significantly to equity and access.[3] When we look at the demographics of the students we serve, in the forty-three WP school district high schools, 14 percent are students with disabilities, 29 percent are English learners, 30 percent are Hispanic students, 9 percent are students of color, and 47 percent are eligible for free and reduced meals (Ketcham and Davis 13).

It's not just that WP provides opportunities to students and districts to earn college credit. Accessing those credits also gives students access to college. Our data show that "consistently, WP students continue their education after high school at a higher rate than the state average. In 2015–16 the state average was 59.4% compared to 63% of WP graduates" (Ketcham and Davis 16). HECC's analysis of WP students' college readiness reveals that "WP are no worse off academically than the overall entering freshman class . . . WP Freshmen at OSU [Oregon State University] had a 3.23 GPA while the overall OSU freshmen comparison GPA was 3.05. This pattern holds true for WP students who attended U of O [the University of Oregon] (3.11 vs. 2.95) and Oregon Tech (3.22 vs. 2.92)" (18). Programs like WP, which break the mold of typical DE models by expanding access to an increasingly diverse population of students, welcome in those who too often are left outside the gates, thus realizing DE's goal of creating a college-going culture among underrepresented populations.

More Teachers Means More Access

One of the barriers to access identified by the Accelerated Learning Committee (a committee established in 2013 by the Oregon Legislature) was "inadequate numbers of qualified instructors able to teach college courses in highschools [*sic*]," with "qualifications" defined as a master's degree (Ketcham and Davis 2). The committee recommended that postsecondary institutions consider other qualifications that could be equivalent to the master's degree in the content area (Oregon Legislature 13).

WP teachers are selected based on experience rather than degree attainment[4] because that approach allows us to maximize access, but we also work with teachers in quarterly all-day professional learning communities (PLCs). These events are structured not as lectures—where we bestow upon our subordinates training in college-level writing pedagogy—but rather as collaborative opportunities where we can *all* share our expertise. High school teachers get additional training in writing theory, but we also benefit from learning about their pedagogical needs and the strategies they've developed over the years to meet them. Inviting teacher presentations and contributions at PLCs has been critical to the success of our partnership and has minimized the assumption that we are the sole experts. As Peter Kittle explains, "Without being able to establish the kinds of professional relationships that are predicated on mutual respect for teaching abilities, subject matter knowledge, and academic values, any ideas being propounded by college writing teachers will be seen as just another mandate from above" (143).

Our professional relationship with the teachers extends to the resources available to them: as Christine Denecker has noted, "the most powerful element for moving students from point A to point B [may lie] with those who carry out dual enrollment composition instruction" (31). To ensure that there is no mismatch between the WP and Western Oregon University (WOU) expectations and pedagogical practices, we have created an online teachers' guide for all teachers to use; it contains a number of accessible composition theory articles, pedagogical scaffolds that we often use in our FYC courses, and sample student texts from past WP students. There are also several resources that were created by the high school teachers themselves.

Working collaboratively to develop the program helps mitigate the "tensions and inconsistencies between secondary and postsecondary writing instruction" (Denecker 29). As frustrated as college faculty get by the preparation of their students, we often don't clearly define what we expect students to know by the time they get to college. Our professional development space has provided a forum where high school and college faculty can discuss expectations, writing theory and practice, and challenges of teaching within the boundaries of our curricular demands. In this way, we build consistency in our values together, and that translates to what gets taught in the classroom. Building these relationships with our high school colleagues is one way to further the social justice work of our program. Their experiences teaching these students help us refine the program to better meet their needs and, in turn, also help us rethink how our on-campus courses can better serve a diverse student body.

The collaborative nature of the PLC and the resources developed ultimately support all students. Regardless of whether they choose to accept their WP credits or earn WP credits at all, they benefit from the improvements in the instruction of writing in high school and the ease of transition into college writing.

Low Cost and Risk Free

In addition to the student population WP serves, the mechanisms of our program are designed to address some of the barriers that typically prevent marginalized students from participating. First, the cost per year for all credits is $30, which is substantially cheaper than other DE programs. AP tests run between $60 and $90 per test, and some dual-credit classes cost $100 or more. In all other accelerated learning models available in Oregon, students are required to register and pay for the course in the beginning of the term and have the grade they earn transcripted—even if it is a failing grade. WP students do not register or pay until they have seen the grade that will be transcripted; they can decide, in other words, if they want to continue their college careers with accelerated learning grades lower than an "A." According to a November 2017 letter to the Higher Education Coordinating Commission, "Students and schools see significant value in the practice and in growing evidence that it narrows the equity gap" (Willamette). In fact, this risk-free approach encourages more students to attempt college credit.

Only passing portfolios (grade "C" or better) are uploaded to the system for transcription. If a student completes all the work and the teacher finds it doesn't meet the minimum threshold, then the student doesn't earn college credit or pay a fee. Likewise, the failing grade will not appear on their transcript. This risk-free practice, which is not altogether different from directed self-placement or informed self-placement, as Pamela Bedore and Deborah Rossen-Knill call it, is one way to strengthen a college-going culture, since it encourages more students to envision college in their future. When students choose their grade, they take responsibility and ownership of their writing placement. They can "learn from the past to make decisions about the future" (Blakesley 29). The act of providing students with agency, as David Blakesley argues, is what brings us closer to the goal of higher education: preparing citizens who are capable of taking deliberate action because they can also reflect on their past. Students know whether they are ready to proceed to the next course or should retake it on a college campus. This practice is one that empowers students.

Because this option is not available to college students, it could be argued that the WP course is not truly equivalent to the college course. We respectfully disagree with this position. Instead—and considering the purpose of WP—this option removes the uncertainty of receiving college credit, which is another barrier for a number of students. The policy is grounded in equity and access, in allowing students to pursue college credit without the burden of a large financial investment. We would challenge the claim that allowing students to choose whether to transcript their course undermines its validity as a "true" college course. Like most CBE programs, WP courses are designed to be more student-centered. Allowing students to choose for themselves whether they want to pay a small fee to have their credits transcripted promotes their individual agency over their learning. If this means that WP courses are not equivalent to a college course, then the flaw is with the college course.

Shifting Our Values: Competency over Seat Time

Similar to all competency-based programs, Willamette Promise abandons consideration of credit hours entirely, instead using a portfolio to directly assess students' learning on the basis of their ability to demonstrate mastery of the outcomes of the course through measurable competencies. Since WP does not operate based on seat time but instead on competency, students have more flexibility with how much time they spend on the WP portfolios.

Nationwide, however, some DE programs operate using time-based systems (most commonly referred to as seat time), like most of higher education. Time-based systems produce inequities and are not reflective of the highly individualized nature of learning. According to C. H. Farrington and Margaret H. Small:

> Under this traditional [seat time] model, a small proportion of students in urban schools do well, but significant numbers fail to graduate, and the majority of those who do are inadequately prepared for college or the workplace . . . But even in a well-resourced classroom with a highly qualified teacher in a caring and challenging school environment, a heterogeneous group of students will be stratified in their achievement when learning time is held constant. Those who demonstrate achievement above a bare minimum level will be awarded course credit at the rate of one Carnegie unit per 120 hours of seat time, whether or not they have mastered requisite skills and content knowledge. (29)

Time alone is not a good measure of learning, and when students fail, they are disincentivized to continue learning given the looming amount of seat time ahead of them.

The availability of proficiency-based accelerated learning options, such as WP, provides additional pathways to graduation and other ways of reaching districts where students struggle to demonstrate what they've learned, given the constraints of the time-based system. As Rebecca Klein-Collins argues, "Credit hours do not inherently convey the amount of student learning that has taken place" while "competencies, on the other hand, are seen as having inherent meaning or object value" (9). Learning outcomes aligned with measurable competencies allow, as Peter Ewell argues, "such goals [to] describe not only what is to be learned but also the specific levels of performance that students are expected to master" (6). Direct assessment is not altogether different from the Advanced Placement Exam or the College-Level Examination Program Exam or on-campus placement tests in math or writing. All are designed to allow students to demonstrate mastery of or competency in the learning material, and all are separate from considerations of seat time.

Specifically, WP students submit a portfolio of work (the average portfolio is approximately forty pages in length) to demonstrate mastery of the college-level learning outcomes at certain competency benchmarks. The same cut score (a grade of C) separates the competent from the not yet competent for the on-campus courses at both WOU and WP. The rubrics used align with the learning outcomes of both the WP course and the WOU campus course—but are also aligned with the WPA standards on writing. Because the WP curriculum is integrated into the high school classroom, there is also much more flexibility in the pace at which students can move through the process, allowing more students to have a realistic chance of success. In fact, flexibility is an important principle in CBE programs.

MOVING FORWARD

Equity and access are values that must be at the heart of curricular initiatives in composition studies. Willamette Promise is designed with these values at the core. Our data indicate that we are spreading access to college courses to disadvantaged districts and to students of diverse racial, cultural, and socioeconomic backgrounds. Our practice of allowing students to choose whether to pay for their credits ensures that they have a risk-free way to try out a college course. Even if they choose not to take the credits, they still benefit from exposure to the college curriculum and the experience of knowing that they can do the work. This is invaluable.

Furthermore, this program speaks to a core value implicit in the Conference on College Composition and Communication's (CCCC's) "CCCC Statement on Preparing Teachers of College Writing." In the section on instructors in DE/DC programs, the statement recommends graduate coursework on and experience working with at-risk student populations. This speaks to a growing commitment, not just from the CCCC but from the National Alliance of Concurrent Enrollment Partnerships (NACEP) as well, to improve dual-credit opportunities for all students, especially those historically left out. It is exactly this population of students that Willamette Promise was designed to serve. We see this program as a powerful alternative to traditional DE, one grounded in social justice and one that challenges composition studies to consider new ways these programs could function. We posit that educators at all levels along with writing program administrators need to more carefully consider the social justice work DE programs can perform and the ways they can rectify some of the disparities within our educational system. That is work worth continuing.

NOTES

1. Competency-based education (also known as proficiency-based) can trace its roots back to the 1980s and outcomes-based reform philosophies. The focus is on the outcomes students are expected to demonstrate to achieve proficiency.
2. The term used in Oregon for the different options students have to earn college credit.
3. In Oregon, various accelerated learning (i.e., DE/DC) programs use the title "Promise"; they originally developed with grants replicating the Eastern Promise initiative—the first DC/DE program that was proficiency-based and collaboratively developed between various school districts and institutions of higher education.
4. 86 percent of participating teachers have a master's or doctoral degree and 7 percent have graduate credits.

WORKS CITED

American Association of State Colleges and Universities. "The Open Door: Assessing the Promise and Problems of Dual Enrollment." *AASCU State Policy Briefing*, vol. 1, no. 1, 2002, pp. 1–10.

Bedore, Pamela, and Deborah F. Rossen-Knill. "Informed Self-Placement: Is a Choice Offered a Choice Received." *WPA: Writing Program Administration*, vol. 28, no. 1–2, 2004, pp. 55–78.

Blakesley, David. "Directed Self-Placement in the University." *WPA: Writing Program Administration*, vol. 25, 2002, pp. 9–39.

Brey, Cristobal, Lauren Musu, Joel McFarland, Sidney Wilkinson-Flicker, Melissa Diliberti, Anlan Zhang, Claire Branstetter, and Xiaolei Wang. "Status and Trends in the Education of Racial and Ethnic Groups." *National Center for Education Statisics, US Dept. of Education*, 2019. https://nces.ed.gov/pubs2019/2019038.pdf. Accessed May 14, 2022.

Conference on College Composition and Communication (CCCC). "CCCC Statement on Preparing Teachers of College Writing." *NCTE*, 2015. www.ncte.org/cccc/resources/positions/statementonprep. Accessed May 14, 2022.

Denecker, Christine. "Transitioning Writers across the Composition Threshold: What We Can Learn from Dual Enrollment Partnerships." *Composition Studies*, vol. 41, no. 1, 2013, pp. 27–50.

Ewell, Peter T. "Accreditation and Student Learning Outcomes: A Proposed Point of Departure." National Center for Higher Education Management Systems, Council for Higher Education Accreditation Occasional Paper, Sept. 2001, pp. 1–25.

Farrington, C. H., and Margaret H. Small. "Removing Structural Barriers to Academic Achievement in High Schools: An Innovative Model." American Educational Research Association Annual Meeting, 2006.

Friedman, Lawrence B., Lisa Hoogstra, Andrew Swanlund, Shazia R. Miller, Manyee Wong, Daniel O'Brien, and Natalie Tucker. "Research Study of Texas Dual Credit Programs and Courses." American Institutes for Research, March 2011, pp. 1–80. https://www.air.org/sites/default/files/2021-06/TX_Dual_Credit_Report_with_appendices_FINAL_ADA_Checked_031711_0.pdf. Accessed May 14, 2022.

Hoffman, Nancy, Joel Vargas, and Janet Santos. "New Directions for Dual Enrollment: Creating Stronger Pathways from High School through College." *New Directions for Community Colleges*, vol. 145, 2009, pp. 43–58.

Hughes, Katherine L., and Joanne Wang Golann. "Dual Enrollment Policies and Practices: Earning College Credit in California High Schools." Community College Research Center, Teachers College, Columbia University, Aug. 2008, pp. 1–22.

Inoue, Asao B. *Antiracist Writing Assessment Ecologies: Teaching and Assessing Writing for a Socially Just Future.* WAC Clearinghouse, 2015.
Johnstone, Sally, and L. Soares. "Principles for Developing Competency-Based Education Programs." *Change: The Magazine of Higher Learning,* vol. 46, no. 2, 2014, pp. 12–19.
Ketcham, Pat, and Cheryl Davis. "Willamette Promise 3-Year Report: 2014–15, 2015–16, and 2016–17." Center for Education Innovation, Evaluation, and Research, Willamette Service District. Apr. 26, 2018. https://www.wesd.org/cms/lib/OR01915639/Centricity/Domain/111/WP%203%20Year%20Report%20-%20Final%204-18-18.pdf. Accessed May 17, 2022.
Kittle, Peter. "It's Not the High School Teachers' Fault: An Alternative to the Blame Game." In *What Is College-Level Writing,* edited by Patrick Sullivan and Howard Tinberg. NCTE, 2006, pp. 134–145.
Klein-Collins, Rebecca. "Competency-Based Degree Programs in the US: Postsecondary Credentials for Measurable Student Learning and Performance." Council for Adult and Experiential Learning, 2012.
Martinez, Monica, and Judy Bray. *All over the Map: State Policies to Improve the High School.* National Alliance for the American High School, c/o Institute for Educational Leadership, 2002.
Moody, Patricia A., and Margaret D. Bonesteel. "Syracuse University Project Advance: A Model of Connection and Quality." In *College Credit for Writing in High School: The "Taking Care of" Business,* edited by Kristine Hansen and Christine R. Farris. NCTE, 2010, pp. 227–245.
Moreland, Casie, and Keith D. Miller. "The Triumph of Whiteness: Dual Credit Courses and Hierarchical Racism in Texas." In *Haunting Whiteness: Rhetorics of Whiteness in a "Post-Racial" Era,* edited by Tammie Kennedy, Joyce Middleton, and Krista Ratcliffe. Southern Illinois UP, 2016, pp. 182–194.
Museus, Samuel D., Brenda R. Lutovsky, and Carol L. Colbeck. "Access and Equity in Dual Enrollment Programs: Implications for Policy Formation." *Higher Education in Review,* vol. 4, 2007, pp. 1–19.
Oregon Equity Lens. Higher Education Coordinating Commission, Chief Education Office, Oregon Educational Investment Board, 2018. https://www.oregon.gov/highered/about/Documents/Commission/COMMISSION/2017/08-August-9-10/4.0d%20Equity%20Lens-reformat.pdf. Accessed May 14, 2022.
Oregon Legislature SB 222 Legislative Report. https://www.oregonlegislature.gov/citizen_engagement/Reports/ALCLegReport11_1_14.pdf. Accessed May 14, 2022.
Patrick, Kayla. "6 Ways to Make Dual Enrollment Programs Equitable." May 23, 2019. https://edtrust.org/the-equity-line/6-ways-to-make-dual-enrollment-programs-equitable/. Accessed May 14, 2022.
Pierson, Ashley, Michelle Hodara, and Jonathan Luke. "Earning College Credits in High School: Options, Participation, and Outcomes for Oregon Students." REL 2017–216, 2017.
Post, Joanna Castner, Vicki Beard Simmons, and Stephanie Vanderslice. "Round up the Horses, the Cards Are Racing Downhill! Programmatic Catch-up to a Quickly Growing Concurrent Enrollment Program." In *College Credit for Writing in High School: The "Taking-Care-of" Business,* edited by Kristine Hansen and Christine R. Farris. NCTE, 2010, pp. 165–188.
Schneider, Barbara. "Early College High Schools: Double-Time." In *College Credit for Writing in High School: The "Taking Care of" Business,* edited by Kristine Hansen and Christine R. Farris. NCTE, 2010, pp. 141–164.
Schwalm, David E. "High School–College Dual Enrollment." *WPA: Writing Program Administration,* vol. 12, no. 1–2, 1991, pp. 51–54.
Shaughnessy, Mina P. "Diving In: An Introduction to Basic Writing." *College Composition and Communication,* vol. 27, no. 3, 1976, pp. 234–239.

Willamette Promise Advisory Board. Letter. Nov. 7, 2017. https://www.oregon.gov/highered/about/Documents/Commission/COMMISSION/2017/12-Dec-14-17/10.1b%20Letter%20from%20Willamettte%20Promise%20to%20HECC.PDF. Accessed May 20, 2022.
Zinth, Jennifer, and Elisabeth Barnett. "Promising Practices: Rethinking Dual Enrollment to Reach More Students." Education Commission of the States, May 2018.

SECTION FOUR

Perspectives of Student Success

DE FYC for All?

12

DIRECT ASSESSMENT OF STUDENT LEARNING IN THE EASTERN PROMISE

Nancy Knowles

Scholarship on dual enrollment (DE) often relies on indirect longitudinal program assessment to suggest that DE coursework engages high school students in challenging intellectual activity, reduces college costs for families, welcomes first-generation college families into higher education, encourages high school and college faculty to collaborate, and cements the pipeline from secondary enrollment to postsecondary graduation demanded by taxpayers, legislators, and the US economy. If students matriculate to and remain enrolled in college, their success appears to indicate DE program success.[1] While longitudinal research is fundamental to a general understanding of DE program quality, relying solely on such research risks conflating correlation with causality: just because DE and strong graduation rates occur together does not necessarily indicate that DE *causes* those rates. Moreover, longitudinal data, relying on aggregates from large data sets across different kinds of courses, may fail to assess whether students actually meet specific course outcomes. Thus, understanding program quality requires DE programs to triangulate longitudinal data with direct assessment of student work samples to demonstrate what students actually know and can do. In the field of first-year composition (FYC), direct assessment is difficult because writing is a process as well as a product. Unlike disciplinary knowledge that can be assessed directly through multiple-choice tests, authentic writing assessment requires review of work samples, a time-consuming effort. Yet claims about student success in DE FYC cannot be supported without this direct assessment.

From 2012 through 2016, the Eastern Promise Language Arts Professional Learning Community (EPLAPLC) at Eastern Oregon University (EOU) in La Grande, Oregon, employed direct assessment to evaluate FYC (Writing 121: Expository Prose Writing), resulting in data that challenged typical DE success narratives. During these four years,

https://doi.org/10.7330/9781646422531.c012

the EPLAPLC scored 734 student portfolios from nineteen districts, and approximately 50 percent of participating students earned passing scores. The difference between success narratives in scholarship arising from indirect assessments and the partial success evident in the EPLAPLC passing rate inspired deeper scrutiny of factors contributing to student success. EPLAPLC research suggests that institutions administering DE FYC programs cannot assume that teacher qualifications and ongoing professional development alone ensure alignment between instructional practices and student learning. Instead, institutions must allocate resources to direct assessment of student writing; based on the results of that assessment, if DE FYC remains viable, institutions must support supervising faculty in inquiring into barriers to student success that include not only teacher qualifications but also student preparedness and the secondary context. The following discussion presents the EPLAPLC and its portfolio process, analyzes the successes and challenges of this program, and makes related recommendations about improving DE FYC.

EASTERN PROMISE LANGUAGE ARTS PLC (EPLAPLC)

Eastern Promise began in 2011 as a partnership among EOU, Blue Mountain Community College, Treasure Valley Community College, the Intermountain Educational Services District, and individual school districts. The goal was to enhance college-going culture in rural eastern Oregon, partly by making Sponsored Dual Credit available to students who might not have access to a college campus or to high school teachers with the degree qualifications needed to offer other forms of college credit. Scholarship suggests that the best model of DE FYC for support of student learning is inviting high school students to the college campus where they can learn from college faculty alongside fully enrolled college students in a challenging college-level context (Klopfenstein and Lively 62). Because this model is often impractical, much of DE FYC in Oregon is taught in the high schools. In general, in alignment with national standards such as those of the National Alliance of Concurrent Enrollment Partnerships (NACEP), Oregon expects a master's degree in the discipline as minimum qualification for teaching college credit–bearing courses. However, the category of Sponsored Dual Credit recognizes that rural regions may face inequitable barriers to DE credit, so it permits college faculty to partner with under-qualified high school teachers to offer college credit (HECC). The Eastern Promise model employs a professional learning community (PLC) composed of secondary and college faculty to support under-qualified high school teachers in offering courses designed and monitored by college faculty. Similar to other DE programs, Eastern Promise has generated longitudinal data indicating success in high school completion and college enrollment and retention.

The Eastern Promise Language Arts PLC convened for the first time in May 2012 and met quarterly during the academic year to support secondary teachers in offering Writing 121: Expository Prose Writing, the first course in a three-term FYC sequence consistent across most public colleges in Oregon. High school teachers involved in the EPLAPLC represented a variety of districts—some large, with 1,000 students, and some so small that the language arts teacher taught all students from sixth grade up. Because this rural variety of scale meant districts had differing calendars and instructional capacities, shared FYC content was blended into the language arts curriculum as best suited local classrooms, with some districts focusing on FYC during a single semester and others meshing FYC with literature content across a year-long course. Registration occurred in spring term, which permitted all districts to complete required work and allowed Eastern Promise students an opportunity to withdraw from the course without responsibility for a grade, similar to other college students. Almost all secondary teachers involved had a master's degree in teaching but not in the discipline of English. Many had been teacher-leaders in EOU's National Writing Project site. At the initial meeting, participants developed course outcomes based on the national (Council of Writing Program Administrators) and state (Oregon Writing and English Advisory Committee) outcomes. At subsequent meetings, participants addressed administrative issues, met with library faculty, and exchanged syllabi, assignments, and instructional strategies.

METHODOLOGY: EPLAPLC PORTFOLIO

To ensure that students taught by under-qualified secondary teachers met course outcomes and as part of ongoing professional development for participating teachers, the EPLAPLC used a portfolio as an authentic direct end assessment.[2] Western Oregon University's DE program scores 20 percent of portfolios for program assessment (Terriere 93). To my knowledge, this is the only other portfolio process in Oregon.[3]

Each portfolio included a research-based argumentative paper, a draft of that paper, a timed writing sample, and a reflective essay. These documents represented the "tip of the iceberg," as significantly more writing was expected in the course overall. The portfolio was scored using a rubric with a five-point scale keyed to course outcomes (appendix 12.A). Students submitted portfolios electronically using the learning management system of one of the colleges involved, and EPLAPLC members scored them online. Each portfolio was scored by at least two EPLAPLC members, with a third scoring to resolve different decisions regarding passing. Portfolios were assigned mostly randomly, with an eye to pairing inexperienced and experienced readers. Inter-rater reliability was tracked by identifying the number of portfolios of the total where scores were within one point of each other, indicating a relatively consistent score. Teachers did not score their own students' portfolios. All readers were asked to spot-check integration of sources.

The portfolio score determined whether the student could pass FYC, and the high school teacher then determined the grade based on the student's performance in the course overall. After the first year, the EPLAPLC was better able to schedule the portfolio so that students could get a sense of their score and revise and resubmit as needed or withdraw from the college course.

ANALYSIS OF EPLAPLC DATA

As mentioned previously, from 2012 through 2016, the EPLAPLC collected and scored 734 student portfolios from nineteen districts to evaluate student work in FYC (Writing 121 Expository Prose Writing) (see table 12.1). Approximately 50 percent of participating students earned passing grades.

Successes

College-Level Skills

The average 50 percent passing rate is partly a success in that half of the participating students had the skills necessary to produce college-level documents.

Elimination of Patchwork Plagiarism

An additional success occurred in the EPLAPLC response to significant patchwork plagiarism in 2013. Half of the failures that first year (a quarter of the total portfolios) resulted from patchwork plagiarism, where students copied and pasted entire chunks of language from their sources into their writing without quotation marks and/or citation, a behavior most secondary teachers did not realize was happening. Being

Table 12.1. Eastern Promise Language Arts PLC WR 121 Data

	2013	*2014*	*2015*	*2016*
Number of schools	9	14	14	9
Number of portfolios	110	222	264	138
Passing rate	53%	61%	47%	35%
Failures due to patchwork plagiarism	25%	< 1%	1%	0
Failures due to ethical use of sources	—	—	14%	23%
Inter-rater reliability	86%	84%	87%	88%

confronted with this gap in instruction during a high-stakes assessment caused secondary teachers anxiety, but they responded by eliminating patchwork plagiarism from student portfolios almost completely thereafter, a significant accomplishment.

Inter-Rater Reliability

Another strength of the group was inter-rater reliability, which consistently hovered above 80 percent. Reliability indicated that scorers, whether secondary or postsecondary, shared a similar understanding of expectations, which protected the rigor of those expectations. The process of scoring portfolios likely supported the reliability of the scores by exposing secondary teachers to the quality of work in peer classrooms.

Secondary-Postsecondary Collaboration

Another success was the partnership itself. Secondary and postsecondary faculty brought significant expertise to the table and were willing, again and again, to address the challenges of the work.[4] Teacher dialogue supported improved practice not only in the FYC courses taught by the twenty or so teachers involved but also in other courses, where teachers attempted to better articulate into and beyond WR 121—what Donald H. Dutkowsky, Jerry M. Evensky, and Gerald W. Edmonds call "spillover effects" (246)—and through dialogue with peers in our respective institutions, which included enhancing the articulation and scaffolding in the language arts curriculum from ninth (and in some cases sixth) grade up, encouraging collaboration on research assignments between secondary language arts classrooms and other secondary disciplines, and improving the preparation of college writing instructors to receive students matriculating from high school to college. EPLAPLC members were supported by Eastern Promise leaders, who stood behind the group's problem solving and insistence on quality, despite the low passing rate. The EPLAPLC also benefited from the support of college library faculty and registrars.

Challenges

Despite successes, the 50 percent pass rate was also a 50 percent fail rate—shocking for high school students, parents, and teachers used to students passing and for postsecondary institutions known for supporting access to college for at-risk student populations. Some failures, of course, do occur in FYC courses: typically at EOU around 10 percent fail WR 121 and 25 percent fail WR 115 Introduction to College Writing, the college course for under-prepared students that precedes WR 121. Although the EPLAPLC succeeded in eliminating most patchwork plagiarism from student portfolios in the span of one year, the failures in EPLAPLC WR 121 resulted primarily from unsupported generalizations and integration of sources. The failure rate might be attributed to a number of factors related to teacher and student preparedness and the high school context.

Lack of Disciplinary Expertise

The high inter-rater reliability in portfolio scoring indicates that secondary teachers scored relatively consistently with college faculty and were good at catching problems in student portfolios generated in other teachers' classrooms, but they were often unprepared for problems the portfolio process uncovered in their own students' writing, as teacher comments on the rough drafts submitted with the portfolios sometimes indicated. This issue may occur in any classroom where teachers work closely with students, but it also may have resulted from secondary teachers' lack of master's degrees in the discipline of English, the minimum qualification usually expected of college-level instructors. FYC teachers, regardless of level, need background in composition as "a subject of study" rather than merely as an activity (Adler-Kassner and Wardle 15), as well as a connection to the ongoing dialogue in the discipline so their instruction is not just a set of practical activities reorganized and redeployed each term but a framework informed and modified by current theory in the field as part of reflective practice (Carillo).[5] A teacher who knows the current theory is better able to make decisions about which activities to implement and in which order as well as how to problem-solve issues that arise each time real students attempt the assignments that look good on paper. While EPLAPLC teachers participated in professional development, they did not do so as composition scholars but as teachers seeking practical strategies for classroom application. A better approach might have been to pair practical strategies with theory, reflection, and teacher research—as might have occurred in graduate-level composition coursework—or, better yet, to support secondary teachers in seeking advanced degrees in rhetoric and composition.

Writing Disconnected from Scholarship

The high school context in which students are taught by teaching specialists rather than disciplinary scholars may also impede student motivation because students may experience writing as busywork rather than as authentically grounded in scholarly dialogue. As Mariolina Rizzi Salvatori argues about her own instructional practices, strategies cannot be abstracted from "the theoretical framework" in which they make sense (446; see also Carillo 131). FYC benefits from the university context where students learn to establish their own voices as scholars in training. Treating writing as part of scholarship is especially difficult in contexts where scholarly writing is practiced only in the language arts classroom. As the 2014 survey of EPLAPLC members indicated, college-level research was not addressed in other courses, which meant that the college-level integration and citation requirements expected in WR 121 came across to students as exceptional rather than as a normal component of scholarly discourse.

Placement

Some of the portfolio failure might also be attributed to EPLAPLC issues with placement into FYC, among other structural issues. NACEP Student Standard 3 (S3) requires that students "meet the course prerequisites," which can be demonstrated by placement, and EOU policy requires that students enroll in English and math courses as dictated by placement. However, because placement software was not initially available at a distance, EPLAPLC secondary teachers were responsible for identifying eligible students, only to have assessments sometimes compromised by the district's need to fill seats efficiently. Then, when the EPLAPLC moved to using EOU's ACCUPLACER software to place students, the institution maxed out the number of assessments available. Eventually, placement became linked to Common Core Smarter Balanced assessments (and ironically, some districts wanted students to take FYC *before* taking eleventh grade Smarter Balanced assessments to improve test scores). As a result of the lack of a good way to handle placement, the EPLAPLC read and failed more portfolios than should have been submitted.

Portfolio Process

Another structural issue was the portfolio process itself. Portfolios are cumbersome and time-consuming to prepare and score, and although most EPLAPLC secondary teachers did not meet minimum qualifications to offer college credit, they resented being asked to engage in this process when college teachers were not. Although the EPLAPLC explored integrating college portfolios into the process, the schedule for the portfolio did not map well onto the college calendar. In addition, stakeholders were frustrated by the fact that the portfolio represented only a portion of the work students completed and, given the difficulty of the research paper, may not have indicated all the skills students possessed. However, in reviewing the process each year, EPLAPLC members were not willing to use a less authentic assessment mechanism or to part with key components of the existing portfolio.

Local Student Support Services

Other structural features common to the educational context in which Eastern Promise FYC occurred came to light as part of a survey of EPLAPLC members conducted in 2014. Among the structural problems identified were lack of peer tutoring, access to college-level databases, access to computer labs, and qualified K–12 library professionals. Only three of sixteen districts involved in the survey had qualified library professionals to support their work, and one individual was often shared by an entire district. These survey results indicate that high school contexts are not necessarily equivalent to college contexts and that offering college courses in such contexts necessitates additional supports for students, such as bringing students to the college library or inviting college librarians to the high school, both of which the EPLAPLC did.

Enrollments Exceeding Caps

An ongoing structural problem in larger high school contexts was enrollments exceeding EOU enrollment caps of twenty-five students, already higher than the twenty recommended by national standards (NCTE "More"). While an additional five or ten students in a class that relies on multiple-choice testing might be permissible, the addition of as many as fifteen students above the course cap made teacher response to drafts nearly impossible. In addition, some of the big courses included multiple levels of learners, requiring teachers to differentiate activities for FYC students from those for other language arts students. When teachers communicated with their district administrators regarding the excess enrollment problem using research regarding best practices, their concerns were not addressed by those administrators, who perhaps had few course options for students.

Lack of Academic Freedom

Like workload, academic freedom appears as a barrier to rigor, as demonstrated in Katie McWain's research findings, which were echoed in the experience of one EPLAPLC high school teacher who was an asset in the DE landscape, having taught previously at the college level. She was put on administrative leave for asking students to analyze lyrics of a popular song occasionally used by college teachers in 100-level college coursework. Despite documents governing the relationship between school districts and college-level academic freedom and content, the district replaced that qualified teacher with a substitute for the remainder of the school year, thereby diminishing the quality of instruction.

Stress

These environmental constraints put pressure not only on the quality of student work but also on the efficacy and health of high school teachers. For example, many stakeholders in the high school environment expect students to pass, sometimes in flagrant disregard for state standards and teacher requirements. When EPLAPLC secondary teachers attempted to help high school students navigate a college-level course in which failure is possible, they risked spending additional time only to have students ignore their assistance, fail, and complain, with parents in tow. Add this kind of interaction to the problems with academic freedom and course caps and put the teacher in a situation where college-level instruction is a job requirement even though the teacher is underqualified, and the resulting vulnerability and stress can (and did) drive highly qualified teachers out of the profession.

Lack of Maturity

The relative consistency of student failure across all but a few EPLAPLC WR 121 sections indicates that in addition to common structural problems, there may be other common factors at work, one being student maturity.[6] In finding "no significant differences" in the skills of students entering college with or without the various forms of DE FYC and suggesting maturity as a factor, Kristine Hansen and her colleagues found that the quality of student work samples hovered in the middle of the scoring rubric, including problems with evidence, counter-arguments, and documentation (72–76). These results align with EPLAPLC findings that student maturity may influence reasoning and audience awareness, which are related to the most significant causes of EPLAPLC portfolio failure—including unsupported generalizations, unethical integration of sources, and an intolerant tone, all of which may arise from failure to understand an audience's needs.

RECOMMENDATIONS

Based on four years of EPLAPLC work, it seems pertinent to echo recommendations that already appear in the NACEP Standards: DE FYC programs must be supervised by adequately compensated college faculty who are scholars in the discipline of English studies and must involve secondary-postsecondary teacher talk, and teachers of DE FYC must maintain routine connection to the discipline of composition to understand the ever-evolving philosophies and research that inform discipline-based instruction. The remaining recommendations represent additions to the scholarship:

1. *DE FYC programs must include authentic student work samples in program* **assessment** *to ascertain whether outcomes are met.* While NACEP Standard Evaluation 2[7] is not specific about type of assessment, longitudinal assessment cannot substitute for authentic direct assessment.
2. *DE FYC programs must address the difference between secondary and post-secondary* **educational contexts**. To deliver on the NACEP expectation of consistency and equivalency, DE FYC programs should invest in access to qualified librarians and college databases, require equivalent class sizes, and infuse writing as scholarly activity and research-based argumentation across disciplines so that FYC strategies can be applied outside and mirrored back onto the language arts classroom. Common Core expectations may already be moving in this direction.
3. *DE FYC programs must address the developmental* **maturity** *of high school students.* While the three months between high school graduation and traditional matriculation to college may not confer maturity, the shift away from a familiar community to a college environment may spur growth and critical thinking. If DE FYC is to operate in the secondary context, program leaders and faculty must identify and implement strategies that enhance reasoning skills by helping students encounter diverse ideas outside those espoused by their home communities and by applying research-based argumentation across disciplines.
4. *DE FYC programs must continue to invest in* **innovation** *in course delivery.* If talented students cannot enroll for credit on a college campus or receive an equivalent education delivered at the high school, there may yet be other models that support access to college-level instruction. For example, one model that Eastern Promise has considered offering is blending an online college course with support from the high school teacher. While online learning is not optimal for building foundational

reading and writing skills among potentially under-prepared students, the online course provides college-level content and instruction in a college context where high school students can work alongside college students, interacting as peers, who can potentially reflect and reinforce development of critical thinking skills.

CONCLUSION

As of 2016, the EOU English/writing program is largely out of the business of offering DE credit for FYC. Based on four years of direct assessment of DE FYC student work samples—and in alignment with Hansen and colleagues and the NCTE's policy research brief, "First-Year Writing: What Good Does It Do?"—faculty argue that more exposure to real college composition is better than less, and we risk undermining the value of our discipline and cheating rural high school students of the learning they could have had in college by providing a substandard approximation of college coursework before students get to college. Moreover, FYC taught by composition scholars remains a "shared experience" vital to welcoming first-year students into the college context (Nicolini in Budden et al. 77).

And yet . . . rural students who are ready for college-level coursework need access to the challenge in order to advance. Some high school students can produce documents equivalent to or better than those written by first-year college students, and they should not be left, frustrated, marking time in the high school classroom. As Ben Levin argues, education should not be bound by artificial grade-level barriers (127) but instead should ensure that students continue to be productively challenged and engaged. If such students cannot access a college course taught by college faculty alongside college-level peers, districts could use the approach recommended here: hire composition specialists, treat coursework across disciplines as scholarship, stage moments where students encounter values outside their home communities, require students to transfer research-based argumentation outside FYC, invest in peer tutoring and college-level databases, ensure that FYC students have access to computer labs and qualified library professionals, maintain national enrollment caps and classrooms of single levels of learners (including direct assessment of student work samples in program assessment), and protect academic freedom. While some of these strategies would require a significant financial investment, some, particularly changes to instructional practice, could be implemented simply through administrative leadership and the cost of teacher talk.

Such curricular revision recognizes that high school contexts are not college contexts but that high schools may be able to approximate them. For students to understand FYC in particular and to competently enact the skills and knowledge the discipline provides, DE FYC needs to be embedded in and relevant to scholarly work occurring at the high school across disciplines.

NOTES

1. Many sources attest to the benefits of DE, including Allen; Edmonds and Squires; Fincher-Ford; Karp et al.; Karp and Hughes; Spurling and Gabriner; and Taylor and Pretlow.
2. While EOU requires a portfolio as end assessment for WR 115 Introduction to College Writing, the college course for under-prepared students that precedes WR 121, other on-campus FYC courses do not.
3. Oregon community colleges like Rogue and Linn-Benton use/have used timed writing as end assessments, required to pass WR 121; however, timed writing, though more efficient, is not an authentic assessment and cannot demonstrate students' ability to meet all course outcomes, which include drafting based on feedback and research.
4. For the benefits of teacher talk, see Anson; Denecker; Farris; Hansen; and Tinberg and Nadeau, for example.
5. These recommendations align with NACEP Faculty Standard 3 (F3) requiring "discipline-specific professional development" (NACEP).
6. Scholarship indicating student maturity as a factor includes Taczak and Thelin; Tinberg and Nadeau; and Ferguson, Baker, and Burnett.
7. NACEP Program Evaluation Standard E2: "The college/university conducts and reports regular and ongoing evaluations of the concurrent enrollment program effectiveness and uses the results for continuous improvement" (NACEP).

APPENDIX 12.A

EASTERN PROMISE LANGUAGE ARTS PLC
WR 121 PORTFOLIO RUBRIC

	Exemplary *5*	*Very Good* *4*	*Satisfactory* *3*	*Developing* *2*	*Unsatisfactory* *1*
1. Read/ think critically: make inferences, acknowledge multiple perspectives, recognize bias	Sophisticated inferences, acknowledgment of multiple perspectives, avoidance and/or recognition of bias	Discussion capitalizes on inferences, multiple perspectives, avoidance and/or recognition of bias	Discussion is strengthened by inferences, multiple perspectives, avoidance and/or recognition of bias	Some attempt to make inferences, acknowledge perspectives, avoid and/ or recognize bias	Faulty or little evidence of inferences, one perspective, biased or presenting biased information
2. Present clear and focused ideas/ content, including evidence, analysis, and synthesis	Clear, focused argument and content with sophisticated evidence, analysis, synthesis	Clear and focused argument and content with strong evidence, analysis, and synthesis	Clear and reasonably focused ideas/content including evidence, analysis, and synthesis	Appropriate ideas exist but are not focused or developed effectively	Trivial, simplistic, invalid, unethical, or scattered content
3. Organize ideas/content effectively	Sophisticated logical structure	Logical order, fluid transitions, single-topic paragraphs	Logical order and single-topic paragraphs	Some logical order and single-topic paragraphs	Failure of paragraph order and/or structure to present ideas clearly
4. Employ appropriate voice in addressing the audience, honoring multiple perspectives and paying attention to rhetorical concerns associated with purpose and context	Sophisticated voice, appropriate for audience, purpose, and/ or context and honoring multiple perspectives	Strong, consistent voice, appropriate for academic audience, purpose, and/or context and acknowledging multiple perspectives	Consistent voice appropriate for academic audience, purpose, and/or context	Some attempt to employ voice appropriate for audience, purpose, and/or context	Voice/content may be inappropriate for audience, purpose, and/ or context; content may not address or honor multiple perspectives

continued on next page

Appendix 12.A—*continued*

	Exemplary *5*	*Very Good* *4*	*Satisfactory* *3*	*Developing* *2*	*Unsatisfactory* *1*
5. Proofread for Standard Written English, including conventions, sentence fluency, and word choice	Evidence of sophisticated choices regarding conventions and style	Evidence of effective proofreading eliminating most error and presenting fluid, effective sentences	Evidence of effective proofreading to reduce error and strengthen style	Some attempt to proofread but still failing to address significant error patterns and/or stylistic problems	Awkward, redundant, vague, wordy, and/or simplistic language, significant error patterns
6. Integrate credible sources ethically	Evidence of sophisticated scholarly research and integration	Ethical integration, correct punctuation, and citation of scholarly	Ethical integration of sources, including scholarly	Some ethical integration of sources but lacking scholarly	No credible sources or failure to integrate or cite ethically
7. Employ writing processes including planning, revising, editing, and reflection	Evidence of sophisticated processes and reflection supporting excellence	Evidence of strong processes and reflection used effectively	Evidence of processes and reflection employed to strengthen writing	Some evidence of processes and reflection	No evidence of writing processes and/or reflection

WORKS CITED

Adler-Kassner, Linda, and Elizabeth Wardle. *Naming What We Know: Threshold Concepts of Writing Studies.* Utah State UP, 2015.

Allen, Drew. *Dual Enrollment: A Comprehensive Literature Review and Bibliography.* CUNY Collaborative Programs, Aug. 2010. https://www.cuny.edu/academics/evaluation/library/DE_LitReview_August2010.pdf. Accessed Feb. 3, 2017.

Anson, Chris. "Absentee Landlord or Owner-Tenants? Formulating Standards for Dual-Credit Composition Programs." In *College Credit for Writing in High School: The "Taking Care of" Business,* edited by Kristine Hansen and Christine R. Farris. NCTE, 2010, pp. 245–271.

Budden, Herb, Mary B. Nicolini, Stephen L. Fox, and Stuart Green. "What We Talk about When We Talk about College Writing." In *Teaching Writing in High School and College: Conversations and Collaborations,* edited by Thomas C. Thompson. NCTE, 2002, pp. 73–93.

Carillo, Ellen C. *Securing a Place for Reading Composition: The Importance of Teaching for Transfer.* Utah State UP, 2015.

Council of Writing Program Administrators. *CWPA Position Statement on Pre-College Credit for Writing.* CWPA, 2013.

Denecker, Christine. "Transitioning Writers across the Composition Threshold: What We Can Learn from Dual Enrollment Partnerships." *Composition Studies,* vol. 41, no. 1, Spring 2013, pp. 27–50. EBSCOhost. Accessed Sept. 23, 2019.

Dutkowsky, Donald H., Jerry M. Evensky, and Gerald S. Edmonds. "Economic Literacy Spillovers into the High School General Economics Course from Teaching the Advanced Economics Course: An Econometric Analysis." In *Bridging the High School–College Gap:*

The Role of Concurrent Enrollment Programs, edited by Gerald S. Edmonds and Tiffany M. Squires. Syracuse UP, 2016, pp. 246–257.

Edmonds, Gerald S., and Tiffany M. Squires, eds. *Bridging the High School–College Gap: The Role of Dual Credit Programs.* Syracuse UP, 2016.

Farris, Christine. "The Space Between: Dual-Credit Programs as Brokering, Community Building, and Professionalization." In *Delivering College Composition: The Fifth Canon*, edited by Kathleen Blake Yancey. Boynton/Cook, 2006, pp. 104–114.

Ferguson, Colin, Pete Baker, and Dana Burnett. "Faculty Members' Perceptions of Rigor in Dual Enrollment, Accelerated Programs, and Standard Community College Courses." *New Directions for Community Colleges*, no. 169, 2015, pp. 83–91.

Fincher-Ford, Margaret. *High School Students Earning College Credit: A Guide to Creating Dual-Credit Programs.* Corwin, 1997.

Hansen, Kristine. "The Composition Marketplace: Shopping for Credit versus Learning to Write." In *College Credit for Writing in High School: The "Taking Care of" Business*, edited by Kristine Hansen and Christine R. Farris. NCTE, 2010, pp. 1–39.

Hansen, Kristine, and Christine R. Farris, eds. *College Credit for Writing in High School: The "Taking Care of" Business.* NCTE, 2010.

Hansen, Kristine, Brian Jackson, Brett C. McInelly, and Dennis Eggett. "How Do Dual Credit Students Perform on College Writing Tasks after They Arrive on Campus? Empirical Data from a Large-Scale Study." *Writing Program Administration*, vol. 38, no. 2, 2015, pp. 56+. Gale Academic Onefile. Accessed Sept. 23, 2019.

Higher Education Coordinating Commission (HECC). "College Credit While in High School." *State of Oregon.* Sept. 15, 2019. https://www.oregon.gov/highered/policy-collaboration/Pages/college-credit-high-school.aspx. Accessed May 15, 2022.

Karp, Melinda Mechur, Juan Carlos Calcagno, Katherine Hughes, Dong Wook Jeong, and Thomas Bailey. "The Postsecondary Achievement of Participants in Dual Enrollment: An Analysis of Student Outcomes in Two States." Community College Research Center, Columbia University, 2007.

Karp, Melinda Mechur, and Katherine L. Hughes. "Study: Dual Enrollment Can Benefit a Broad Range of Students." *Techniques: Connecting Education and Careers*, vol. 83, no. 7, 2008, pp. 14–17.

Klopfenstein, Kristin, and Kit Lively. "Dual Enrollment in the Broader Context of College-Level High School Programs." In *Dual Enrollment: Strategies, Outcomes, and Lessons for School-College Partnerships: New Directions for Higher Education 158*, edited by Eric Hofmann and Daniel Voluch. Jossey-Bass, 2012, pp. 59–68.

Levin, Ben. *More High School Graduates: How Schools Can Save Students from Dropping Out.* Corwin, 2012.

McWain, Katie. "Finding Freedom at the Composition Threshold: Learning from the Experiences of Dual Enrollment Teachers." *TETYC*, vol. 45, no. 4, May 2018, pp. 406–424.

National Alliance of Concurrent Enrollment Partnerships (NACEP). *National Concurrent Enrollment Partnership Standards.* NACEP, May 2017. http://www.nacep.org/docs/accreditation/NACEP_Standards_2017.pdf. Accessed May 1, 2019.

National Council of Teachers of English (NCTE). "First-Year Writing: What Good Does It Do?" *NCTE*, 2013. http://mjreiff.com/uploads/3/4/2/1/34215272/nctepolicybrief.pdf. Accessed Feb. 3, 2017.

National Council of Teachers of English (NCTE). "More Than a Number: Why Class Size Matters." *NCTE Position on Class Size and Teacher Workload.* NCTE, 1999.

Oregon Writing and English Advisory Committee (OWEAC). *OWEAC Policy on Dual-Credit Programs*, May 11, 2007. https://oweac.files.wordpress.com/2007/10/oweac-policy-on-dual6-approved.pdf. Accessed Feb. 4, 2017.

Salvatori, Mariolina Rizzi. "Conversations with Texts: Reading in the Teaching of Composition." *College English*, vol. 58, no. 4, 1996, pp. 440–454.

Spurling, Steven, and Robert Gabriner. "The Effect of Dual Credit Programs upon Student Success at City College of San Francisco: Findings." City College of San Francisco, 2002. http://files.eric.ed.gov/fulltext/ED470634.pdf. Accessed Feb. 4, 2017.

Taczak, Kara, and William H. Thelin. "Re-Envisioning the Divide: The Impact of College Courses on High School Students." *TETYC*, vol. 37, no. 1, 2009, pp. 7–23.

Taylor, Jason L., and Joshua Pretlow, eds. *Dual Enrollment Policies, Pathways, and Perspectives.* New Directions for Community Colleges 169. Jossey-Bass, 2015.

Terriere, Jordan E. "When High School Teachers Teach College Writing: Oregon Approaches to Dual Credit Teacher Qualifications, Support, and Professional Development." 2015. Oregon State University, MA thesis.

Tinberg, Howard, and Jean-Paul Nadeau. "What Happens When High School Students Write in a College Course? A Study of Dual Credit." *English Journal*, vol. 102, no. 5, 2013, pp. 35–42.

13

READY TO WRITE?

A Mixed Methods Study of Dual Enrollment Composition Students' Writing Self-Efficacy and Writing Experiences

Erin D. Scott-Stewart

Dual enrollment (DE) programs are highly variable within and among the fifty states; programs differ based on class location, instructor credentials, content offered, and participant demographics (Marken et al. 3–4; Shivji and Wilson; Rivera, Kotok, and Ashby 15). Available research points to multiple benefits of participation, including increased high school (HS) graduation rates, higher HS grade point averages, greater satisfaction with HS, more opportunities to rehearse college student roles in authentic courses, increased college entry rates, higher persistence rates, and decreased time and cost to degree. In addition, findings suggest that DE has the potential to provide these benefits to marginalized students (Karp 26–27; An 120; Rivera, Kotok, and Ashby 25). However, DE composition research is an emerging field that must address the increasing proliferation of and participation in DE, writing difficulties of newly degreed workforce entrants, and increasing literacy demands of the workplace.

Recent data suggest that about one-third of US HS students are DE participants, and earlier data point to participation almost doubling, to 1.3 million students in eight years (Shivji and Wilson; Marken et al. 3; Kleiner and Lewis 7). Minimum DE participation typically involves first and sometimes second FYC courses that predominately fall under the "general education" designation. Although writing is not a mere job skill mastered once and for all in FYC (Alexander), surveyed US employers indicate that over 20 percent of "new workforce entrants with four-year [degrees] are 'deficient'" in "written communications" and "basic knowledge of writing" (Casner-Lotto and Barrington 11); also, American firms "spend . . . $3.1 billion annually to remediate employees' writing deficiencies" (Quible and Griffin 32). Moreover, research strongly suggests that professional positions will increasingly require effective, highly

https://doi.org/10.7330/9781646422531.c013

literate problem solvers (Smith et al. 381). Because multiple studies point to self-efficacy for writing (SEW) as a strong, positive predictor of writing performance, stakeholders who are aware of students' SEW and its influencers will be more equipped to generate policies and curricula that better prepare students for twenty-first-century workplace literacies (Pajares 147; Usher and Pajares 757).

The literature review grounding this study describes standard FYC curricula in Louisiana, summarizes hypothesized sources of self-efficacy (mastery experiences and social persuasion), and details studies of DE composition and undergraduates' SEW. This work examines DE students' perspectives of FYC courses to determine how the DE curricula compare to the standard FYC curricula and how the students' perceptions of curricula might influence SEW. This study also includes an analysis of students' writing performance in advanced English courses in literature; these courses were beyond FYC requirements and included topics such as fiction, poetry, and British literature.

The data analysis revealed that DE FYC course curricula frequently do *not* mirror typical FYC curriculum and despite employers' assessments of recent college graduates' writing, most students reported high SEW. Those with low SEW seemed further hindered by DE courses that lacked the curriculum necessary for building SEW and improving writing performance. For advanced English courses, data suggest an achievement gap, with Black students underperforming their peers. Overall, misaligned curriculum could be particularly problematic for students with low SEW and for disadvantaged students who are less likely to receive high-quality English language arts (ELA) instruction in K–12 (Darling-Hammond 208).

SOURCES OF SELF-EFFICACY FOR WRITING

Albert Bandura defines self-efficacy, a component of social cognitive theory, as "beliefs in one's capabilities to organize and execute the courses of action required to produce given attainments" (3). Research suggests that students with high self-efficacy set higher goals, persist through difficulties, use effective strategies, and experience lower anxiety (138). Although studies suggest that students report artificially high SEW, research still points to SEW as the strongest predictor of writing performance (Usher and Pajares 780–781; Hansen et al., "Advanced" 480). Bandura also asserts that self-efficacy changes as the result of four sources of information; two are emphasized here. Mastery experiences, or taking on challenges, are "most effective," and the level of difficulty perceived in tasks can increase or decrease self-efficacy (80). Social persuasion or feedback is also of interest. Contrary mastery experiences quickly subvert self-efficacy derived from false social persuasion, and negative social persuasion that precedes mastery experience can undermine confidence, causing individuals to quit or avoid challenges (105).

Writing Self-Efficacy for Undergraduates

Research suggests that "SEW makes an independent contribution to [predicting] writing outcomes and plays the meditational role that . . . theorists [like Bandura] hypothesize" (Pajares 145). Study results support an inverse relationship between writing anxiety and SEW, leading investigators to advocate for integrating writing centers into FYC to help students decrease anxiety and increase SEW and writing performance (Martinez, Kock, and Cass 354–359). While reading self-efficacy and SEW were both highly correlated with writing performance, SEW accounted for larger score variances, lower apprehension, and more enjoyment—which points to writing performance being influenced by a "constellation" of beliefs (Prat-Sala and Redford, "Writing Essay" 16–17; Sanders-Reio, Alexander, and Reio 10). Consequently, this study seeks to understand how mastery experiences and social persuasion in DE writing might influence SEW.

Dual Enrollment Writing Research

Existing research points to crucial inconsistencies in the content and rigor of DE FYC courses, with classes on HS campuses particularly vulnerable. For HS DE teachers, greater labor demands related to curriculum, standards, larger classes, grading, and parental and administrative pressure seem to negatively affect course curriculum. These differences in labor requirements are seemingly compounded by a lack of collaboration between K–12 and college personnel (Denecker 32; McWain 410–417). On college campuses, younger DE students reported lower SEW than typical FYC writers; also, they struggled with writing for specific audiences and revising their work based on feedback (Taczak and Thelin 8–9; Tinberg and Nadeau 40). Thus, multiple studies reveal faults in DE FYC structures that suggest that DE writers might have lower SEW and lower writing performance, but one study (Hansen et al., "How" 67) found no statistically significant writing performance differences between DE and non-DE writers in college courses.

Despite the availability of various options to earn FYC credit, including Advanced Placement (AP), ACT/SAT score exemptions, and traditional on-campus courses, DE is perceived as having the most potential to narrow achievement gaps (Rivera, Kotok, and Ashby 15). Thus, it is increasingly important to understand how preexisting student characteristics relate to DE students' writing performance, SEW, and perceptions of their DE FYC courses. With greater understanding, stakeholders can make more informed decisions about DE FYC policies and curricula. Therefore, these research questions were addressed: are there statistically significant differences in curriculum, SEW, and writing performance based on FYC credit pathway, gender, race/ethnicity, and parents' education? How do DE FYC students describe their SEW and writing experiences? How do the qualitative findings complement the quantitative results?

EMBEDDED MIXED METHODS RESEARCH DESIGN

This embedded mixed methods study used multiple data sets to answer multiple research questions (Plano Clark and Ivankova 85). A document analysis provided an overview of FYC curricula at five postsecondary institutions in Louisiana and informed this study's survey and interview protocols. Overall, the curricula were designed for students to compose analyses and arguments in three or more four- to eight-page papers per semester. There were no creative writing assignments. Prioritized quantitative methods were used to investigate differences in curriculum, SEW, and performance for DE versus non-DE writers while considering gender, race/ethnicity, and parents' education (Cowan et al. 6). Open-ended survey items and interviews provided DE students' perspectives of FYC writing experiences and SEW to complement the quantitative results (Plano Clark and Ivankova 85).

Samples

The participants—attendees at a large Research I university in Louisiana—entered college between fall 2015 and spring 2017. The survey sample (n = 1,027, 86 DE FYC participants), the institutional data (n = 467, 395 with DE FYC participants), and the interview sample (n = 14, all with DE FYC credit) was composed largely of white females, which is somewhat reflective of the university's population (see table 13.1).

Table 13.1. Participant demographic data

	Survey (n = 1,027)		*Institutional Data (n = 467)*		*Interviews (n = 14)*	
	n	%	n	%	N	%
Credit pathway						
DE	86	8%	395	85%	14	100%
Non-DE	941	92%	72	15%	0	0%
Gender						
Male	298	29%	123	26%	4	17%
Female	729	71%	344	74%	10	83%
Race						
Black	15	10%	88	19%	4	17%
White	795	77%	345	74%	10	83%
"Other"	127	12%	34	7%	0	0%
Parents' education						
Some HS	72	7%	24	5%		
HS diploma	219	21%	133	28%		
College degree	476	46%	178	38%		
Advanced degree	22	20%	81	17%		
No data available	58	6%	51	11%		

Data Collection

After IRB approval, survey invitations were emailed to students with FYC credit who entered the university from fall 2015 to spring 2016 (n = 1,027). Respondents gave informed consent to begin the Qualtrics survey. Subsequently, email interview invitations were sent to former DE students who entered between fall 2015 and spring 2017 (n = 2,120); fourteen students volunteered for interviews (ten 2015–2016 entrants and four 2016–2017 entrants). The university provided additional student data after the survey closed, so the potential interview pool was expanded with DE writing students who entered in 2016–2017. This allowed for a larger, more appropriate qualitative sample size (Onwuegbuzie and Collins 289). Interviewees emailed informed consent. Interviews were recorded with Google Voice, transcribed by Rev .com, and analyzed in Excel.

Instruments

Derived from existing instruments, the quantitative survey asked students from different FYC pathways to gauge SEW (*I can express my arguments clearly in essays.* $\alpha = 0.95$) and report type and number of FYC assignments (*e.g., analysis, argument*) (Prat-Sala and Redford; Kiuhara, Graham, and Hawken). With institutional data, advanced English (beyond FYC) and writing-intensive course GPAs were used to measure writing performance. Open-ended survey items and interviews yielded qualitative data for SEW (*How do you view yourself as a writer?*), mastery experiences (*Looking back on your DE composition experiences, what would you improve about the course?*), and social persuasion (*Looking back on your DE composition experiences, what feedback was most helpful to you?*) (Campbell et al.; Lunsford, Fishman, and Liew; Hansen et al., "How" 70–72).

Analyses

Quantitative analyses were conducted in Statistical Package for Social Sciences (SPSS) 24. Institutional data were analyzed for differences in performance based on the same criteria: FYC pathway, gender, race/ethnicity, and parents' education. Qualitative findings were used to understand how mastery experiences and social persuasion might influence SEW and to complement the quantitative results. In a grounded theory methodology, "initial" coding involved naming "segment[s] of data" to keep "participants' voices" prominent, and focused coding was used to "develop the most salient categories" to produce an "emerging" framework of DE students' experiences (Charmaz 46). The researcher completed this coding cycle five times over a six-month period. These coding cycles involved extensive peer review after the third and fifth cycles. Integration occurred during discussion (Plano Clark and Ivankova 114).

QUANTITATIVE RESULTS: CURRICULUM, SEW, AND WRITING PERFORMANCE

Using logistic regression procedures, the survey data were used to determine the likelihood that students engaged in a typical FYC curriculum—argument writing (typical) and creative writing (not typical)—for all credit pathways except ACT/SAT exemptions. Over 90 percent of respondents ($n = 567$) reported writing at least three argument papers, with some noticeable percentage differences (see table 13.2). The model included gender, race, parents' education, and FYC credit pathway as predictors, but credit pathway was the only statistically

Table 13.2. Number of arguments written by credit pathway

Credit Pathway	*Wrote 1–2 Arguments*	*Wrote 3+ Arguments**	*Odds Ratios*	*Total*
Dual enrollment[†]	4 (5%)	79 (95%)[†]	–	83 (15%)
AP exemption	5 (3%)	138 (97%)	0.690	143 (25%)
Traditional[†]	44 (13%)	297 (87%)[†]	2.970[†]	341 (60%)
Total arguments	53 (9%)	514 (91%)	–	567 (100%)

**Represents typical FYC curriculum; † Statistically significant difference, p < 0.05*

Table 13.3. Creative writing assignments by credit pathway

Factor	*0 Creative Writing Assignments*	*1+ Creative Writing Assignments*	*Odds Ratios*	*Total (n = 566)*
Gender				
Male	122 (85%)	22 (15%)	516	144 (25%)
Female	302 (72%)	120 (28%)	–	422 (75%)
Credit Pathway				
Dual enrollment	48 (58%)	35 (42%)	–	83 (15%)
AP exemption	84 (58%)	59 (42%)	0.927	143 (25%)
ENGL 1001/transfer	292 (86%)	48 (14%)	0.226*	340 (60%)
Total creative writings	424 (100%)	142 (100%)	–	566 (100%)

** Statistically significant difference, p < 0.05*

significant predictor ($\chi^2(6) = 14.969$, $p < 0.05$). It explained 5.6 percent of the variance in arguments assigned (see table 13.2). Respondents with traditional FYC credit were about three times more likely than DE students to report writing three or more arguments.

For creative writing, credit pathway and gender were the statistically significant predictors ($\chi^2(6) = 61.687$, $p < 0.05$), explaining 15.3 percent of the variance. DE participants were over four times more likely to write creatively than traditional students, and male students were half as likely as females to write creatively (see table 13.3). Overall, the quantitative results for arguments and creative writing suggest that DE respondents were less likely to engage in standard FYC curriculum.

An ANOVA procedure was used to determine if there were differences in SEW based on credit pathway, gender, race, and parents' education. There were no statistically significant interactions; however, there were statistically significant differences in SEW based on FYC credit pathway with very small effect sizes, $F(3{,}992) = 10.882$, $p < 0.05$,

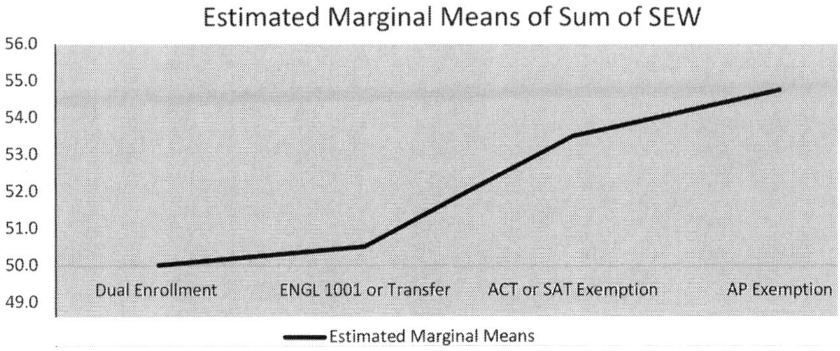

Figure 13.1. Estimated marginal means for self-efficacy by credit pathway

Table 13.4. Average English GPA by race/ethnicity

Group	*White*		*Black*		*"Other"*		*Total*
	n	GPA	n	GPA	n	GPA	n
	345	3.152*	88	2.699†	34	3.163*	451

** Subset 1; † Subset 2*

partial $\eta^2 = 0.032$. Pair-wise comparisons revealed that students with test exemptions reported statistically significantly higher SEW scores than their peers (see figure 13.1). While difficult to parse, the reasons for this might involve confidence derived from the test exemptions themselves and might also represent an overestimation of actual ability (Hansen et al., "Advanced" 462).

A two-way ANOVA was conducted to determine if there were differences in advanced English GPAs. With no significant interactions, main effects revealed statistically significant differences in English GPA by race, with post-hoc tests suggesting that Black students underperform their peers (see table 13.4). While this finding is congruent to national writing assessment results for eighth and twelfth graders and with research, it also points to potential racial bias in teaching and evaluating Black students in P–20 education (Jacoby-Senghor, Sinclair, and Shelton 52–53; Marken et al. 11).

QUALITATIVE FINDINGS: DE PARTICIPANTS' SEW AND SOURCES OF SEW

Fourteen interviewees were asked to describe their SEW; ten viewed themselves as capable writers, two as exceptional, and one as struggling.

One respondent's answer was not sufficient for evaluation. Survey and interview respondents described mastery experiences and social persuasion that informed SEW.

Interviewees who described themselves as capable writers spoke of mastery experiences related to specific writing abilities and provided qualifying statements. For example, a junior said, "I wouldn't call myself a creative writer [or] the best writer, but I'm not terrible . . . I know . . . to have a thesis [and] transition sentences." Similarly, a sophomore shared, "I don't think I'll ever be writing for the *New York Times* or *Vogue* . . . but I am . . . perfectly capable [of] getting a point across." While these quotations are representative of more than two-thirds of the interview sample, two other respondents unequivocally described themselves as exceptional writers and detailed their writing processes. A sophomore engineering major based her self-assessment on subsequent performance and feedback in a writing-intensive course; she also described her writing process as follows: "I'm pretty good at writing formal papers. I [took] an English course [here] . . . and got an A-plus . . . I tend to sit down and write a paper . . . [over] like two days. I've been told that I express myself well on a page and I have a . . . good grasp of grammar . . . I feel confident in writing." In contrast to her peers, a sophomore education major described having low SEW; she expressed a strong dislike for writing and portrayed her DE writing course as lacking rigor, saying it was not "anything hard." Like the participants with high SEW, she seems to have predicated her judgment on difficulties in post-FYC mastery experiences, saying, "I still had problems in my [college] class; [I] just struggled with writing. I think I always will. I'm just not a very good writer." Most interviewees described moderate to high SEW, but their responses advance the idea that DE courses that lack appropriate content and rigor might be less problematic for students with moderate to high SEW but more detrimental to those with low SEW. Overall, the students who reported moderate SEW referenced skills practiced but provided qualifying statements. In contrast, the interviewees who reported high SEW made direct, unqualified statements regarding their writing excellence; described their writing processes; and referenced positive post-FYC feedback, including grades.

Supporting the interviewees' assessments of SEW are survey takers and interviewees' descriptions of mastery experiences (skills practiced) and social persuasion (feedback). Like interviewees with moderate SEW, about one quarter of survey respondents described mastery experiences involving appropriate FYC curriculum. Conversely, others critiqued their courses, citing misaligned curriculum and lack of rigor.

The collective qualitative responses suggest that many DE FYC students can clearly articulate the skills practiced in those writing courses. Survey respondents referenced mastery experiences involving "general writing skills"; "how to [structure] a well thought out paper"; learning to "give supporting details"; "[using] and [citing] sources"; grammar, usage, and mechanics; writing thesis statements; and critiquing writing. But survey takers also perceived their mastery experiences as inadequate due to the number and type of FYC assignments. One male junior explained, "Only having two papers was difficult when it came to raising your grade," a female sophomore would have liked "more nonfiction writing . . . and [fewer] personal narratives," and a junior wanted less "HS work." Responses also suggest a perceived lack of rigor, with one sophomore explaining, for example, "I would have made [DE composition] classes harder . . . so it wasn't as severe a jump [when I got to college]." Taken together, the survey takers' critiques about mastery experiences in DE FYC point to inconsistencies in curricula across DE programs.

When discussing feedback, DE respondents to the open-ended survey items (n = 86) and interviewee respondents (n = 14) overwhelmingly viewed instructor feedback as effective in improving their writing. Survey takers pointed to the effectiveness of "one-on-one" help and to "corrections written on graded papers." Again, the interviewees echo the survey respondents by referencing effective instructor feedback; one participant was particularly detailed, sharing: "After each [paper, we met] with her individually and discuss[ed] our paper . . . She [gave] detailed feedback . . . allow[ed] us to revamp our papers . . . This one-on-one was amazing! I got much more feedback than . . . if she had done it any other way . . . She was able to . . . ask us questions and lead us more towards the answers . . . than just writing [comments] on the side of our papers." This student's response is representative of others and describes how mastery experiences and social persuasion might work in tandem to increase SEW.

For some interview and survey participants, having both a HS teacher and a college instructor was helpful when the HS teacher was available to provide more real-time feedback; conversely, this model was problematic for participants when the two instructors gave conflicting feedback. One survey respondent shared, "My HS teacher gave the best feedback. She would help us through the [writing] process unlike my . . . professor who had hundreds of students." In contrast, for a sophomore education major, receiving conflicting feedback negatively affected her grade, forcing her to bypass the HS teacher and negotiate revisions directly with the college instructor. She shared, "I [told] the college professor that I sent them to my [HS] teacher [first] . . . so he actually said . . . 'just start sending them to me, and I'll give you my feedback.' "

Unlike instructor feedback, which was consistently viewed as more effective, responses about peer feedback suggest inconsistent use and effectiveness and a potential lack of trust. Survey takers rarely mentioned peer feedback as helpful, which might be related to the overwhelming effectiveness of and/or greater trust in teacher feedback. In other cases, peer feedback was mentioned *instead* of instructor feedback as the most helpful aspect of DE writing courses, suggesting that for some, instructor feedback might have been less available or less helpful. For the interviewees, half of the participants pointed to effective peer feedback structures while others described ineffective or nonexistent processes. Survey and interview respondents believed peer review effectiveness was based largely on their peers' writing ability. For instance, a sophomore survey taker briefly described peer review days as effective because she "had very smart peers," and others characterized peer review as helpful because it "[involved] people [their] age" who could relate to them. Describing peer reviews in great detail, another sophomore explained that sessions were helpful when more capable writers did the review. She shared, "So we'd have peer review days, and that really helped when other students who were at my level or above would [review my work] . . . I'd say, 'Just trash my paper!' " This comment illustrates that for students, the peers' writing and evaluation abilities were critical in determining how effectively peer review might function in a class.

On the other hand, a small minority cited inconsistent, ineffective peer feedback. These perceptions seemed to also be based on peers' writing abilities. One respondent representatively shared, "Out of all the [essays] we wrote, we only did two peer swaps . . . One of them was a complete mess. I swapped with a student who is not very good at English." Others noted a lack of peer review, with one saying "we did not really" use it. Taken together, the peer review findings point to inconsistencies within and across DE programs.

DISCUSSION

In this mixed methods study, the "qualitative findings provided confirmation and nuance for understanding quantitative results" (Grossman and Porche 716). Taken together, the results provide an overview of how former DE students experience FYC curriculum, measure SEW in relation to peers from other FYC pathways, and describe sources of SEW. The results also suggest a racial achievement gap in post-FYC English courses. Most significant, the findings here suggest that while students' SEW might be a strong, positive predictor of how those students fare on college writing tasks, their writing performance in higher education might not be adequate for the twenty-first-century workplace.

Student perspectives offered here suggest an increased likelihood of major curricular differences in DE classes, namely those taught by HS teachers. These differences include requiring fewer arguments and more creative assignments while providing ineffective or no peer review. These findings support existing research which suggests that misalignment between DE and traditional FYC curricula are due in part to HS teachers' conflicting priorities and heavy labor demands as they attempt to fill disparate teaching roles without much collaboration with college instructors and program administrators (Denecker 32; McWain 410–417). The issues with curriculum seem to be particularly detrimental to students with lower SEW because the DE courses do not provide the mastery experiences and social persuasion needed to increase SEW and writing performance.

The high SEW reported in the survey was supported by DE interviewees, who mostly described themselves as average or above average writers and who discussed mastery experiences (writing activities) and social persuasion (feedback) that might have influenced their SEW. However, students still made many recommendations for improving mastery experiences and social persuasion—both of which influence self-efficacy. Thus, the findings from this study offer some support for Bandura's hypothesis about the sources of self-efficacy (2–3). In addition, the findings suggest that the participants might be relatively advantaged students who would classify themselves as capable writers despite their FYC credit pathway.

Similar to existing data, the quantitative results yielded no statistically significant differences in advanced English GPAs for students using different credit pathways (Hansen et al., "How" 72–73). However, Black students in advanced English classes had lower GPAs than their peers; these findings mirror the most recent National Assessment for Educational Progress (NAEP) writing achievement data for eighth and twelfth graders and also point to persistent educational inequities in the US. These inequities include racial bias in the teaching of Black students (Cherng, Halpin, and Rodriguez 189–191; Egalite and Kisida 74; Gershenson, Holt, and Papageorge 35; Jacoby-Senghor, Sinclair, and Shelton 52–53; National Center for Education Statistics 2; Darling-Hammond 208).

Most participants in this study reported high SEW, but research indicates that students can overestimate their writing abilities (Hansen et al.,

"Advanced" 480). Thus, while their writing performance might be adequate for college writing tasks, it may be inadequate for the twenty-first-century workplace; this disparity suggests a disconnection between the writing demands of school versus the writing demands of the workplace.

LIMITATIONS

Limitations are related to self-selection bias; sample size; inclusion of participants from a single institution; cross-sectional, concurrent data collection; and limited race/ethnicity categories. The samples are large in relation to similar studies, but larger, more representative samples from more institutions might yield more generalizable results—especially considering that students with negative FYC experiences are less likely to participate in writing research or take advanced English courses. Inclusion of such students might have yielded lower average SEW scores and a more balanced picture of DE writing curricula. Further, with concurrent, cross-sectional data collection, there were, respectively, no opportunities to adjust the qualitative instruments based on quantitative results or gauge changes in participants' attitudes over time. Finally, due to constraints of the statistical procedures, students who did not classify as Black or white were combined into an "other" category, which precluded a more nuanced analysis.

CONCLUSION: IMPLICATIONS FOR PRACTICE AND FUTURE RESEARCH

Ultimately, these results have implications for instruction in DE FYC courses but also—and perhaps more important—for how literacy instruction in schools aligns with literacy demands of the twenty-first-century workplace. While students mostly view themselves as capable writers, employers do not share this view of their college graduates' communication skills (Casner-Lotto and Barrington 11; Quible and Griffin 32). This suggests that the "high wall" separating school learning from professional competencies must be dismantled through communication and collaboration among instructors and school administrators at all educational levels *as well as* with employers and human resources professionals (Gatta and Deprez 286). Such partnerships might use existing resources to promote and implement authentic intellectual literacy experiences that have value beyond school (Newmann, Marks, and Gamoran 287).

Through these collaborative efforts, schools can expand the reach of existing writing center resources for use in DE courses, especially those taught on HS campuses (Martinez, Kock, and Cass 359). Indeed, higher education writing centers and libraries may well represent huge untapped resources for providing DE students with more opportunities for writing practice and access to quality feedback while reducing HS teachers' workload and providing the academic support students need to close writing achievement gaps. Also, some HS DE teachers recommend participation in the National Writing Project (NWP), describing it as a "transformative experience in their pedagogical development that [allows] them to advocate for better writing instruction at their home schools" (McWain 420). Large-scale NWP participation might result in more appropriate content and rigor in HS ELA and DE FYC courses, which might improve students' SEW and writing performance, better prepare them for workplace communication, and provide more equitable access to quality literacy instruction. In addition, the suggested achievement gaps noted here lend additional weight to the calls for K–12 and higher education faculty to have opportunities to "critically reflect" on and overcome racial biases that are detrimental to the success of minority students (Kumar, Karabenick, and Burgoon 542).

Emerging DE composition research is generally qualitative and based on instructor and researcher perspectives, so more quantitative and mixed method studies with larger, more representative samples of students are needed. More longitudinal studies would also be useful, and new studies can link individual SEW scores directly to writing assignment scores to further investigate the connection between SEW and performance. Finally, more studies of collaboration are needed to generate best practice models of school-employer partnerships.

WORKS CITED

Alexander, Jonathan. "From the Editor." *College Composition and Communication*, vol. 68, no. 1, 2016, pp. 4–9. *JSTOR*. www.jstor.org/stable/44783524. Accessed May 15, 2022.

An, Brian P. "The Role of Academic Motivation and Engagement on the Relationship between Dual Enrollment and Academic Performance." *Journal of Higher Education*, vol. 86, no. 1, 2015, pp. 98–126. doi: 10.1353/jhe.2015.0005.

Bandura, Albert. *Self-Efficacy: The Exercise of Control*. New York: W. H. Freeman, 1997.

Campbell, Jennifer, Richard Colby, Kelli Custer, Doug Hesse, Eliana Schonberg, Rebekah Shultz-Colby, and John Tiedmann. *The University of Denver Longitudinal Study of Undergraduate Writing*. University of Denver, 2010, pp. 4–7. https://www.du.edu/writing/media/documents/du_longitudinal_study_writing_overview.pdf. Accessed May 15, 2022.

Casner-Lotto, Jill, and Linda Barrington. *Are They Really Ready to Work? Employers' Perspectives on the Basic Knowledge and Applied Skills of New Entrants to the 21st Century U.S. Workforce*. Conference Board, Corporate Voices for Working Families, Partnership for 21st Century Skills, and Society for Human Resource Management, 2006. https://files.eric.ed.gov/fulltext/ED519465.pdf. Accessed May 15, 2022.

Charmaz, Kathy. *Constructing Grounded Theory*. Sage, 2006.

Cherng, Hua-Yu Sebastian, Peter F. Halpin, and Luis A. Rodriguez. "Teaching Bias? Relations between Teaching Quality and Classroom Demographic Composition." *American Journal of Education*, vol. 128, no. 2, 2022, pp. 171–201.

Cowan, Charles D., Robert M. Hauser, Robert A. Kominski, Henry M. Levin, Samuel R. Lucas, Stephen L. Morgan, Margaret Beale Spencer, and Chris Chapman "Improving the Measurement of Socioeconomic Status for the National Assessment of Educational Progress: A Theoretical Foundation." Recommendations to the National Center for Education Statistics, Nov. 2013. https://nces.ed.gov/nationsreportcard/pdf/researchcenter/socioeconomic_factors.pdf. Accessed May 15, 2022.

Darling-Hammond, Linda. "Inequality in Teaching and Schooling: How Opportunity Is Rationed to Students of Color in America." In *The Right Thing to Do, the Smart Thing to Do: Enhancing Diversity in the Health Professions, Summary of the Symposium on Diversity in Health Professions in Honor of Herbert W. Nickens, M.D*, edited by Brian D. Smedley, Adrienne Y. Stith, Lois Colburn, and Clyde H. Evans. National Academies Press, 2001, pp. 208–233. doi: 10.17226/10186.

Denecker, Christine. "Transitioning Writers across the Composition Threshold: What We Can Learn from Dual Enrollment Partnerships." *Composition Studies*, vol. 41, no. 42, 2013, pp. 27–50.

Egalite, Anna J., and Brian Kisida. "The Effects of Teacher Match on Students' Academic Perceptions and Attitudes." *Educational Evaluation and Policy Analysis*, vol. 40, no. 1, 2018, pp. 59–81.

Gatta, Mary, and Luisa S. Deprez. "Creating a 21st-Century Workforce Development System." In *Transforming the U.S. Workforce Development System: Lessons from Research and Practice*, 1st ed., edited by David Finegold. Labor and Employment Relations Association Series. Labor and Employment Relations Association, University of Illinois at Urbana-Champaign, 2010. pp. 261–285.

Gershenson, Seth, Stephen B. Holt, and Nicholas W. Papageorge. "Who Believes in Me? The Effect of Student–Teacher Demographic Match on Teacher Expectations." *Economics of Education Review*, vol. 52, 2016, pp. 209–224.

Grossman, Jennifer M., and Michelle V. Porche. "Perceived Gender and Racial/Ethnic Barriers to STEM Success." *Urban Education*, vol. 49, no. 6, 2014, pp. 698–727. doi: 10.1177/0042085913481364.

Hansen, Kristine, Brian Jackson, Brett C. McInelly, and Dennis Eggett. "How Do Dual Credit Students Perform on College Writing Tasks after They Arrive on Campus? Empirical Data from a Large-Scale Study." *Writing Program Administration*, vol. 38, no. 2, 2015, pp. 56–92.

Hansen, Kristine, Suzanne Reeve, Jennifer Gonzalez, Richard R. Sudweeks, Gary L. Hatch, Patricia Esplin, and William S. Bradshaw. "Are Advanced Placement English and First-Year College Composition Equivalent? A Comparison of Outcomes in the Writing of Three Groups of Sophomore College Students." *Research in the Teaching of English*, vol. 40, no. 4, 2006, pp. 461–501. doi: http://www.jstor.org/stable/40171711.

Jacoby-Senghor, Drew S., Stacey Sinclair, and J. Nicole Shelton. "A Lesson in Bias: The Relationship between Implicit Racial Bias and Performance in Pedagogical Contexts." *Journal of Experimental Social Psychology*, vol. 63, Mar. 2016, pp. 50–55. *EBSCOhost*. doi: 10.1016/j.jesp.2015.10.010.

Karp, Melinda Mechur. " 'I Don't Know, I've Never Been to College!' Dual Enrollment as a College Readiness Strategy." *New Directions for Higher Education*, no. 158, 2012, pp. 21–28. doi: 10.1002/he.

Kiuhara, Sharlene A., Steve Graham, and Leanne S. Hawken. "Teaching Writing to High School Students: A National Survey." *Journal of Educational Psychology*, vol. 101, no. 1, 2009, pp. 136–160. doi: 10.1037/a0013097.

Kleiner, Brian, and Laurie Lewis. *Dual Enrollment of High School Students at Postsecondary Institutions: 2002–03.* US Department of Education, National Center for Education Statistics, 2005.

Kumar, Revathy, Stuart A. Karabenick, and Jacob N. Burgoon. "Teachers' Implicit Attitudes, Explicit Beliefs, and the Mediating Role of Respect and Cultural Responsibility on Mastery and Performance-Focused Instructional Practices." *Journal of Educational Psychology*, vol. 107, no. 2, May 2015, pp. 533–545. EBSCOhost. search.ebscohost.com/login.aspx?direct=true&db=eric&AN=EJ1061911&site=eds-live.

Lunsford, Andrea A., Jenn Fishman, and Warren M. Liew. "College Writing, Identification, and the Production of Intellectual Property: Voices from the Stanford Study of Writing." *College English*, vol. 75, no. 5, 2013, pp. 470–492.

Marken, Stephanie, Lucinda Gray, and Laurie Lewis. "Dual Enrollment Programs and Courses for High School Students at Postsecondary Institutions: 2010–11." US Department of Education, National Center for Education Statistics, 2013. http://nces.ed.gov/pubs2013/2013002.pdf. Accessed May 15, 2022.

Martinez, Christy Teranishi, Ned Kock, and Jeffrey Cass. "Pain and Pleasure in Short Essay Writing: Factors Predicting University Students' Writing Anxiety and Writing Self-Efficacy." *Journal of Adolescent and Adult Literacy*, vol. 54, no. 5, 2011, pp. 351–360.

McWain, Katie. "Finding Freedom at the Composition Threshold : Learning from the Experiences of Dual Enrollment Teachers." *Teaching English in the Two-Year College*, vol. 45, no. 4, 2018, pp. 406–425.

National Center for Education Statistics. *The Nation's Report Card: Writing 2011.* Institute of Education Sciences, US Department of Education, 2011.

Newmann, Fred M., Helen M. Marks, and Adam Gamoran. "Authentic Student Pedagogy Performance." *American Journal of Education*, vol. 104, no. 4, 2012, pp. 280–312.

Onwuegbuzie, Anthony J., and Kathleen M. T. Collins. "A Typology of Mixed Methods Sampling Designs in Social Science Research." *Qualitative Report*, vol. 12, no. 2, 2007, pp. 281–316.

Pajares, Frank. "Self-Efficacy Beliefs, Motivation, and Achievement in Writing: A Review of the Literature." *Reading and Writing Quarterly*, vol. 19, 2003, pp. 139–159. doi: 10.1080/10573560390143085.

Plano Clark, Vicki L., and Nataliya V. Ivankova. *Mixed Methods Research: A Guide to the Field.* Sage Publications, 2015.

Prat-Sala, Mercè, and Paul Redford. "Self-Efficacy in Essay Writing Scale." *PsychTESTS*, 2010, pp. 1–2. doi: 10.1348/000709909x480563.

Prat-Sala, Mercè, and Paul Redford. "Writing Essays: Does Self-Efficacy Matter? The Relationship between Self-Efficacy in Reading and in Writing and Undergraduate Students' Performance in Essay Writing." *Educational Psychology*, vol. 32, no. 1, 2012, pp. 9–20. doi: 10.1080/01443410.2011.621411.

Quible, Zane K., and Frances Griffin. "Are Writing Deficiencies Creating a Lost Generation of Business Writers?" *Journal of Education for Business*, vol. 83, no. 1, 2007, pp. 32–36. doi: 10.3200/JOEB.83.1.32–36.

Rivera, Luis E., Stephen Kotok, and Nathan Ashby. "Access to Dual Enrollment in the United States: Implications for Equity and Stratification." *Texas Education Review*, vol. 7, no. 2, July 2019, pp. 14–29. http://dx.doi.org/10.26153/tsw/229=82.

Sanders-Reio, Joanne, Patricia A. Alexander, and Thomas G. Reio Jr. "Do Students' Beliefs about Writing Relate to Their Writing Self-Efficacy, Apprehension, and Performance?" *Learning and Instruction*, vol. 33, 2014, pp. 1–11. doi: 10.1016/j.learninstruc.2014.02.001.

Shivji, Azim, and Sandra Wilson. "Dual Enrollment: Participation and Characteristics." US Department of Education, National Center for Education Statistics, 2019.

Smith, M. Cecil, Larry Mikulecky, Michael W. Kibby, Mariam Jean Dreher, and Janice A. Dole. "What Will Be the Demands of Literacy in the Workplace in the Next

Millennium?" *Reading Research Quarterly*, vol. 35, no. 3, 2004, pp. 378–383. doi: 10.1598/rrq.35.3.3.

Taczak, Kara, and William H. Thelin. "(Re)Envisioning the Divide: The Impact of College Courses on High School Students." *Teaching English in the Two-Year College*, vol. 37, no. 1, 2009, pp. 7–23.

Tinberg, Howard, and Jean-Paul Nadeau. "What Happens When High School Students Write in a College Course? A Study of Dual Credit." *English Journal*, vol. 102, no. 5, 2013, pp. 35–42.

Usher, Ellen L., and Frank Pajares. "Sources of Self-Efficacy in School: Critical Review of the Literature and Future Directions." *Review of Educational Research*, vol. 78, no. 4, 2008, pp. 751–796. doi: 10.3102/0034654308321456.

14

SIDESTEPPING THE SHAME/ BLAME BINARY

Hearing and Responding to Dual Enrollment Students' Voices in the Composition Classroom

Anna Bogen

I am worried that I will not be able to write enough or understand what I am writing.

—Student 23, Ohio Technical College/Ohio High School, September 2017

When I think about dual credit, I get an ulcer. Honestly.

—Author Sybil Priebe, May 2016

Over the past decade, dual enrollment (DE) programs have brought an increase in both opportunity and, as seen in the quotations above, anxiety. In Ohio, the College Credit Plus (CCP) program offered free DE courses to 71,485 students (grades 7–12) during the 2017–2018 academic year. Most of these classes (82%) were offered by two-year colleges (Ohio Department of Higher Education *Annual Report* 4, 13–15). DE, therefore, has rapidly become a key element of the community college experience across Ohio, forcing faculty to reconsider not only the dynamics of the college classroom but also wider questions around the high school–college boundary. Within English departments in particular, the expansion of DE has forced a sometimes uncomfortable reconsideration of thorny questions about what constitutes college-level writing (Sullivan and Tinberg). The stakes are high for all parties, in part because the issues DE raises are as emotional as they are academic. The study, which is the focus of this chapter, takes this emotional aspect as a starting point to investigate DE students' affective understanding of "college-level writing." Using student response data from a 2017–2018

https://doi.org/10.7330/9781646422531.c014

case study of DE students in first-year composition (FYC), I examine two major affective categories that emerged around the idea of college-level writing: shame and blame. Ultimately, although both categories reflect a negative student experience, I argue that shame and blame have a significant role to play in helping faculty understand and support DE students in the FYC classroom and within the wider "new normal" of the changing community college landscape.

MOMENTUM AND GAP: THE SCHOLARSHIP OF DUAL ENROLLMENT

Dual enrollment has been credited with many advantages, particularly in quantitative higher education research, where studies have shown a strong link between DE and a range of positive outcomes—including earlier enrollment, better performance in college, and shorter overall time to degree (Allen and Dadgar; An; Burns et al.; Wang et al.). Ben Struhl and Joel Vargas's 2012 study on DE in Texas sums up this line of thinking: "After studying tens of thousands of Texas students who completed college courses in high school, we found that these students attended and completed college within the state at much higher rates than students with similar backgrounds who did not take college courses in high school" (5). Although there are still questions about how DE creates these positive effects, scholars have continued to focus on DE's role as a transitional/liminal space that helps students gain what Xueli Wang and colleagues have termed "academic momentum" (165). For Melinda Mechur Karp, for example, DE can act as a "college readiness strategy" ("I Don't Know" 21), where students learn about the "academic demands of the [college student] role, including the normative classroom expectations held of college students" ("Learning" 32). While some studies have shown a more neutral effect from DE (Allen and Dadgar; An; Burns et al.), DE's generally positive public reception and its positioning as a useful "transition" to improve higher education outcomes have been used as justification for nationwide expansion of the model.

This embrace of DE has left English departments, particularly in the two-year sector, scrambling to respond to a "new normal." Composition studies, however, has often questioned both the theory and practice of DE's assumed "transitional" role. For example, scholars such as Douglas Hesse, Howard Tinberg and Jean-Paul Nadeau, and Kristine Hansen have perceptively highlighted the larger economic forces propelling DE. Hansen, for example, worries that DE could lead students to see education as "shopping for credits," devaluing traditional on-campus FYC in favor of "outsourced" high school options (1). For Sybil Priebe, quoted at the beginning of this chapter, the economic pressures brought to bear by DE potentially give too much power to stakeholders "who see dollar signs and enrollment numbers" rather than learning (438). Carolyn Calhoun-Dillahunt summed up this view when she described DE as "one of the trends that put first-year writing—and the students and programs . . . that such courses support—at risk" (281).

Alongside economic considerations, DE composition scholarship presumes a clash of high school and college writing cultures, often described as a "gap" or "border" that students (and faculty) must traverse. Mary Jo Reiff and Anis Bawarshi's influential study of transfer, for example, although not directly focused on DE, categorizes students as "boundary guarders" or "boundary crossers," depending on their willingness to shed previous writing strategies. Similarly, Christine Denecker sees DE as "a space for examining the disconnect between high school and college writing expectations," concluding that dialogue among teachers on both sides of the divide is key to "ameliorating gaps" (29, 41). Christine R. Farris, who also uses the "gap" metaphor in her article "Minding the Gap and Learning the Game: Differences That Matter between High School and College Writing," argues that responsible DE requires "coming to an understanding of how our notions of good writing and our institutional constraints differ across the school culture divide" (273).

These examples demonstrate that composition scholars have important reservations about DE and share a common rhetoric focused on the gaps in writing instruction between college and high school. This can run the risk of relying on unhelpful stereotypes that cast high school writing as formulaic, template-driven, and unimaginative while its college equivalent is expansive, open, and conceptual. Susan Fanetti, Kathy M. Bushrow, and David L. DeWeese claim, for example: "High school education is designed to be standardized and quantifiable. College Education is designed to be theoretical" (77–78). Moreover, this type of generalization runs the risk of marginalizing or even stigmatizing credentialed high school DE faculty. Tracy Tensen, a high school teacher with an MA who teaches DE through a community college, found that despite her credentials, she constantly faced skeptical assumptions from the college faculty, leading her to wonder, "So how do I prove I am worthy to teach community college composition? Would I be a 'bet-ter' instructor on the community college campus" (17)? The absurdity of this idea is underlined in a study by Joanne Addison and Sharon James McGee, which found that, in general, faculty expectations in both cultures were closer than we might think: "The degree of alignment between high school and college faculty, or the fact that more high school faculty in our sample reported engagement in deep-learning practices (better teaching practices?) than college faculty, may be surprising" (157–159).

The use of the adverb "surprising" clearly indicates here that Addison and McGee are well aware of college faculty's potential biases against high school writing. Additional research is needed to tease out the reality of high school–college writing differences on the ground. In the meantime, our students are caught in the middle of these discussions. In general, the student perspective remains under-researched in DE, although some important small-scale studies exist. Karp's 2007 study of DE students and her 2012 follow-up article examine students' changing perceptions of the role of college students as they took DE classes. Similarly, Denecker's important 2013 article, "Transitioning Writers across the Composition Threshold: What We Can Learn from Dual-Enrollment Partnerships," draws on student and high school teacher perspectives (voices often left out of other scholarship) to explore the DE classroom as a place of transition. Finally, M. Allison Kanny, who studied a group of five DE students in Los Angeles, reports students feeling a sense of stigma. All three of these studies, by using student views to focus on the high school–college boundary, allow for a more nuanced picture of the DE experience. If the gap still can't be generalized, these studies at least make it clear that students are engaging and sometimes struggling with the high school–college boundary. Studies with a student-focused component, therefore, have great potential to help us flesh out the still too general perspectives of DE that cast it as either a momentum-providing savior or a deficit-revealing threat, what Miles McCrimmon has usefully labeled the "Pollyanna vs. Doomsday" binary (216). In particular, additional studies may provide the specific examples necessary to bolster stronger, more useful claims about the real state of the high school–college "gap" without relying on stereotype or stigma. Moreover, including student views has the potential, as these studies show, for creating specific interventions for DE classrooms, where many faculty from both sides of the divide have found themselves without sufficient support. My study, while also small-scale and specific, aims to add to the growing number of student-based studies of DE.

METHODOLOGY

For the purposes of this study, I designed and carried out an academic year–long study of DE students enrolled in FYC. Not only did I want to know what these students thought college writing was, I also wanted to know how they used that "knowledge" and what importance they assigned to it. I therefore began with a very broad research question, how do DE students view "college writing"? Student responses guided the study as it developed.

The research site for the study included a small Ohio technical college (hereafter referred to as OTC) and a nearby Ohio high school (hereafter referred to as OHS). The students in the study were all juniors or seniors enrolled full-time at OHS and taking English Composition I online through OTC's learning management software, Canvas. Although OTC is a relatively small technical college (2,374 students were enrolled as of 2018), it serves a wide area encompassing a city and surrounding rural counties, mainly through its large CCP program. CCP, which made up 34 percent of OTC's total enrollment in 2017, the year the study began, has since expanded (as of 2019) to 35 percent (Haas). OHS's student population is largely white (92.1%), with just under 20 percent qualifying as "economically disadvantaged" by state standards. Although OHS received a C grade overall on its Ohio Department of Education "report card," a higher number of students at OHS passed the state test in English language arts (84.4%) than the state average (Ohio Department of Education, "College"). In addition, to qualify for the CCP program, all students tested out of remedial English and were required by the state of Ohio to attain a minimum score of 18 (English) and 22 (reading) on the ACT, a score higher than normal OTC requirements. Moreover, many of the students enrolled in the study had previous DE experience. According to the former director of OTC's CCP program, students are encouraged to take other, more "low-stakes" college-level courses before English composition to prepare them for college expectations before taking a writing-intensive course (Wade). Students in the study also referred to this practice, describing other college courses they had taken.[1]

The research site created two aspects the study design had to take into account: students had some prior knowledge of "college classes," and, equally significant, they were taking an online class composed entirely of CCP students from the same high school. These factors complicate the theory that DE allows students to practice the "college role." I chose to study this group of online students with this heterogeneity firmly in mind; as the title of this collection implies, DE is a "kaleidoscope" rather than a monolith, and it is impossible to find a perfect cohort of study participants to fit every permutation of DE. The online nature of the course, while complex from a pedagogical standpoint, did provide me with a simple format for eliciting thoughtful and direct written responses from individual students, and I took advantage of this from a data-gathering perspective.

During the two semesters the study ran, I asked students to complete a series of thirteen written reflections (approximately one every two or three weeks) focused on different aspects of college writing, based on guiding questions (see appendix 14.A for a complete list of questions). These guiding questions covered a range of topics, including the role of a college student, the writing process, peer review, grammar/style, and genre. Each reflection was designed as an "open" assignment, and students were encouraged to write between one and two pages in response. The reflections were graded pass/fail to avoid the appearance of "right" or "wrong" answers. Although all students had to complete the reflections as part of the course, the study only used data from students who had agreed to participate. In addition, because many of the students were underage, their parents' permission was obtained as part of the Institutional Review Board process.

After gathering data, I then anonymized, numbered, and coded students' written reflections using grounded theory's constant-comparative method as laid out in Juliet Corbin and Anselm Strauss's *Basics of Qualitative Research.* In the "open coding" phase, I read through the data and created memos focusing on themes that emerged. They included:

> "Time/stress": Responses in this category focused on students' limited time and the stress this caused them when facing a college-level workload.
>
> "Formatting/grammar": Responses in this category covered comments students made about grammar or formatting in relation to college-level writing.
>
> "Independence": Responses in this category focused on students' perception of personal responsibility and work ethic in relation to college-level work. I also coded a subset of these responses as "Parents" because of references to parental involvement.
>
> "Deficit": Responses in this category focused on students' sense of their own inadequacy vis-à-vis the college student role.

Next, I used the categories to manually code the remaining responses. I chose to focus on and refine the "deficit" category in particular for two reasons: first, because it was by far the largest category to emerge from the first responses, and second, because it surprised me in its contradiction of the "entitled" high school student stereotype that emerges in some DE/FYC research. I refined this category into subcategories, which I labeled "shame" and "blame." I chose the terms because they capture the sense of deficit at the heart of the larger category; in addition, the deficit language also clearly placed responsibility on different people, with "shame" responses targeting students themselves and "blame" responses focusing on others, usually high school teachers.

Guided by Corbin's point that "asking questions and making comparisons continue to be major analytic strategies" (5) throughout the coding process, I then used the "shame" and "blame" polarities as a way to guide the rest of my coding, narrowing down my research question to the following: how do students see the boundary between college and high school writing, and how do they see themselves vis-à-vis that boundary? In the next section, I explain my initial findings about all three categories.

BOUNDARY AND DEFICIT

It was clear from the initial coding that students overwhelmingly identified a difference between high school and college writing. This was perhaps unsurprising, given the students' participation in a course taught directly by a college professor; indeed, the recognition of this boundary suggests a degree of audience awareness on the part of the students. Moreover, students clearly positioned themselves on one side of the boundary as eager but novice "college writers." For example, one student described wanting to learn "the skills that it takes to write an amazing paper" (Student 16), while another suggested that "this class is everything I thought it was going to be and is really going to help me prepare for college and my career after college" (Student 14).

The flattery implied in the responses above highlights an interesting point about the students' recognition of the high school–college writing boundary; although they were firmly convinced that a boundary existed, their ideas about what the differences were often vague and unformed. For example, students described formatting as one of the major differences between high school and college writing. OTC generally uses APA formatting in composition classes because most of our majors are in scientific or technical fields, whereas the English department at Ohio High School teaches MLA. Even though this reasoning was clearly explained to students, many of them seized on the difference in formatting as tangible evidence of "college writing." For example, Student 11 stated: "I had no clue what APA format was coming in to this class, and now that I know what I'm doing, I'll be prepared for any future class I'll have to take. We were only ever taught MLA, and I feel that I would not have the help next year that I'm getting now. I'm being taught how to use APA, and when I attend Bowling Green [State University, Ohio] I'm assuming they'll expect me to know how to use it." Another student commented, "I also need to know how to write papers in different formats so that when I get to college I don't struggle to keep up in classes that require me to write long papers in different formats" (Student 14). This emphasis on format, an easily graspable "difference," shows clearly how students' reading of the "boundary" does not necessarily reflect any real understanding of what that boundary might be.

For these students, the difference between high school and college writing was incredibly specific—it was the difference between *their* high school classes and *their* first writing class at OTC. True, in the students' obsession with formatting, we could see some justification of the "formulaic high school writing" stereotype, but students did not credit their high school teachers with stressing the importance of formatting; indeed, quite the opposite. Students were angry at what they perceived as high school teachers' *failure* to teach the correct formatting techniques. Seeing this anger emerge during the coding process further encouraged me to look at students' emotional responses to the high school–college boundary, leading to "shame" and "blame."

SHAME AND BLAME

Strategy 1: Shame

In her pioneering work on shame resilience, Brené Brown defines shame as "an intensely painful feeling or experience of believing we are flawed and therefore unworthy of acceptance and belonging" (45). Although student responses rarely reached quite this painful a pitch, the word *shame* captured a quality in the responses that ties strongly to Brown's definition—that of the "experience of being flawed." Responses that consistently described students as flawed or failed "college writers" were coded as "shame," in total 104 response sections by 21 students. They ranged in tone from mild self-reproach—Student 4: "I need to pick up better study habits"—to clear distress: "I thought that I knew what to do, as I went on and wrote more and more, I thought my paper was just getting worse and worse" (Student 6). Many expressed anxiety about reaching a "college standard" in the class. Words like "worry/ied," "struggle/d" and "nervous" occurred frequently in early semester responses, with students apologizing for their perceived or expected failures well before any assessment took place: "I tried to complete the paper to the best of my abilities. Some parts of it may not be up to college standard, and I would appreciate any feedback or help you can provide me with" (Student 17); "I did not know if I wrote my paper to the correct standard . . . my overall composition was not up to par because of my general lack of understanding" (Student 13). Importantly, the responses occurred *before* assessment, and these students were not responding to bad grades but *anticipating* a failure to live up to a mysterious "standard." In fact, they had been asked to write about what went well in their drafting process as well as the challenges they faced. Many students had difficulty naming the positive parts of their work without downplaying them: "On a positive note, I do believe I did a couple of things that could be considered correct" (Student 13); "there were only a few things that went well . . . overall I feel the quality of my work was not very good" (Student 19).

Other trends within the "shame" data included students self-identifying as a "bad" writer in one or more areas (22%) or as "bad" overall student (13%). While the writers above focused largely on their anxiety over not meeting a "college standard," these comments went further in personalizing that failure. Sometimes there was a healthy suggestion that this "flaw" could be overcome, as in this student who self-identified as lazy: "Something I need to work on is my effort when doing assignments. I often do not put in 100% which is something I will need to start doing" (Student 6). Most students, however, seemed to view their weaknesses as more permanent, something that might lead to failure in the class: "I have never been very good at parts of speech. This is a quiz I would probably still fail if I was expected to take a quiz over it" (Student 17). Finally, several students self-identified as perfectionistic, a trait that negatively affected their feelings about their work: "If I missed one little think [*sic*] I do not think the paper would have made any sense" (Student 5); "it is always very challenging for me not to conduct any research [when writing a personal essay] because I want to be as correct as I can. I do not want someone to read my paper and think, wow she is completely wrong" (Student 4). Responses in this category fit Brown's definition of shame largely because of the personalization as well as the fear that individual "flaws" could lead to a lack of acceptance, in the latter student's case through an imagined, current-traditionalist reader.

What, then, should we make of this cluster of responses around shame? Discerning students' motivations is tricky here; responses were written down, and while students were encouraged to be honest and open, there is certainly at least some mix of sincerity and performativity in their comments. In her article "Writing Shame," Elspeth Probyn cuts to the heart of the emotional and bodily sensations that accompany writing, no matter how practiced the author: "There is a shame in being highly interested in something and unable to convey it to others, to evoke the same degree of interest in them and to convince them that it is warranted. The risk of writing is always that you will fail to interest or engage readers. Disappointment in yourself looms large when you can't get the words quite right or get the argument across" (72). Probyn's description of writing shame parallels the students', especially in the fear of disappointing or confusing the reader. For Probyn, writing shame is positively connected to ethical writing practices, and a strand of DE scholarship seems to suggest the need for student modesty; Reif and Bawarshi's "boundary crossers," for example, are valued because they are willing to admit ignorance, while Hesse expresses fear that DE could encourage the "Lake Woebegone effect," in which too many high school students will consider themselves "above average" merely because they are enrolled in college classes. But is this sort of shame really helpful or ethical for DE writers? The word *confident* was also common in the responses, almost always used with a negative ("not confident," "unconfident"), and a certain degree of confidence is necessary to succeed in writing.

Moreover, the anxiety and fear of failure that haunt these "shame" responses are likely to inhibit students' ability to learn. As Anne Elrod Whitney points out, writing shame often leads not to better writing but to writing *avoidance*, a finding that corroborates Carol Dweck's work on learning and self-theories. Dweck and her collaborator, Heidi Grant, found that students with an "entity" self-theory (a mind-set that sees intelligence as "fixed" and therefore potentially open to shame) are vulnerable to developing a "helpless" reaction to challenge (408). Without further research, it is impossible to tell whether my students' "shame" responses are the result of a preexisting fixed mind-set or a step on the way to developing such a mind-set. It is clear, though, that this is a place where intervention from writing instructors could be helpful. Furthermore, the data suggest faculty need to be more transparent in their expectations for student writing rather than rely on students to have the emotional maturity to admit vulnerability in the classroom. Consistently and explicitly acknowledging the contextually dependent nature of "good" writing can also perhaps help ameliorate students' anxieties here.

However, it is also important to acknowledge the possibility of a performative element to these "shame" responses, since it is impossible to judge students' sincerity. Ultimately, whether conscious of it or not, students could be performing roles as humble college students. "Performing shame" in this way could be intended to produce a protective effect, in the pessimistic logic that anyone who has ever submitted a paper for publication knows all too well: if I denigrate my own work, it will hurt less if I am criticized or rejected. Student 4 put this strategy into words: "I always feel like the quality of my work is not the best, but when I get my papers back I am always surprised by how well I ended up doing." Because of the large number of responses and students' general candor, I suspect that ultimately, through their negative self-talk, these students *were* expressing a real sense of inadequacy. However, it is impossible to say for certain whether they were instead/also humbling themselves in the hope of receiving understanding and support from the professor. Because I focused on emotion rather than learning, this study did not cross-reference students' comments against their success in the course, so it is impossible to tell if the expression of shame affected student grades. This leaves an enticing question for future study.

Strategy 2: Blame

As with shame, "blame" was a strategy that twenty-two of the twenty-three student participants employed. Most of the ire in these responses was directed toward high school teachers (77%), but a substantial minority (17%) also blamed their peers for not helping them reach a college standard through peer review and workshopping. The "blame" responses were a little more specific than the "shame" responses when it came to defining college writing, and the largest subcategories of complaint found within this group included high school teachers not teaching specific genres (26%), not teaching or correcting grammar (25%), and spending too much time focusing on literature (17%). All three of these subcategories illuminate the students' conceptions of "college writing" in a similar way to the formatting issues discussed earlier, suggesting that for these students, "college writing" meant "writing happening in this particular college class," defined against "writing happening in any high school class."

In an interesting twist, the first composition course students took followed a traditional "modes" model that has since been discontinued at OTC in favor of a rhetorical genre-based model. In English Composition I, therefore, students wrote a series of short essays before moving into research and argument in English Composition II. Although neither course was taught using templates, timed "standardized" writing, or the five-paragraph essay, the courses still shared features in common with what some DE scholars have characterized as "high school–style writing": papers were short and based on personal experience, a steps-based writing process was emphasized, and students were expected to complete quizzes on various grammar topics. The responses coded as "blame," however, showed that students clearly categorized *any* assignment from the OTC class as "college writing" and *any* assignment from their high school, including college stalwarts like the researched argument paper or rhetorical analysis, as "high school writing."

Moreover, when faced with assignments in the college class, many students expressed frustration about facing a new genre: "I myself and others that I know . . . did not really know what they were doing because we have never written a description paper before" (Student 6); "I struggled with most of the process of the paper because I feel like this is one I never tried before" (Student 8). Students' unwillingness to face challenge is evident here, once again reflecting Dweck's "entity" self-theory. More problematic, many students took their unfamiliarity with new genres as a sign of their high school teachers' deficiencies: "Our English classes are awful. We write a couple of papers in high school but are not taught how to write them" (Student 7); "we also never learned the different styles . . . we still should have learned more than just a research paper" (Student 5). Occasionally, a high school teacher was even criticized for teaching students too much, as in Student 2's remark that "I was taught how to make outlines, for papers, but they were way more advanced and detailed than they needed to be." The phrase "needed to be" here encapsulates the fixed view of non-overlapping college and high school genres that the "blame" responses tended to emphasize.

This blaming of high school teachers is not unique to DE classes and forms another way in which the DE classroom gives us useful insight into FYC as a whole. Indeed, most college writing instructors will recognize this type of "blame game" around the high school–college writing boundary. Peter Kittle even describes how a genre he calls the "testimony of conversion" can be seen in scholarship about high school and college teaching: "I was a blind, sinful high school teacher until I saw the light and became a born-again writing instructor" (140). As others have pointed out, blaming high school teachers for FYC students' perceived deficiencies is not only unfair but unproductive, since it fails to take into account the constraints on high school faculty (for example, the need to teach literature as well as writing) or the ways high school teachers prepare students for writing beyond just a college class (for example, by teaching workplace genres or high-stakes standardized test preparation).

Perhaps unsurprisingly, the "blame" responses are considerably harder to read than the "shame" responses, since they frequently showed students at their worst, particularly when they dismissed or insulted their teachers. However, like the "shame" responses, it is impossible to tell how many of the "blame" responses are sincere and how many are part of a defensive performance. Certainly, some high school teachers (and college faculty!) are "terrible," make their classes read boring books, and don't teach enough genre variety; but we must remember that student responses were targeted toward the audience of a college professor whom they had only encountered online. The "college" attributes students professed to enjoy were often things their peers admitted to also doing in high school (pre-writing, researching a topic of their choice), as were the aspects they did not like, such as peer review, which occurred in both environments and was hated across the board. Clearly, whatever the true state of teaching at Ohio High School (and I suspect it is like teaching in every educational institution—some excellent, some terrible, and some in the middle), students felt pressure from the DE class to perform the role of a college student and to displace their fear of failing. One way to do both was to publicly abandon allegiance to high school instruction. Ultimately, however, the only element that defined their view of college writing was that it *wasn't* taught by their high school teachers.

IMPLICATIONS AND APPLICATIONS

Although both the "shame" and "blame" strategies have potential worth as emotional catharsis for students, they are unhealthy ways to handle the high school–college transition. As such, they provide insight into some of the potentially damaging emotional effects of DE and of FYC in general. However, as I stressed earlier, it is important to remember that the student responses gathered in this study do not represent every DE or FYC student. In this area, composition studies needs more research into specific student populations. The students surveyed, for example, took their DE class online at a community college in a rural community where few students leave Ohio for college and degrees from four-year universities are fairly rare. The students' sense of shame, therefore, as well as their attempt to displace it in the form of blame, are almost certainly the result of combined pressures coming from lack of academic opportunity, social class, parental expectation, regional norms, and a host of other societal factors. Rather than generalize my findings to all students, I hope they serve as an inspiration for other studies, whether small-scale like this one or well-funded longitudinal work beyond the reach of a small technical college. The more data we gather about different groups of students impacted by DE, the better positioned we will be as a field to advocate for them, ourselves, and FYC in general.

Collaboration

Almost universally, DE scholarship has called for greater collaboration between high school teachers and college faculty, and I will add my voice here, but with a note of caution. The self-righteous dismissal of their high school teachers that students showed in this study has sometimes been echoed by college faculty. Understandably, many faculty feel insecure faced with DE, and with good reason, but the precarity of our own survival in a tight job market and an under-valued field must not lead us to stereotype or marginalize high school teachers. Rather, respectful collaborations between high school and college faculty can serve to unite us in the face of shared administrative pressure. Scholarship has already shown many such thriving partnerships, such as the formal discussions/grading sessions that Denecker describes at the University of Findlay and Melissa Dennihy's "Bridging the Space" program for high school and college teachers in New York. At OTC, where we partnered with fifteen high schools as of 2019, faculty are beginning to "cross over" more and more, as credentialed high school teachers are adjuncts on campus over the summer and college faculty travel to high schools during the year. A recent workshop focused on teaching techniques for DE students brought faculty together to share materials, techniques, and stories.

Emphasizing Connections

Along with collaboration between high school and college faculty, the results of my study also suggest that college composition instructors should emphasize the *connection* between high school and college writing to students. Students need to know that high school teachers deserve respect and that adequate "preparation" for college does not mean identical assignments or expectations but a contiuum of useful and increasingly challenging skills and concepts. As Dennihy describes, all too often college faculty find themselves telling students to "unlearn what they learned in high school," advice that relies on the unhelpful view of "college classrooms as spaces where students' previous educations had to be renounced" (157). Dennihy reminds us how even that most reviled "high school" writing assignment, the five-paragraph essay, can be revisioned by faculty as "a springboard for grappling with more advanced assignments" rather than a scourge to be eliminated from the college classroom (162). I hope that sharing this sense of continuity with students can be key to mitigating self-defeating shame/blame responses.

Along with emphasizing these connections, student responses from this study suggest that we should look much more closely into another stereotype: that of the overconfident, entitled FYC student who claims to have learned all there is to know about writing in high school and must therefore be "un-taught" and disabused of their arrogance in college. Shame was much more prevalent among my study participants than arrogance, and even the most unpleasant "blame" responses were clearly motivated by a fear of not measuring up. While it may be true that the student population studied here is less prone to this type of behavior than those from more privileged backgrounds, it is still important to remember that fear and insecurity drive our students just as much as the "Lake Woebegone effect." Shame and blame responses suggest that we should emphasize to high school students that what they have learned so far is directly related to what they will learn in the future, that writing is a lifelong skill praticed in many different ways, and that they don't have to immediately or perfectly perform the "college writer" role.

Rhetorical Awareness "Awareness"

Finally, my research suggests that the DE classroom and the high school–college writing binary can be of particular use to FYC instructors in teaching rhetorical awareness. I was surprised by students' clear attempts to measure up to what they thought the "college standard" was, and even though their ideas about that standard were often very different from what I actually required of them, they clearly grasped the idea that they needed to write differently for different situtations. Indeed, even some of the most misguided attempts to flatter the instructor (Student 11: "We cannot express how nice it is to finally learn something useful!") showed an attempt to please and interest a new audience—in this case, a college professor. Such moves indicate the beginning of rhetorical awareness, as found in the Conference on College Composition and Communication's (CCCC's) statement on Postsecondary Writing Instruction, which indicates that a good FYC course "emphasizes the rhetorical nature of writing; considers the needs of real audiences; recognizes writing as a social act." While I am not arguing that mere presence in a DE course taught by a college professor will magically create sophisticated rhetorical awareness in students, explicitly drawing students' attention to their own audience awareness is a useful place to begin, creating rhetorical awareness "awareness," as it were.

Writing differently for different disciplines, professors, and situations is one of the major skills required to succeed in college, and DE FYC students are perfectly positioned to start gaining that awareness early. This awareness can also aid in the development of the meta-cognitive reflection that researchers like Reiff and Bawarshi have identified as a key component of transfer, therefore allowing FYC to become "a potential site for disrupting the maintenance of strict domain boundaries" (331). Teachers could even use the high school–college writing divide as the subject of an early reflection, as I did here, perhaps leading into a wider unit on genre, such as the first unit of Kathleen Blake Yancey and her colleagues' popular "teaching for transfer" curriculum—which proposes "genre," "audience," "rhetorical situation," and "reflection" as the first of the "key terms" FYC students should learn.

CONCLUSION

I began this chapter by noting that the expansion of DE is forcing faculty to reconsider the dynamics of the college classroom. As I conclude, I want to examine this reconsideration more broadly—DE not only challenges us to reconsider our classroom practices, but it also acts as a useful microcosm of the high school–college transition that is a key part of FYC as a whole. Many scholars have commented on FYC's central role as "a transition point for students entering the university" (Reiff and Bawarshi 331). DE composition may be a relatively new and quickly expanding form of FYC, but it ultimately remains, crucially, not a separate type of instruction but part of FYC itself. As a result, faculty teaching FYC in any incarnation can benefit from the insights gained through studying DE students' transitions.

Nevertheless, many important questions remain unanswered in terms of the value, purpose, and administration of DE. Furthermore, the challenges it poses to both secondary and higher education are real and demand continuing scholarly and public discussion. An increasing part of that discussion must focus on listening to, sharing, and amplifying students' voices. As college and high school faculty, we must support students without leaving them "caught in the middle" of our own struggles over status, resources, or worldview. Several years ago, I had a thirteen-year-old student write one of the best college papers I've ever received; it doesn't look as though that kind of paradox is going away anytime soon. Whatever our feelings about DE, that student and others like her are waiting.

NOTE

1. Here and in the discussion that follows, student responses are identified by the number assigned to the student, between 1 and 23.

APPENDIX 14.A

REFLECTION GUIDING QUESTIONS FOR STUDENTS

1. How do you see the different roles of college students and high school students? Based on this introductory module, what challenges do you think you will need to address in order to succeed as a college student in this course?
2. Reflect on your typical writing process in high school. How is it similar/different to the process we've focused on in this module? What changes might you need to make in your process to succeed in this class?
3. This week, please reflect on the grammar quizzes that you've just been reminded of. Which of these grammar topics are you confident about? Which are challenging for you? How will you study? Finally, describe any grammar teaching that you've received in school so far.
4. Describe the process of writing your draft. What went well? What was challenging? How do you feel overall about the quality of your work?
5. How do you feel about descriptive versus illustrative writing? What are the major differences that you see? Which one feels easier for you and why?
6. Describe the process of writing your *final* draft. What went well? What was challenging? How do you feel overall about the quality of your work?
7. Describe the process of writing your draft. What went well? What was challenging? How do you feel overall about the quality of your work?
8. How did the peer review you received help you revise your paper (or not)? What do you think you need to work on, based on this peer review? How do you see peer review as fitting into the college writing classroom?
9. Compare your experience of taking an online class with a face-to-face class. Next, compare this class so far with the English classes you've taken in the past.
10. How did you feel about writing the definition paper? How does the definition paper compare to your earlier papers? Set yourself a goal related to the last two papers of the class.
11. Reflect on your high school experience with writing, particularly in terms of sentence-level style. What sorts of advice/tips have you received? What have you learned about what the "style" of a formal essay should be?
12. What analytical writing or schoolwork have you done in the past? When you hear the word "analysis," what does that mean to you? How do you feel about this type of writing?

13. Please write approximately 1 page reflecting on the course as a whole. Guiding questions are listed below, but you may also include other points. Please remember that this is NOT an evaluation of the course or the teacher (you'll get to do this too!) but a reflection on your own learning.

Questions: What was the most/least valuable thing you learned during this course? How did this course differ from your high school classes? How did you find the online format? What one thing would you change about this course if you could?

WORKS CITED

Addison, Joanne, and Sharon James McGee. "Writing in High School/Writing in College: Research Trends and Future Directions." *College Composition and Communication*, vol. 62, no. 1, 2010, pp. 147–179.

Allen, Drew, and Mina Dadgar. "Does Dual Enrollment Increase Students' Success in College? Evidence from a Quasi-Experimental Analysis of Dual Enrollment in New York City." *New Directions for Higher Education*, no. 158, 2012, pp. 11–19.

An, Brian P. "The Role of Academic Motivation and Engagement on the Relationship between Dual Enrollment and Academic Performance." *Journal of Higher Education*, vol. 86, no. 1, 2015, pp. 98–126.

Brown, Brené. "Shame Resilience Theory: A Grounded Theory Study on Women and Shame." *Families in Society: The Journal of Contemporary Social Services*, vol. 87, no. 1, 2006, pp. 43–52.

Burns, Kathleen, William A. Ellegood, Jill M. Bernard Bracy, Mimi Duncan, and Donald C. Sweeney II. "Early College Credit Programs Positively Impact Student Success." *Journal of Advanced Academics*, vol. 30, no. 1, 2019, pp. 27–49.

Calhoun-Dillahunt, Carolyn. "2018 CCCC Chair's Address." *College Composition and Communication*, vol. 70, no. 2, 2018, pp. 273–293.

Corbin, Juliet, and Anselm Strauss. *Basics of Qualitative Research: Techniques and Procedures for Developing Grounded Theory*. 3rd ed. Sage, 2008.

Denecker, Christine. "Transitioning Writers across the Composition Threshold: What We Can Learn from Dual Enrollment Partnerships." *Composition Studies*, vol. 41, no. 1, 2013, pp. 27–50.

Dennihy, Melissa. "'Forget What You Learned in High School!' Bridging the Space between High School and College." *Teaching English in the Two-Year College*, vol. 43, no. 2, 2015, pp. 156–169.

Dweck, Carol, and Heidi Grant. "Self-Theories, Goals and Meaning." In *The Handbook of Motivation Science*, edited by James Y. Shah and Wendi Gardner. Guilford, 2008, pp. 405–416.

Fanetti, Susan, Kathy M. Bushrow, and David L. DeWeese. "Closing the Gap between High School Writing Instruction and College Writing Expectations." *English Journal*, vol. 99, no. 4, 2010, pp. 77–83.

Farris, Christine R. "Minding the Gap and Learning the Game: Differences That Matter between High School and College Writing." In *College Credit for Writing in High School: The "Taking Care of" Business*, edited by Kristine Hansen and Christine R. Farris. NCTE, 2010, pp. 272–281.

Haas, Bob. Personal Interview. Oct. 8, 2018.

Hansen, Kristine. "The Composition Marketplace: Shopping for Credits versus Learning to Write." In *College Credit for Writing in High School: The "Taking Care of" Business*, edited by Kristine Hansen and Christine R. Farris. NCTE, 2010, pp. 1–39.

Hesse, Douglas. "Afterword: Of Cellists and Writers, Getting Better and Getting On." In *College Credit for Writing in High School: The "Taking Care of" Business*, edited by Kristine Hansen and Christine R. Farris. NCTE, 2010, pp. 283–292.

Kanny, M. Allison. "Dual Enrollment Participation from the Student Perspective." *New Directions for Community Colleges*, no. 169, 2015, pp. 59–70.

Karp, Melinda Mechur. " 'I Don't Know, I've Never Been to College!' Dual Enrollment as a College Readiness Strategy." *New Directions for Higher Education*, no. 158, 2012, pp. 21–28.

Karp, Melinda Mechur. "Learning about the Role of a College Student through Dual Enrollment Participation." Community College Research Center Working Paper no. 7, 2007.

Kittle, Peter. "It's Not the High School Teacher's Fault: An Alternative to the Blame Game." In *What Is College-Level Writing*, edited by Patrick Sullivan and Howard Tinberg. NCTE, 2006, pp. 134–145.

McCrimmon, Miles. "Contesting the Territoriality of 'Freshman English': The Political Ecology of Dual Enrollment." In *College Credit for Writing in High School: The "Taking Care of" Business*, edited by Kristine Hansen and Christine R. Farris. NCTE, 2010, pp. 208–227.

Ohio Department of Higher Education. *Annual Report: Year Three of the College Credit Plus Program 2017–2018*. Ohio Department of Higher Education, 2019.

Ohio Department of Education. "College Credit Plus: About." https://www.ohiohighered.org/collegecreditplus#:~:text=College%20Credit%20Plus%20is%20Ohio's,from%20Ohio%20colleges%20or%20universities. Accessed May 15, 2022.

Ohio Department of Education. "Pleasant High School." Ohio School Report Cards, 2019. www.reportcard.education.ohio.gov/school/achievement/030304.

Priebe, Sybil. "TYCA to You: Dual Credit." *Teaching English in the Two Year College*, vol. 43, issue 4, May 2016, pp. 438–448.

Probyn, Elspeth. "Writing Shame." In *The Affect Theory Reader*, edited by Melissa Gregg and Gregory J. Seigworth. Duke University Press, 2010, pp. 71–90.

Reiff, Mary Jo, and Anis Bawarshi. "Tracing Discursive Resources: How Students Use Prior Genre Knowledge to Negotiate New Writing Contexts in First-Year Composition." *Written Communication*, vol. 28, no. 3, 2011, pp. 312–337.

Struhl, Ben, and Joel Vargas. "Taking College Courses in High School: A Strategy for College Readiness." Jobs for the Future, 2012. www.jff.org/resources/taking-college-courses-high-school-strategy-college-readiness/. Accessed May 15, 2022.

Sullivan, Patrick, and Howard Tinberg, eds. *What Is "College-Level" Writing?* NCTE, 2006.

Tensen, Tracy. "Playing Both Sides: The Struggles of a Dual Enrollment Instructor." *English Journal*, vol. 102, no. 2, 2018, pp. 17–19.

Tinberg, Howard, and Jean-Paul Nadeau. "Contesting the Space between High School and College in the Era of Dual Enrollment." *College Composition and Communication*, vol. 62, no. 4, 2011, pp. 704–725.

Tinberg, Howard, and Jean-Paul Nadeau. "What Happens When High School Students Write in a College Course? A Study of Dual Credit." *English Journal*, vol. 102, no. 5, 2013, pp. 35–42.

Wade, Tiffany. Personal interview. September 12, 2019.

Wang, Xueli, Hsun-yu Chan, Allen L. Phelps, and Janet I. Washbon. "Fuel for Success: Academic Momentum as a Motivator between Dual Enrollment and Educational Outcomes of Two-Year Technical College Students." *Community College Review*, vol. 43, no. 2, 2015, pp. 165–190.

Whitney, Anne Elrod. "Speaking My Mind: Shame in the Writing Classroom." *English Journal*, vol. 107, no. 3, 2018, pp. 130–132.

Yancey, Kathleen Blake, Tara Taczak, and Liane Robertson. *Writing across Contexts: Transfer, Composition, and Sites of Writing*. Utah State UP, 2014.

AFTERWORD
Reflections and Aspirations

Keith D. Miller and Shirley K Rose, Arizona State University

We expect that most readers will have finished reading this collection at the same place our editors began it, when they wrote "to be honest, we are not entirely sure how we feel about dual enrollment." If so, that is testament to the success of the collection of scholarship assembled here. The editors' admission has captured the ambivalence about dual enrollment (DE) composition courses that many of their readers share. It also has modeled for readers how to approach this topic with an open mind and willingness to spend time reflecting on new ideas and new information without expecting to come to definitive conclusions or to necessarily be ready to decide on action steps. Some of the scholarship presented here has challenged claims made by advocates of DE while other scholarship undermines unquestioned assumptions and prejudices held by opponents of DE. This examination of DE programs and practices provides, to use the editors' metaphor of the kaleidoscope, a refracted lens for viewing high school and college composition that allows us to see what we might not have otherwise been able to see.

The editors of this collection have pointed out that composition studies has largely ignored dual enrollment programs, despite their existence in one form or another since the 1950s. There are perhaps a wide range of reasons for this ignorance, but the variegated scholarly work assembled here has demonstrated that there is much we can learn from these programs, even if we have been ambivalent about them. They have made a strong case for their claim that the future of dual enrollment programs will affect all college writing programs and college writing teachers, regardless of whether they participate directly in offering or teaching these courses. They have proven their point that "DE FYC conversations are, in fact, FYC conversations that affect the entire field."

https://doi.org/10.7330/9781646422531.c015

How will this collection change that conversation? Contributors have helped readers view the "gap" between high school and college composition as a discursive construction that need not be taken for granted but can be questioned and subject to critique. They have shown us that understanding faculty development issues in DE programs also provides new perspectives on persistent concerns for other adjunct faculty who teach college composition. These chapters help us shift our perspective from concern that college composition studies' sphere of influence is shrinking to awareness that its reach is expanding.

The work collected here has also helped us see that because DE programs often replicate structural inequities, they expose barriers and roadblocks in students' pathways to college attainment. As Joseph Jones ably explains (chapter 3, this volume), some of these obstacles arise in part because the historical relationship between English teachers in high schools and colleges is, in his words, "mostly unmarked by sustained efforts at shared responsibility." He makes this point in part by summoning noteworthy historians of composition instruction, including Albert Kitzhaber, who in 1960 advocated greater dialogue and cooperation between these two sets of teachers that could help overcome what Kitzhaber deemed the vague definition (or non-definition) of FYC.

In her foreword to this volume, Christine Farris sketches her own laudable, pioneering work in Indiana to promote collaboration and collegiality between high school and college teachers of writing. She also advocates such collaboration on issues beyond those directly tied to DE. Along with Kristine Hansen, Farris co-edited a landmark collection of essays about DE in 2010, some of which weigh and communicate efforts to cross or bridge the institutional division that separates high schools from colleges. Christine Denecker directly espoused such dialogue and teamwork in an essay she published in 2013.

Fortunately—partly in response to the work of Farris, Hansen, and Denecker—some of the essayists in this volume worked alongside high school teachers (in a variety of settings) while often striving to reconsider and re-conceptualize English instruction. Unfortunately, however, despite Kitzhaber's call in 1960, the excellence of Farris's work, the notable Hansen/Farris collection, and Denecker's astute argument, no one has spawned a mass movement nationwide that could overcome the lamentable gap that often separates English teachers in high schools from those in colleges. Nor, unfortunately, did these scholars greatly advance, on a national scale, what Scott Campbell (chapter 6, this volume) calls the "de-terretorialization" of English instruction in high schools and colleges.

So how can we foster greater cross-pollination of ideas between these two sets of teachers, cross-pollination that would enhance the strengths of both groups? Is it conceivable to transform those who are geographically close into a single set of colleagues who are aware of the arbitrariness of "steps" of education from one grade level to the next? How about transforming them into a set of colleagues who could renegotiate and improve English education in general? Essayists in this volume point to possible venues and opportunities for such collaborative work.

We would like to use the remainder of this afterword to make further suggestions. Both of us are seasoned veterans in the classroom. One of us (Keith) hesitated to teach online until 2017, when his chair coaxed him to jump into the only online MA program supplied by our behemoth department. At least three-quarters of the students in that program were and are high school English teachers, scattered from Florida to Hawaii. Their eagerness to learn was astonishing, as was the quality of their work, even as the horrific plague of COVID-19 suffused the nation throughout spring 2020.

After reading the chapters in this collection, we admit that ignoring DE hasn't worked as a strategy for making it go away, and we recognize that there is little we could do to eliminate it if we wished to. Acknowledging that reality, we're ready to turn our attention to making the best of the situation. We find ourselves eager to brainstorm with colleagues to explore ways our department could move forward to establish academic program offerings centered largely on studies of DE. For example, could an online MA program in writing studies designed for teachers of DE help us serve a need and be consistent with our university's commitment to improving college attainment and completion in our state, where only a relatively small percentage of teens go on to earn a college degree? In the refracted light of this edited collection's kaleidoscopic lens, we're inspired to envision a program that would rely heavily on collaborative efforts with our departmental colleagues in English education and colleagues at area community colleges (many of them our own PhD graduates) to develop and offer a program of study designed for in-service teachers. We envision working together to interrogate and (re)design curricula, assignments, grading criteria, and classroom activities for various pre-DE, DE, and post-DE courses alike. We can picture qualified, veteran DE teachers, including high school teachers, creating and teaching some of these courses. And we think other universities could develop and proffer similar MA programs.

We can also envision a doctoral-level graduate program focused around DE and involving various qualified faculty from universities, two-year colleges, and high schools. For these kinds of programs, in-person, hybrid, or online classes could be offered on weeknights, Saturdays, and/or during the summer to accommodate students who are full-time teachers. School systems could provide financial incentives, and universities could supply scholarships to well-qualified applicants in need of financial assistance.

We like to dream.

WORKS CITED

Denecker, Christine. "Transitioning Writers across the Composition Threshold: What We Can Learn from Dual Enrollment Partnerships." *Composition Studies*, vol. 4, no. 1, 2013, pp. 21–50.

Hansen, Kristine, and Christine R. Farris. *College Credit for Writing in High School: The "Taking Care of" Business.* NCTE, 2010.

Kitzhaber, Albert. "Death—or Transfiguration." *College English*, vol. 21, no. 7, 1960, pp. 367–373.

INDEX